THE ORDER *of the* OLD TESTAMENT

THE ORDER *of the* OLD TESTAMENT

INTERPRETING THE CANONICAL CONTEXT OF THE LAW, PROPHETS, AND WRITINGS

MARIO MELENDEZ

Baker Academic
a division of Baker Publishing Group
Grand Rapids, Michigan

Published by Baker Academic
a division of Baker Publishing Group
Grand Rapids, Michigan
BakerAcademic.com

Printed in the United States of America

Library of Congress Cataloging-in-Publication Data

Names: Melendez, Mario, 1986– author

Title: The order of the Old Testament : interpreting the canonical context of the law, prophets, and writings / Mario Melendez.

Description: Grand Rapids, Michigan : Baker Academic, a division of Baker Publishing Group, [2026] | Includes bibliographical references and index.

Identifiers: LCCN 2026015829 | ISBN 9781540969453 paperback | ISBN 9781493456215 ebook | ISBN 9781493456222 pdf

Subjects: LCSH: Bible. Old Testament—Canonical criticism

Classification: LCC BS1171.3 .M45 2026

LC record available at https://lccn.loc.gov/2026015829

Baker Publishing Group publications use paper produced from sustainable forestry practices and postconsumer waste whenever possible.

26 27 28 29 30 31 32 7 6 5 4 3 2 1

Catalina,
may you find joy in the Word of God as your mother and I do.
May our lives and teachings lead you to a life
of holiness and contentment in the Lord.

CONTENTS

ACKNOWLEDGMENTS

I am indebted to the teachings and mentorship of Dr. Archie England at New Orleans Baptist Theological Seminary. You have guided a generation of Old Testament lovers, and we honor you in our teaching and preaching. I would also like to acknowledge Oklahoma Baptist University and Dr. Matt Emerson for being supporters of me in writing this book.

ABBREVIATIONS

General and Bibliographic

AT	author's translation
b.	Babylonian Talmud (when preceding a tractate name)
BCE	before the Common Era
BHS	*Biblia Hebraica Stuttgartensia*
bk(s).	book(s)
ca.	*circa*, about
CE	Common Era
cent.	century
chap(s).	chapter(s)
esp.	especially
ESV	English Standard Version
IVP	InterVarsity Press
JPS	Jewish Publication Society
LXX	Septuagint (the Old Testament in Greek)
m.	Mishnah (when preceding a tractate name)
NASB	New American Standard Bible
NIV	New International Version
OT	Old Testament
RSV	Revised Standard Version

Old Testament / Hebrew Bible

Gen.	Genesis
Exod.	Exodus
Lev.	Leviticus
Num.	Numbers
Deut.	Deuteronomy
Josh.	Joshua
Judg.	Judges
Ruth	Ruth
1 Sam.	1 Samuel
2 Sam.	2 Samuel
1 Kings	1 Kings
2 Kings	2 Kings
1 Chron.	1 Chronicles
2 Chron.	2 Chronicles
Ezra	Ezra
Neh.	Nehemiah
Esther	Esther
Job	Job
Ps(s).	Psalm(s)
Prov.	Proverbs
Eccles.	Ecclesiastes
Song	Song of Songs
Isa.	Isaiah
Jer.	Jeremiah
Lam.	Lamentations
Ezek.	Ezekiel
Dan.	Daniel
Hosea	Hosea

Joel	Joel
Amos	Amos
Obad.	Obadiah
Jon.	Jonah
Mic.	Micah
Nah.	Nahum
Hab.	Habakkuk
Zeph.	Zephaniah
Hag.	Haggai
Zech.	Zechariah
Mal.	Malachi

New Testament

Matt.	Matthew
Mark	Mark
Luke	Luke
John	John
Acts	Acts
Rom.	Romans
1 Cor.	1 Corinthians
2 Cor.	2 Corinthians
Gal.	Galatians
Eph.	Ephesians
Phil.	Philippians
Col.	Colossians
1 Thess.	1 Thessalonians
2 Thess.	2 Thessalonians
1 Tim.	1 Timothy
2 Tim.	2 Timothy
Titus	Titus
Philem.	Philemon
Heb.	Hebrews
James	James
1 Pet.	1 Peter
2 Pet.	2 Peter
1 John	1 John
2 John	2 John
3 John	3 John
Jude	Jude
Rev.	Revelation

INTRODUCTION

"CONTEXT, CONTEXT, CONTEXT," exclaimed the old professor. "You must read Scripture in light of its historical, cultural, canonical, and linguistic contexts." If you're a student of Scripture, or have taken hermeneutics courses, you've undoubtedly heard your professor make a similar proclamation. Yet, as one begins to delve into the depths of biblical studies of the Old Testament, one context rarely discussed in hermeneutics books is the canonical context, specifically how each book connects with the surrounding material.

The canonical context of the Old Testament can be very confusing for students and professors alike. While hermeneutics books provide great content about the other hermeneutical contexts (historical, cultural, linguistic), rarely is there such in-depth conversation about the canonical context. The Old Testament has been historically organized in two major canonical orders: the fourfold order and the threefold order. The fourfold order follows the Septuagint (LXX) Greek translation of the Old Testament (3rd–1st cent. BCE). The order is based loosely on genre: law, history, poetry/wisdom, prophecy. This fourfold order is the structure that most English Bibles follow. The threefold order follows the Hebrew Bible, commonly referred to by the term "Tanakh" (TaNaK), an acronym formed from the first letters of its three parts: Torah (Law), Nevi'im (Prophets), and Ketuvim (Writings).[1] Table 1 shows the two canonical arrangements side by side.

1. To distinguish between the threefold and fourfold arrangements, I will refer to the threefold canon as the Hebrew Bible or the Tanakh and use the Hebrew titles Torah, Nevi'im, and Ketuvim for its divisions. I will refer to the fourfold canon as the Old Testament and use the labels Pentateuch, Historical Books, Wisdom Books, and Prophetic Books for its divisions.

Table 1. Fourfold and Threefold Divisions Compared

LXX/English Fourfold Canon	Tanakh Threefold Canon
Pentateuch	**Torah (תּוֹרָה)/Law**
1. Genesis (Γένεσις)	1. Genesis (בְּרֵאשִׁית)
2. Exodus (Ἔξοδος)	2. Exodus (שְׁמוֹת)
3. Leviticus (Λευιτικόν)	3. Leviticus (וַיִּקְרָא)
4. Numbers (Ἀριθμοί)	4. Numbers (בְּמִדְבַּר)
5. Deuteronomy (Δευτερονόμιον)	5. Deuteronomy (דְּבָרִים)
Historical Books	**Nevi'im (נְבִיאִים)/Prophets**
1. Joshua (Ἰησοῦς Ναυῆ)	**Former Prophets (נְבִיאִים רִאשׁוֹנִים)**
2. Judges (Κριταί)	6. Joshua (יְהוֹשֻׁעַ)
3. Ruth (Ῥούθ)	7. Judges (שֹׁפְטִים)
4. 1 Kings (1 Sam.) (Βασιλειῶν Α′)	8. 1 Samuel (שְׁמוּאֵל א)
5. 2 Kings (2 Sam.) (Βασιλειῶν Β′)	9. 2 Samuel (שְׁמוּאֵל ב)
6. 3 Kings (1 Kings) (Βασιλειῶν Γ′)	10. 1 Kings (מְלָכִים א)
7. 4 Kings (2 Kings) (Βασιλειῶν Δ′)	11. 2 Kings (מְלָכִים ב)
8. 1 Chronicles (Παραλειπομένων Α′)	**Latter Prophets (נְבִיאִים אַחֲרוֹנִים)**
9. 2 Chronicles (Παραλειπομένων Β′)	12. Isaiah (יְשַׁעְיָהוּ)
10. Ezra-Nehemiah (Ἔσδρας Β′)	13. Jeremiah (יִרְמְיָהוּ)
11. Esther (Ἐσθήρ)	14. Ezekiel (יְחֶזְקֵאל)
	15. The Twelve Minor Prophets (שְׁנֵים עָשָׂר)
	• Hosea (הוֹשֵׁעַ) • Nahum (נַחוּם)
	• Joel (יוֹאֵל) • Habakkuk (חֲבַקּוּק)
	• Amos (עָמוֹס) • Zephaniah (צְפַנְיָה)
	• Obadiah (עֹבַדְיָה) • Haggai (חַגַּי)
	• Jonah (יוֹנָה) • Zechariah (זְכַרְיָה)
	• Micah (מִיכָה) • Malachi (מַלְאָכִי)
Wisdom Books	**Ketuvim (כְּתוּבִים)/Writings**[a]
1. Job (Ἰώβ)	16. Psalms (תְּהִלִּים)
2. Psalms (Ψαλμοί)	17. Proverb (מִשְׁלֵי)
3. Proverbs (Παροιμίαι)	18. Job (אִיּוֹב)
4. Ecclesiastes (Ἐκκλησιαστής)	19. Song of Songs (שִׁיר הַשִּׁירִים)
5. Song of Songs / Song of Solomon / Canticles (Ἆσμα Ἀσμάτων)	20. Ruth (רוּת)
Prophetic Books	21. Lamentations (אֵיכָה)
1. Isaiah (Ἠσαΐας)	22. Ecclesiastes (קֹהֶלֶת)
2. Jeremiah (Ἰερεμίας)	23. Esther (אֶסְתֵּר)
3. Lamentations (Θρῆνοι)	24. Daniel (דָּנִיֵּאל)
4. Ezekiel (Ἰεζεκιήλ)	25. Ezra (עֶזְרָא)
5. Daniel (Δανιήλ)	26. Nehemiah (נְחֶמְיָה)
6. Hosea (Ὠσηέ α′)[b]	27. 1 Chronicles (דִּבְרֵי הַיָּמִים א)
7. Joel (Ἰωήλ δ′)	28. 2 Chronicles (דִּבְרֵי הַיָּמִים ב)
8. Amos (Ἀμώς β′)	
9. Obadiah (Ἀβδιού ε′)	
10. Jonah (Ἰωνᾶς ϛ′)	
11. Micah (Μιχαίας γ′)	
12. Nahum (Ναούμ ζ′)	
13. Habakkuk (Ἀβακούμ η′)	
14. Zephaniah (Σοφονίας θ′)	
15. Haggai (Ἀγγαῖος ι′)	
16. Zechariah (Ζαχαρίας ια′)	
17. Malachi (Μαλαχίας ιβ′)	

a. The traditional Jewish order of books in the Ketuvim is presented here, which differs from the order in *BHS*.

b. The traditional English order of the twelve Minor Prophets is presented here. The Greek numerals after the book names indicate the order in the Septuagint.

Perhaps the canonical context isn't discussed or debated deeply in courses and textbooks due to a Christian assumption and affirmation of the fourfold canon, but there is a resurgence of interest in the threefold order within biblical studies. This resurgence may be due to growth in several fields: literary considerations of the Hebraic canonical structure, archaeological considerations from ancient writings such as the Dead Sea Scrolls, and Jewish-Christian considerations such as a desiring to recapture the early beliefs and practices of the first Christian generation. In this book, I endeavor to unravel the enigma of the Hebrew order and further aid Christian understanding of and possible adoption of the threefold order.

I attended four different theological institutions in preparation for my academic career. The quote about the importance of context, which opens this chapter, is something that was stressed at all my institutions. In fact, I have said this very thing when teaching hermeneutics. However, now as an Old Testament professor at Oklahoma Baptist University, I have come to recognize the hermeneutical quandary of the canonical context. Although I hold two master's degrees in biblical studies and a doctorate in biblical interpretation, I was never exposed to the potential reasons for the Tanakh's structure, nor was I introduced to hermeneutical reasons for the church to accept it. The topic of this book came into my personal research when a student pressed me to help him find a "newer" way to articulate the book of Ecclesiastes in a sermon series. I began my quest of understanding Ecclesiastes as a "sermon series," for the book is attributed to Qohelet, which means "preacher." I did not find any satisfying answers to the book's purpose in sermon form until my wife and I took a research trip to Israel. As we traveled, I asked various rabbis and researchers I met what they did with Ecclesiastes in their pulpits and lecterns. A Karaite[2] yeshiva[3] teacher gave the most satisfying answer, "Ecclesiastes is a series of sermons by King Solomon to non-Yahweh people that culminates in them knowing that Yahweh is the answer." He encouraged me to find the support for his position in a Hebrew grammar written by Aaron ben Asher, a ninth-century Masorete. In the pages of this old grammar book, I found support for his position as well as an intriguing concept for understanding the threefold testament. Ben Asher's concept led me to continue researching other

2. Karaite Judaism, founded in the 8th cent. CE in Babylon, is a Jewish religious movement that rejects the Talmud as authoritative, adhering solely to the Tanakh (Hebrew Bible) for religious guidance and practice. Adherents emphasize a literal interpretation of Scripture and reject the oral traditions that form the basis of rabbinic Judaism. As a result, Karaites have developed their own methods of interpretating the Tanakh.

3. A yeshiva is a Jewish educational institution where traditional Jewish studies, particularly focused on Torah and Talmudic learning, are taught. In Karaite yeshivas, only the Tanakh is studied.

understandings of the threefold canonical structure and how this structure might help Christians better understand our sacred text.

In my quest to grasp the Tanakh's threefold structure, I have discovered six key approaches to understanding how and why the threefold order came to be. Each one of these approaches offers a different reason for organization, and more importantly, each provides a different hermeneutical perspective and impact. The purpose of this book is to introduce these various approaches and hopefully offer many good reasons to accept and employ the Tanakh order for interpreting Scripture. The six approaches to understanding how and why the threefold order came to be are as follows:

- the Triple Canon approach (also called unfolding Scripture or historical progression)
- the Genre Author approach (also called authorial/literary diversity)
- the Theological Development approach
- the Spiritual Guidance approach
- the Messianic Trajectory approach
- the Sacred Structure approach (also called architectural structuring or temple structure)[4]

Since the Tanakh was finalized in the ninth century, Ben Asher's concept of the Sacred Structure approach is presented last. While all these approaches are helpful, I believe Ben Asher's concept offers the best hermeneutical insight and provides a fresh means of comprehending the threefold text.

Purpose of This Book

Over the last twenty years or so, many Old Testament survey textbooks have used the Hebrew Tanakh order instead of the fourfold order found in most English Bibles.[5] You may have even used one of these new books because your professor prefers this order. None of these books, however, introduces all the

4. Stephen Dempster introduces some of these approaches in his two-part journal article. See Dempster, "'Extraordinary Fact'"; Dempster, "'Extraordinary Fact,' Pt. 2."

5. You may have used one of these: Walter Brueggemann and Tod Linafelt, *Old Testament Survey: The Canon and Christian Imagination* (Westminster John Knox, 2021); John Collins, *Introduction to the Hebrew Bible* (Fortress, 2004); John Drane, *Introducing the Old Testament* (Fortress, 2001); William Dumbrell, *The Faith of Israel: A Theological Survey of the Old Testament*, 2nd ed. (Baker Academic, 2002); John Goldingay, *Introduction to the Old Testament* (InterVarsity, 2015); Paul House and Eric Mitchell, *Old Testament Survey*, 3rd ed. (B&H, 2023). There are many more.

noted approaches or their hermeneutical impact, although some scholars are working on this concept and trying to bring the Tanakh order to the foreground for Christians. I first introduce and define each approach and then present adherents of the approach and any potential pitfalls. Each chapter concludes by applying the approach to three texts as an illustration.[6] The final chapter of this book compares the various hermeneutical approaches on a final set of texts.

I believe that the Tanakh order seen in many recent OT academic works and adopted by some institutions can be helpful for Christians. The Tanakh order presents a more succinct hermeneutic, permitting one to quickly articulate and teach the OT and introduce the biblical text as Jesus knew it.

There are some variations in how the books of the Tanakh are arranged, but I follow the commonly held Masoretic ordering of the books reflected in the JPS translation, which has been the authoritative order within Orthodox Judaism since the fifteenth century. Though as Beckwith observes, let us not forget that "this stability of order is a relatively modern phenomenon, and owes a good deal to the invention of printing. It was preceded by an era of fluidity, both among Jews (the chief guardians of the Hebrew Bible) and among Christians (the chief guardians of the Greek)."[7] The aim of the current work is to present the threefold concept, not necessarily the variations within this arrangement.[8] Again as Beckwith points out,

> In Jewish and Hebrew sources, it is true, the five books of the Law always appear in their natural, chronological order, and likewise the first four books of the Prophets; these are invariably the historical books Joshua, Judges, Samuel and Kings, which continue the historical sequence from the point where the Law leaves it. But the remaining books of the Prophets—the oracular books—have in the Jewish and Hebrew sources no settled order; which is likewise the case with the Hagiographa.[9]

While the purpose of this book is to introduce the threefold canon and hopefully convince Christian readers of its utility, this work is by no means a complete survey of all the views concerning the writing, gathering, and ordering of the Tanakh. My treatment also omits the books of the Old Testament Apocrypha. Although many within Christendom hold these books

6. The texts used in the discussion of each view were selected by fellow members of the southwest region of the Evangelical Theological Society.

7. Beckwith, *Old Testament Canon*, 181–82.

8. The primary area of variation is the ordering of the Ketuvim. For instance, the Aleppo Codex places Chronicles first in the Ketuvim, whereas the Babylonian Talmud places it last, and as already mentioned, *BHS* presents the books in a different sequence. For a fuller treatment of the debated order of the books within the Tanakh, see Croy, *Sequencing the Hebrew Bible*.

9. Beckwith, *Old Testament Canon*, 182.

to be Scripture, they are not included in my discussion because they do not appear in the Masoretic ordering of the Hebrew Bible.

Preview of This Book

The most commonly held view of the three sections of the Tanakh is the Triple Canon approach, also known as the "historical progression" theory. This is the only approach that I was taught in school. In the first chapter, we explore the transformative journey of Scripture across centuries and highlight pivotal moments that canonized its content. To grasp the origins of the texts, we quickly cover views on the oral traditions that preceded their written forms and the cultural and religious contexts in which they emerged. The three major milestones to consider are the fifth century BCE, third century BCE, and first century CE.

The second view we consider is a balance between genre- and author-based organization. Some scholars distinguish the three sections by author (Moses, prophets, other people), while others identify the three sections by genre (law, prophecy, and other). I think both concepts are best understood as being intricately intertwined, showing the rich complexity of the Tanakh. Therefore, in chapter 2 we navigate through Scriptures' tripartite organization using the Author Genre approach, revealing the diverse literary genres and distinct authorial voices that shape its narrative: from the foundational Torah as law authored/influenced by Moses to the prophetic texts of the Nevi'im brimming with visionary insights and moral teaching and to the contributions of nonprophetic authors within the Ketuvim, illuminating the multifaceted nature of the Tanakh.

The third approach for grasping the Tanakh structure is built on the field of OT theology and Israelite religion studies. In this Theological Development approach, which we discuss in chapter 3, the Tanakh is organized to show a development of belief, enabling us to see the variations in theological development encapsulated within each section of the Tanakh. A classic example of theological development is the progression from polytheism, to henotheism, to monotheism.[10] We will cover similar evolving beliefs, ideologies, and doctrinal shifts throughout different epochs, shedding light on the growth and transformation of theological concepts within the text.

A fourth way that people have conceived of the Tanakh order is the Spiritual Guide approach, in which the timeless wisdom, moral teachings, and spiritual

10. Although the terms *henotheism* and *monotheism* both refer to the worship of one god, a henotheist does not deny the existence of other gods, whereas a monotheist believes that there is only one god.

truths embedded in the text offer guidance and illumination to readers across diverse cultures and eras. According to the American Bible Society, one of the main reasons why people read the Bible is to gain spiritual insight for life decisions.[11] In chapter 4, we see how the Tanakh's various parts have been used to provide spiritual guidance.

The penultimate view we cover in chapter 5, the Messianic Trajectory approach, is articulated by those who are often called "canonicalists." They read all the books of the Hebrew Bible as a progression pointing toward the Messiah, Christ Jesus, viewed as the fulfillment of the Torah, the hope of the Nevi'im, and the wisdom of the Ketuvim. Although the canonicalists are cited, we must not forget that the messianic hope expressed in the Tanakh is a view that preceded Christianity.

The final ordering concept, the Sacred Structure approach discussed in chapter 6, sees the Tanakh as parallel to the structure of the temple. After the fall of the temple in 70 CE, diaspora Jews formulated a concept of the Bible as being a reflection of, and substitute for, the temple. Thus, many Middle Eastern communities called Scripture *Miqdashyah* (Yahweh's Temple). By drawing intriguing parallels between biblical narratives and ancient temple practices, this approach uncovers symbolic connections, rituals, and spiritual motifs within the text, revealing a deeper layer of significance and resonance with the sacred spaces of antiquity. Aaron ben Asher summarized the analogy this way: "The Torah, *Nevi'im* and *Ketuvim* [. . .] are as the Holy of Holies, the Holy [Place] and the Courtyard of the Tent of Meeting."[12] Viewed through this analogy, one can perceive the Tanakh as God's invitation (Ketuvim), God's word (Nevi'im), and God's presence (Torah).

Results of This Book

Our journey concludes by discussing the implications of viewing the threefold canon through these six approaches. We examine how these approaches to the Tanakh can enrich interpretation, spiritual practices, and scholarly engagement with the biblical text.

- If you accept the Triple Canon approach, I hope that you will find assurance in seeing how God has worked throughout the history of God's people to preserve God's Word.

11. American Bible Society, "State of the Bible USA 2023," 10.
12. Ben Asher, *Sefer Diqduqei ha-Te'amim*, 3–4.

- If you accept the Genre Author approach, I pray that you will be encouraged by knowing that God's authors used specific literary forms to convey God's word to us.
- If you accept the Theological Development approach, may you find rest in the realized Christ as the Yes and Amen of the revealed theology.
- If you accept the Spiritual Guide approach, may the Word of God be a lamp to your feet and a light for your path.
- If you accept the Messianic Trajectory approach, may you find Jesus to be the Yes and Amen of the Hebrew Bible.
- Finally, if you accept the Sacred Structure approach, may you find Scripture to be the place where all people are invited into the presence of God, just as the temple was the beacon of hope on Mount Moriah.

My quest to help a student grasp Ecclesiastes resulted in a fun journey with hermeneutical impact. I have accepted the final view presented in this book. The Karaite's articulation of Ecclesiastes has led me to see all the Ketuvim as sermon texts to evangelize nonbelievers and invite them into becoming the covenant people of God. The journey of writing this book has led me to appreciate the Tanakh order in my personal walk with the Lord, my course lectures, and my preaching. I hope and pray that reading this book will bring about the same fervor for God's Word in your life.

1

Triple Canon Approach

Tanakh as Historical Acceptance of God's Word

HAVE YOU EVER BEEN TO or seen a picture of the Grand Canyon? I went to the canyon with my father, and as we stood on the cliff edge, the park ranger taught me how to understand the various colored layers visible in the canyon walls! Imagine more than thirty different layers of colors, all various types of rock. The park ranger explained that each layer represents a distinct time period of the earth's history. The Triple Canon approach to the Tanakh is exactly the same outlook as the park ranger's explanation of the Grand Canyon: each layer represents a different time period.

As I mentioned in the introduction, I attended four different theological institutions at three different academic levels, and the view discussed in this chapter was the only one I was taught. I was introduced to this approach by the name Triple Canon Theory, and it is the most commonly held view of the three sections of the Tanakh. In essence, the Triple Canon approach argues that the Tanakh is not only structured via the three canonizing periods, but each section is impacted by the context of that period.

Anyone who holds this understanding of the Tanakh necessarily reads the Bible as a transformative journey of Scripture across centuries while highlighting pivotal moments that canonized its content. Not only is the historical situation of the canonizing period important, but the origins and oral traditions that preceded the written form are pivotal to grasp in order to see how they shaped the final form we have today. In light of this, there are several questions to ask if we are to rightly apply this approach to the Tanakh's canonical context.

- How does this text fit into this section (with the canonical view in mind)?
- When was this section of the canon closed?
- In what historical period was the text written and canonized?
- Who compiled this section?
- What is the political purpose of this section?
- How does this approach inform our hermeneutic of this text?
- What are the benefits of applying this approach to this text?
- What are the potential problems with applying this approach to this text?

These questions are demonstrated in the application section below, but for now keep them in mind as we consider the reasons why some hold to this view and some of the potential problems with this view.

Reasons for Adopting This Approach

One reason for adopting this approach is the comprehensive overview of the historical development / canonical structure of the Tanakh that it provides. Through this approach we are aware of how the different parts of the Tanakh were written, compiled, and edited over centuries and shaped by varying historical contexts. Also, through this view we denote how texts progressively gained religious authority and were used within the Jewish community, highlighting the dynamic interplay between religious practice and Scripture. Finally, this approach to the canonization process illustrates how the religious community responded to external influences (e.g., Persian, Hellenistic) and internal developments (e.g., Israelite religious debates).

Another reason for adopting this approach is that it provides a historical framework for interpreting each passage, rather than using a more theoretical hermeneutic that may overlook the historical context of the respective canonical section. The Triple Canon approach ensures that each text is analyzed within the sociopolitical and cultural circumstances surrounding its canonization: the Torah in the postexilic period, focusing on laws and identity restoration; the Nevi'im during the Hellenistic period, emphasizing prophecy and theological reflections on Israel's history; and the Ketuvim, extending from the second century BCE to the first century CE and showcasing Hebrew religious experiences. This view can lead to a hermeneutic that honors the canonical period of each section, whereas a more theoretical hermeneutic might approach the text with overarching interpretive principles such as literary analysis, theological constructs, or ideological frameworks without necessarily grounding the interpretation in specific historical contexts.

Proponents of This Approach[1]

From the early church father Jerome to modern theologians like Richard Bauckham, many have accepted the narrative of how the Tanakh's structure is intertwined with its canonizing periods. In his *Prologue to the Books of the Kings*, Jerome enumerates the Hebrew Scriptures as follows: "Five of Moses, eight of the prophets, nine of the Hagiographa." In his "Historical Study of the Canonization of the Hebrew Scriptures," Zeitlin tells us that the church fathers studied the canonization process but ignored or misconstrued the testimony of the Jewish Tannaim concerning canonization. Origen and Melito even purposely journeyed to Palestine to ascertain firsthand which books were canonized and which were not.[2] While the specific numbering has been a subject of scholarly discussion, Jerome's clear delineation of three distinct sections provided an early and influential framework for understanding the Tanakh's composition. Jerome's categorization, drawn from his interactions with Jewish scholars, implicitly suggests a recognition of different collections of sacred texts, which scholars would later argue correspond to different eras of canonization.

Centuries later, this foundational observation was developed into a more concrete historical theory. The nineteenth-century historian Heinrich Graetz, for instance, famously proposed that the final section of the canon, the Ketuvim, was officially closed at the Council of Jamnia (Yavne) in the late first century CE.[3] Graetz's theory, based on rabbinic discussions of the time, offered a specific historical moment for the canonization of the Writings, thus solidifying the idea that the Tanakh's three parts correspond to distinct chronological periods of acceptance. Although the notion of a formal, binding "Council of Jamnia" has been largely challenged and revised by later scholarship, Graetz's work was instrumental in popularizing the approach of viewing the Tanakh's structure through the history of its canonization.

1. In each chapter, I have selected the proponents that I associate with each interpretive approach, sometimes with suggestions from fellow scholars. Few if any of these scholars explicitly claim the interpretive approach I've assigned them, and many have varied in their methodological approach over the course of their careers.

2. Zeitlin, "Historical Study," vii.

3. Graetz, *Kohelet, oder der Salomonische Prediger*, 164–67.

The subsequent critiques of Graetz's theory did not dismantle the core idea of a chronologically formed canon but rather refined it. Scholars such as Sidney Z. Leiman and Roger Beckwith, for example, argue against the decisiveness of Jamnia and propose that the canon was likely closed at an earlier date, possibly during the Hasmonean dynasty (ca. 140–40 BCE).[4] Beckwith, in his extensive research, points to evidence from sources such as the book of Sirach and the Gospel of Luke—which refer to "the Law and the Prophets" (Sir. prologue) and "the Law of Moses, the Prophets, and the Psalms" (Luke 24:44)—as indications that the first two sections of the canon were well-established by the second century BCE, with the third section being largely recognized as well. By pushing back the timeline, Leiman and Beckwith reinforce the central tenet that the tripartite division of the Tanakh reflects a sequential process of canonization, even if the precise dating remains a subject of academic debate.

Adding another layer of nuance to this understanding is the work of Albert Sundberg.[5] While acknowledging the historical development of the canon, Sundberg emphasizes a crucial distinction between "Scripture" and a "closed canon." He argues that while many texts were considered authoritative Scripture for centuries, the concept of a closed list of books emerged much later. The significance of Sundberg's contribution is in highlighting that the process of canonization was not as neat or linear as a simple three-stage model might suggest. He notes the lack of explicit ancient sources detailing the rationale behind the selection and closing of the canon. This perspective does not negate the tripartite structure's connection to its canonizing period but rather enriches it by suggesting a more organic and protracted process of acceptance for each section.

Finally, the work of Richard Bauckham provides a hermeneutical framework that underscores the importance of the canon's historical formation for its interpretation. Though primarily a New Testament scholar, Bauckham's assertion that the "Bible is God's message in, to and through very particular historical situations" has profound implications for understanding the Tanakh. His call to find the Bible's universality "in and through its particularity"[6] encourages a reading that respects the canonical shape and the historical context of its development. For Bauckham, the very structure of the Tanakh is part of its theological message. Therefore, recognizing the distinct canonizing periods of the Torah, Nevi'im, and Ketuvim is not just a historical exercise but a prerequisite for a faithful and nuanced application of the text.

4. Leiman, *Canon and Masorah of the Hebrew Bible*; Beckwith, *Old Testament Canon*.

5. Sundberg, *Old Testament of the Early Church*; Sundberg, "'Old Testament': A Christian Canon."

6. Bauckham, *Bible in Politics*, 12.

So from Jerome's early tripartite articulation to Bauckham's canonical hermeneutic, we see consistent and evolving support for the idea that the Tanakh's organization is a direct reflection of its canonizing periods. While the specific dates and the nature of the canonization process have been subject to vigorous debate, the overarching consensus remains. The foundational authority of the Torah, the subsequent prophetic traditions, and the more diverse collection of writings represent not just literary categories but also the historical layers of Israel's reception and recognition of its sacred texts. The very structure of the Tanakh, therefore, stands as a testament to its own history, a divinely inspired library assembled and ordered over centuries.

Hermeneutical Realities of This Approach

When adopting the Triple Canon approach to the Tanakh, one must necessarily accept the redacted form of the text that has been handed down to us. In hermeneutics, "authorship" refers to the original writers of the biblical texts, those who composed the material based on their contemporary context, experiences, and purposes. "Redactors" are those who later compiled and edited/modified (i.e., redacted) texts to reflect the concerns and understandings of a later period.

The acceptance of this view, therefore, results in a potential loss of authorial voice/intent so that the edited/compiled section of the Tanakh could be shaped to fit a later time period and the recipients' particular needs. While this may be a troubling loss, I believe that this approach shows how Scripture was carefully preserved and applied to the era of canonization. As a result, we modern readers must deal with reception theory and the form of the text as handed down through the ages. We must admit, though, that the arrangement of books in many print editions of the Hebrew/Christian Bible may not carry any theological weight, since they don't preserve the original order.[7] Regardless of the format (whether scrolls, codices, or a complete bound Bible), the ancient readers would pick up the text and hold it "conceptually in relation" to other sections of the Testament.[8]

Like the notation of authorship and redaction, adherents to this view must be comfortable with canonical recipients leading the shaping of the Tanakh rather than the original recipient. Sadly, many of my friends who hold to this view get bogged down in the canonical situation of a section and completely miss the historical background of the original writer. For my friends, the

7. King, Philpot, and Osborne, *The Law, the Prophets, and the Writings*, 30.
8. King, Philpot, and Osborne, *The Law, the Prophets, and the Writings*, 44.

theological emphasis shifted from the author to the redactor once the text was canonized. Furthermore, the text now emphasizes themes and concerns relevant to the canonizing period, which may differ from those of the original authorial period.

To be fair to adherents of this approach, focusing solely on the original authorial context would ignore the complex redactional history of the text and result in an oversimplification of the text's interpretation. The texts of the Tanakh often contain layers of editing and compilation by different redactors over time, each contributing to the texts in unique ways. Focusing solely on the original recipients, therefore, may overlook the redactional complexities present in the canonical text we possess.

Torah: Canonization of Moses (5th Cent. BCE)

The canonization of the Torah is traditionally thought to have occurred during the postexilic period, around the fifth century BCE. This process unfolded in a time of significant transformation for the Jewish people as they returned from Babylonian exile and sought to reestablish their religious and social identity under Persian rule. The need for a unified and authoritative text became crucial in this context, providing both legal and theological foundations for the restored community.

In the midst of a war-torn Israel, the Torah assumed a central role in rebuilding the nation and grounding its future generations. The Babylonian exile, which lasted from 586 to 539 BCE, had a profound impact on Jewish identity, worship, and governance centered around the temple in Jerusalem. According to Weinfeld, "The destruction of the Temple created a vacuum that was filled by the Torah . . . the emphasis was transferred from cult to Scripture."[9] So when considering the Torah in light of the exile, we must see it as being organized to replace the temple.

After the Persian conquest of Babylon, King Cyrus issued a decree permitting the exiled Jewish population to return to their homeland (Ezra 1:1–4), and a small portion of the Jews returned to war-torn Judah/Israel to rebuild. They rebuilt not only their country and temple but also their lives. At the heart of this rebuilding was the continued centrality of the Torah. The return from exile was not merely a physical return but a recommitment to the law, to the Torah, which had to be read, taught, obeyed, and transmitted. The text of the Torah therefore needed to be redacted and collected in order to clearly articulate the Hebrew religion and way of life. With its laws, historical

9. Weinfeld, *Deuteronomy and the Deuteronomic School*, 21.

narratives, and covenantal themes, the Torah provided a unifying framework for Jewish life. It functioned as a national history database, a legal constitution, and a theological guide. As Sanders explains, "Torah was not merely law but was story-shaped instruction, an ongoing narrative that governed the people's present conduct and future hope."[10]

One of the most significant figures in the postexilic period was Ezra the priest-scribe. According to the biblical accounts, Ezra led a group of exiles back to Jerusalem and initiated religious reforms that emphasized adherence to the Mosaic law. "The authority of the Torah became fixed in the Persian period," observes McDonald, who credits "Ezra and those associated with him" for their efforts "to make the Torah the constitution of Jewish life."[11] As Neh. 8 describes, Ezra publicly read the Torah to the assembly of returned exiles: "They read from the book, from the Law of God, clearly; and they gave the sense, so that the people understood the reading" (Neh. 8:8).

During this event, the Levites helped interpret the Torah, and the returned Israelites applied it as the foundation of life and practice. Ezra's actions signify not only religious revival but also the establishment of the Torah as a normative and binding text for the Jewish people. "The Law was no longer simply one component of Israel's religious life," argues Christopher Seitz, "but became the comprehensive framework for religious, social, and political existence."[12]

When interpreting passages from the Torah, it is crucial to consider the sociopolitical context of the postexilic Jewish community. The return from exile was not merely a physical restoration but also a theological reaffirmation of their covenant with God. The commandments, rituals, and legal structures within the Torah were central to this process. Brevard Childs summarizes: "The final canonical shaping of the Torah served to crystallize Israel's faith as a norm for future generations, binding the community to a divinely sanctioned past and projecting hope into the future."[13]

Torah Test Case: The Call of Abraham (Gen. 12:1–3)

What Is This Text About?

Genesis 12:1–3 marks a decisive turning point in the narrative of the Tanakh. In this text, God calls Abram to leave his land, family, and heritage, and God promises to make him a great nation, bless him, and make his name great. Most

10. Sanders, *Canon and Community*, 42.
11. McDonald, *Formation of the Biblical Canon*, 1:83.
12. Seitz, *Goodly Fellowship of the Prophets*, 36.
13. Childs, *Introduction to the Old Testament as Scripture*, 128.

notably, God declares, "In you all the families of the earth shall be blessed" (Gen. 12:3). This covenantal moment becomes the theological foundation not only for Israel's identity but also for its mission to the nations. As Walter Brueggemann notes, "This text initiates a new history, not only for Abraham but for the world, because of God's resolve to bless all families of the earth."[14]

How Does This Text Fit into This Section?

According to Brevard Childs, "Genesis 12:1–3 is not simply the beginning of the Abraham cycle, but the structuring principle of the entire Pentateuchal narrative."[15] As such, Gen. 12:1–3 falls within the Torah, which forms the theological and narrative backbone of the Hebrew Bible. Specifically, this text stands at the hinge between the primeval history (Gen. 1–11) and the patriarchal narratives (Gen. 12–50). While the opening chapters of Genesis offer a universal lens on humanity, sin, and judgment, Gen. 12 narrows the focus to a particular person and a chosen lineage. The missional and redemptive focus of the entire canon begins here.

When Was This Section of the Canon Closed?

Although many hold to Mosaic authorship of the Torah, including either written or oral traditions preserved from the patriarchal period, it is widely accepted among scholars that the Torah reached its final form (at the least canonization) during or after the Babylonian exile (6th–5th cent. BCE). This canonization period reflects theological, political, and social concerns that shaped the community's identity. As Jon Levenson observes, "The Abrahamic promise was a key instrument in constructing a postexilic identity: a people in exile, like Abraham, still anchored in divine election."[16] In a time when land, temple, and sovereignty were stripped away, Gen. 12:1–3 offered a theological answer to a pressing national question: Can we still be the people of God in exile? Abraham, who left his homeland and had no temple, was still chosen and blessed by God. Thus, exilic and postexilic readers found in Abraham a paradigm for faithfulness and identity without territorial anchoring.

In What Historical Period Was This Text Written and Canonized?

While the events of Abraham's life may stem from the second millennium BCE, the redaction and canonization of this text reflect postexilic theological

14. Brueggemann, *Genesis*, 116.
15. Childs, *Introduction to the Old Testament as Scripture*, 146.
16. Levenson, *Inheriting Abraham*, 72.

needs. This was a time of rebuilding under Persian rule, when scribal elites such as Ezra played a significant role in renewing covenant fidelity and defining Jewish identity. Socially, Gen. 12 affirms divine election in the face of foreign rule. Politically, it asserts that land and blessing are gifts from God, not the result of imperial conquest. Religiously, as Mark Boda notes, "The Abrahamic covenant served to unite the exilic and postexilic communities under the banner of divine promise, even in the absence of political autonomy."[17]

Who Compiled This Section?

Though theories such as the Documentary Hypothesis (JEDP) suggest multiple sources over time, it is plausible that a redactor, possibly Ezra or another priestly figure, shaped Gen. 12 into its final form for a postexilic audience. The priestly editors emphasized covenant, purity, and divine initiative—elements richly embedded in Gen. 12. Ezra, often traditionally referred to as the "second Moses," may well have been the theological architect behind the Torah's final shape. Rabbinic tradition holds that "Ezra would have been worthy to receive the Torah had Moses not preceded him" (b. Sanhedrin 21b).

What Is the Political Purpose of This Section?

Genesis 12:1–3 not only defines Israel's theological origins but also functions as a charter for its vocation and political identity. The promise of land and nationhood, grounded not in conquest but in divine calling, legitimized Israel's presence and purpose in Canaan—especially during times of displacement. The postexilic community, struggling under foreign powers, needed to be reminded that their chosenness was not invalidated by their lack of sovereignty. This text subtly challenges imperial narratives by rooting Israel's identity in a divine promise rather than in military might.

How Does This Approach Inform Our Hermeneutic of This Text?

The Triple Canon approach invites us to read Gen. 12:1–3 not only as an ancient story but also as a deliberately positioned theological introduction to Israel's role in God's redemptive plan. The text doesn't just introduce Abraham; it also launches a theological trajectory toward universal blessing.

This approach emphasizes the function of the text in its final form. The text becomes an invitation to see Israel's exile not as merely a failure but as a continuation/reliving of the Abrahamic life and mission to bless the nations, even hostile ones.

17. Boda, *Return to Me*, 67.

What Are the Benefits of Applying This Approach to This Text?

1. Theological clarity: This approach highlights God's unwavering mission to bless through Israel.
2. Narrative coherence: It links the promise to Abraham with Israel's story and prophetic fulfillment.
3. Canonical consistency: It shows the continuity of God's plan through the Torah, the Nevi'im, and the Ketuvim.
4. Missional ethic: It also interprets divine election as a call to serve others, not for self-exaltation.

What Are the Potential Problems in Applying This Approach to This Text?

1. Ambiguity: The blending of redaction layers can obscure the original historical setting.
2. Reductionism: Overemphasizing political or canonical context may sideline theological richness.
3. Anachronism: Projecting postexilic concerns onto patriarchal material may distort earlier intentions.
4. Fragmentation: A focus on redaction history might challenge beliefs in the unity and inspiration of the text.

Summary of Test Case

Genesis 12:1–3 stands as a theological and narrative cornerstone within the Tanakh, marking a shift from universal human history (Gen. 1–11) to God's particular covenant with Abraham and his subsequent family. The location of this text introduces a missional trajectory that shapes the entire biblical canon. Its canonization, likely finalized in the exilic/postexilic period, responds to the social and theological crises of exile, offering a model of faithful identity rooted in the divine promise of God's covenantal faithfulness rather than in land or temple. The text's political situation, especially during foreign domination, comforts the returned people and confirms Israel's sense of chosenness and vocation to bless all nations. As Gerhard von Rad concludes, "The patriarchal history is not a nostalgic memory but a mirror in which Israel must continually rediscover itself."[18] Through the Triple Canon approach to the Tanakh, Gen. 12:1–3 is read not merely as a historical record

18. Von Rad, *Genesis*, 148.

but as a purposeful theological prologue to Israel's role in God's redemptive plan, even in the midst of exile. While this approach faces interpretive tensions, such as historical layering, it yields rich insight into the coherence, calling, and hope embedded in the Abrahamic covenant, making it foundational for understanding Israel's story and mission throughout the Tanakh.

Nevi'im: Canonization of Prophetic Messages (3rd Cent. BCE)

The canonization of the Nevi'im took place during the Hellenistic period, approximately between the third and second centuries BCE.[19] This section of the Hebrew Bible consists of the Former Prophets (Joshua, Judges, Samuel, and Kings) and the Latter Prophets (Isaiah, Jeremiah, Ezekiel, and the Twelve Minor Prophets). The process of recognizing these texts as authoritative Scripture was influenced by historical, theological, and cultural factors.

Like the Torah's preservation and articulation of the Hebrew way of life and belief, the prophetic books continue the historical narratives and offer theological reflections on the Torah during a time of foreign rule and cultural challenges. In that time, Walter Brueggemann notes, "the prophets functioned as interpreters of history who rendered the events of Israel's life intelligible in terms of God's covenant and justice."[20] In essence, these prophetic books demonstrate how the Israelites' faithfulness or disobedience to the covenant impacted their fate, both historically and in the contemporary Hellenistic crisis, reinforcing the theological themes found in the Torah.

Differing from the Former Prophets, the Latter Prophets provide divine messages during critical periods in Israel's history. They offer interpretations of historical events, divine warnings, calls for repentance, and messages of hope for restoration. As Brevard Childs observes, "The prophetic writings serve as a theological bridge between the history of Israel and the future hopes of the people, conveying God's judgment and mercy."[21] In this way, the prophetic books interpret Israel's past while shaping its religious future.

Hellenistic rule, in particular, "presented a challenge to Jewish religious identity, provoking a defensive reaction aimed at preserving and defining Judaism's distinctiveness," Martin Hengel explains.[22] According to the Triple Canon approach to the Tanakh, Jewish leaders preserved Jewish belief and life first through the sacred texts of the Torah and then through the Nevi'im.

19. Zeitlin, "Historical Study."
20. Brueggemann, *Theology of the Old Testament*, 154.
21. Childs, *Introduction to the Old Testament as Scripture*, 186.
22. Hengel, *Judaism and Hellenism*, 32.

So by the third to second centuries BCE, the canon of Scripture included the Nevi'im. The prophetic books—with their themes of covenant, judgment, and restoration—became essential for articulating Jewish identity in an era of cultural pressure and uncertainty. As Joseph Fitzmyer makes clear, "The prophetic tradition served as a source of resistance against foreign domination, inspiring hope for divine intervention and renewal."[23] The prophets' emphasis on Israel's unique covenant with God helped counteract Hellenistic cultural assimilation and reinforced Jewish religious distinctiveness. They were publicly read and taught as critical sources for identity, which reinforced their status as Scripture. Géza Vermès points out that the synagogue became a center for preserving and transmitting the prophetic tradition, which was regarded as vital for sustaining the community's faith.[24] Over time, the prophetic writings came to be viewed as containing timeless wisdom and divine instruction, further solidifying their place within the canon.

Interpreting the prophetic books requires an understanding of the historical and cultural context of their canonization. The messages from the Assyrian and Babylonian periods must be read in light of the later Greek invasions and cultural upheavals. For example, the book of Isaiah is often utilized because it contains prophecies addressing both immediate political situations and long-term eschatological hopes. The early chapters warn of Assyrian aggression, while later sections shift toward themes of restoration and the coming of an ideal future ruler. Isaiah 7:14 proclaims, "Therefore the Lord himself will give you a sign: The virgin will conceive and give birth to a son, and will call him Immanuel" (NIV), pointing toward a future hope beyond the immediate crisis.

Similarly, Jeremiah's prophecies focus on the impending Babylonian exile, yet also include promises of a new covenant:

> "The days are coming," declares the Lord,
>   "when I will make a new covenant with the people of Israel. . . .
> I will put my law in their minds
>   and write it on their hearts." (Jer. 31:31, 33 NIV)

In sum, prophetic books speak to both their original audiences and later generations seeking meaning in their own historical circumstances. As John Goldingay observes, "The prophetic corpus challenges readers across generations to see God's ongoing purposes in history, continually shaping community identity and hope."[25]

23. Fitzmyer, *Dead Sea Scrolls and Christian Origins*, 107.
24. Vermès, *Complete Dead Sea Scrolls*, 115.
25. Goldingay, *Old Testament Theology*, 291.

Nevi'im Test Case: God's Choice of David (1 Sam. 16:7)

What Is This Text About?

First Samuel 16:7 is well-known because of one phrase: "Man looks on the outward appearance, but the Lord looks on the heart." In the context, God instructs the prophet Samuel not to judge by outward appearance when choosing a new king for Israel, for David was "ruddy" and the least of the eight brothers. This verse, and the phrase contained therein, emphasizes that divine evaluation is based on inner character and intent, not external qualities such as height, beauty, or strength. It sets the stage for God's choice of David, a young shepherd overlooked by others but chosen by God for his heart.[26]

How Does This Text Fit into This Section?

First Samuel 16:7 is located within the Nevi'im, specifically in the Former Prophets, the subdivision that includes the books of Joshua, Judges, Samuel, and Kings. These books offer a theological history of Israel from the conquest of Canaan to the Babylonian exile. While often called "historical books" in Christian circles, in the Jewish canon they are regarded as prophetic, not because they contain prophetic oracles, but because they interpret Israel's past through the lens of covenant faithfulness or failure, just as the writing prophets do in the Latter Prophets.

The Former Prophets function as theological narratives that reflect on Israel's history under the guidance of divine sovereignty. First Samuel 16:7 encapsulates a central prophetic concern: the nature of God's choice in leadership. God's rejection of Saul and selection of David based on the "heart" rather than on "outward appearance" signals a prophetic redefinition of kingship, emphasizing spiritual integrity over human expectation. This aligns with the prophetic call across the Nevi'im to prioritize covenant loyalty and inward righteousness over formal rituals or worldly strength (cf. Isa. 1:11–17; Mic. 6:6–8).

When Was This Section of the Canon Closed?

The Nevi'im portion of the canon was likely finalized during the Second Temple period, in the third century BCE. Scholars agree that while the material within these books originated in earlier periods, the canonical shaping—especially the final form of the Former Prophets—took place postexile, as part

26. I am aware of the concept of the "heart after God" being "God's heart for David." For more on this, see Sandra Richter, *Epic of Eden*. However, for the sake of this book, I'm sticking with the traditional handling of this text for this particular interpretive approach.

of the theological reflection on Israel's failures and hoped-for restoration. This finalization did not merely preserve historical memory but offered theological interpretation rooted in covenant theology. As John Sailhamer observes, "The ordering of the books of the Hebrew Bible is part of the meaning of the books themselves."[27] The placement of Samuel in the Nevi'im indicates that it is to be read not merely as a history of kings but as prophetic commentary on leadership in light of divine purposes.

In What Historical Period Was This Text Written and Canonized?

The events of 1 Sam. 16 reflect the period of Israel's early monarchy, likely in the eleventh–tenth centuries BCE. This was a period of consolidation under a centralized king, a major shift from tribal confederation to monarchy. The tension between Saul and David reflects broader anxieties about this transition, especially whether kingship would align with God's purposes.

The canonization of 1 Samuel occurred in the exilic or early postexilic period (6th–5th cent. BCE), though it reached its final placement within the Nevi'im around the third century BCE. Politically, this was a time when Israel had lost its sovereignty and lived under successive foreign empires (Babylonian, Persian, and Hellenistic). Theologically, the crisis of exile prompted deep reflection on why the monarchy had failed and what kind of leadership might bring renewal. First Samuel 16:7 answers that question by proposing a divine criterion for leadership centered on moral character and covenant loyalty, presumably with the hope that the people of God will follow the will of God in selecting a leader who is for God, not against God.

Who Compiled This Section?

The Former Prophets, which includes 1–2 Samuel, are often attributed to the Deuteronomistic Historians, a school of exilic scribes influenced by the theology of Deuteronomy. Martin Noth's classic thesis argues that during the exile a single theological editor or school compiled these texts to explain Israel's collapse as a result of covenant unfaithfulness.[28] Later scholars like Frank Moore Cross propose a double redaction theory, adding nuance to this editorial process. These compilers likely shaped the narratives with deliberate theological messaging. David's heart-centered election in 1 Sam. 16 was not merely a historical anecdote. Rather, it expressed a canonical ideal meant to critique prior failures (such as Saul) and offer a theological vision for future leaders.

27. Sailhamer, *Introduction to Old Testament Theology*, 212.
28. Noth, *Deuteronomistic History*.

What Is the Political Purpose of This Section?

First Samuel 16:7 serves an overtly political function. It critiques the superficial and worldly standards of leadership that Saul embodied and reorients authority around divine selection and internal righteousness. In exile or post-monarchic contexts, this text redefines what legitimate leadership looks like in the absence of a Davidic king. In fact, it sets up the Davidic ideal, which plays a critical role in the rest of Samuel and Kings and is central to later prophetic expectations of a messianic figure. David is not perfect, but his selection serves as a theological anchor for interpreting both the monarchy's potential and its failure. This verse articulates the kind of leadership the Former Prophets value: humble, chosen, and aligned with God's heart.

During the third century BCE, under Hellenistic rule, Jewish leadership was largely priestly or scribal. In such a context, texts such as 1 Sam. 16:7 offered hope for national renewal through covenant fidelity, not political conquest. As Jon Levenson explains, "The canon is not merely a repository of past events but a tool for forming future identity."[29] For this reason, the text is politically subversive: it declares that God's approval transcends appearances, titles, or foreign domination. It affirms that leadership aligned with God's will can arise even under oppressive regimes.

How Does This Approach Inform Our Hermeneutic of This Text?

Interpreting 1 Sam. 16:7 using the Triple Canon approach requires that we read it not merely in its historical context but also in its final canonical placement and theological function. Since the Nevi'im section was canonized in the third century BCE, this verse should be understood as addressing concerns relevant to that era: leadership without kingship, faithfulness under foreign rule, and the search for moral guidance in a fragmented community.

The Triple Canon approach discourages purely historical readings. It encourages a theological hermeneutic sensitive to canonical trajectory and literary framing. The emphasis on the "heart" echoes themes developed across the Nevi'im, especially in Jer. 17:10 and Ezek. 36:26, showing a canonical unity around internal transformation as central to Israel's restoration.

What Are the Benefits of Applying This Approach to This Text?

1. Theological anthropology: The text affirms that God evaluates humans based on their hearts, not on appearance. This offers a high view of human responsibility and divine discernment.

29. Levenson, *Hebrew Bible, the Old Testament, and Historical Criticism*, 10.

2. Moral leadership: In a time of political instability, this view proposes an enduring vision of godly leadership that is inwardly faithful rather than outwardly impressive.
3. Canonical consistency: The emphasis on the heart ties this text to broader prophetic themes, helping readers see theological unity across diverse texts.
4. Ethical relevance: The text remains relevant in any age as a critique of superficial leadership, reminding communities to value character over charisma.
5. Liturgical and pedagogical utility: This interpretation makes the text applicable for instruction, prayer, and identity formation, especially in times of political uncertainty.

What Are the Potential Problems in Applying This Approach to This Text?

1. Overspiritualization: Focusing solely on the "heart" may ignore the communal, institutional, and political dimensions of kingship. Leadership is about not just piety but also public responsibility.
2. Idealization of David: This view risks idealizing David in a way that ignores his moral failures, thus flattening the text's narrative tension.
3. Canonical flattening: Canonical readings may obscure the diversity of sources and voices in the Former Prophets, leading to overly harmonized interpretations.
4. Historical distance: The political and cultural assumptions behind this view (e.g., monarchy, divine election) may feel distant to modern readers, limiting its accessibility.
5. Misapplication of "God knows the heart": This theme, while comforting, can be misused to excuse unethical behavior under the assumption that external actions are secondary to inner intentions.

Summary of Test Case

Viewed through the lens of its canonical placement and third-century BCE finalization, 1 Sam. 16:7 emerges not just as a memorable verse about divine perception but as a cornerstone of prophetic theology. The message that God prioritizes the heart over outward appearance provides a theological critique of leadership rooted in covenantal values. Finalized during a time of political displacement and spiritual searching, this verse functioned as a guiding principle for true leadership amid the absence of a Davidic king.

Canonically situated within the Former Prophets, the verse becomes part of a broader narrative aimed at shaping Israel's understanding of divine sovereignty, covenant faithfulness, and moral leadership. Rather than a mere historical detail, David's selection based on the heart exemplifies the prophetic vision for Israel's future, one where spiritual integrity outweighs social stature or political strength.

For modern readers, 1 Sam. 16:7 remains a powerful theological and ethical guide. It challenges communities to value character over charisma, inner faithfulness over outer conformity, and divine alignment over popular approval. Its enduring relevance lies in its call to reimagine leadership not as a position of power but as a vocation marked by humility, integrity, and a heart aligned with God's purposes.

Ketuvim: Canonization of Reflections on Life and Wisdom (1st Cent. CE)

The final stage of the Hebrew Bible's canonization is that of the Ketuvim, a diverse collection of texts that includes poetry, wisdom literature, historical narratives, and philosophical reflections. Their accumulation occurred over an extended period, from approximately the second century BCE to the first century CE, making it the most gradual and complex section of canon formation. Unlike the Torah, which was recognized as authoritative early in Jewish history, and the Nevi'm, which gained widespread acceptance due to its theological significance, the Ketuvim underwent a slower and more varied process of canonization. Different Jewish communities recognized these texts at different times, and some books faced debate over their inclusion. The famous canon list found in Josephus had twenty-two books.[30]

Books such as Psalms and Proverbs had clear liturgical and didactic functions and were widely accepted early on. Brevard Childs concludes that Psalms quickly "functioned as Israel's hymnbook and prayerbook, and Proverbs as the wisdom manual that shaped ethical life."[31] However, some books faced greater scrutiny. For example, Ecclesiastes, with its seemingly skeptical and philosophical tone, raised concerns among scholars because of its questioning of traditional values.[32] Likewise, the spiritual and canonical value of the Song of Songs was debated until the sensual and romantic imagery of this poetic work was later interpreted allegorically as representing the love relationship between God and Israel. As Phyllis Trible explains, "The Song of Songs'

30. Josephus, *Against Apion* 1.37–41.
31. Childs, *Introduction to the Old Testament as Scripture*, 202.
32. Lieb, Mason, and Roberts, *Oxford Handbook of the Reception History of the Bible*, 364–67.

metaphorical reading provided a bridge to understanding its theological significance beyond its literal eroticism."[33] Rabbinic debates over the status of certain books within the Ketuvim are recorded in the Mishnah and Talmud. Bava Batra 14b–15a in the Babylonian Talmud records a famous debate about the inclusion of Ecclesiastes, Song of Songs, and Esther in the canon, revealing the diversity of opinion within Jewish tradition.

By the first century CE, many of these books were widely used in Jewish communities, as this quote from the Babylonian Talmud indicates:

> Our rabbis have taught: there are three kings [of significance for dreams]. . . . There are three larger books of the Hagiographa [of significance for dreams]. If one sees the book of Psalms, he may hope for piety; if the book of Proverbs, he may hope for wisdom; if the book of Job, let him be afraid of punishment. There are three smaller books of the Hagiographa [of significance for dreams]. If one sees the Song of Songs in a dream, he may hope for piety; if Ecclesiastes, he may hope for wisdom; if Lamentations, let him be afraid of punishment; [and one who sees the Scroll of Esther will have a miracle wrought for him]. (b. Berakhot 57b)[34]

I believe that the rabbinic movement played a decisive role in shaping and solidifying the Jewish biblical canon, particularly in the case of the Ketuvim. A potential key moment often associated with this process is the supposed Council of Jamnia, where Jewish leaders reportedly discussed various aspects of Scripture, including the status of Ecclesiastes and Song of Songs. As mentioned earlier in this chapter, the notion of a formal, binding Council of Jamnia has been largely challenged and revised by later scholarship, but even if Jamnia didn't happen, there was indeed a selection process for these books, likely a long, gradual process that culminated in the acceptance of the Ketuvim as Scripture. So by the first century CE, the canon of the Ketuvim was established, forming the final section of the Hebrew Bible.

In contrast to the Torah and Nevi'im, the Ketuvim requires varied interpretive techniques due to its diversity of literary genres and themes. Because these texts span a long historical period and cover a wide array of topics, from the skepticism of Ecclesiastes to the Psalms' hymns of praise, their interpretation is influenced by various historical and philosophical periods, including Hellenistic thought and Second Temple Judaism. As Michael Fishbane points out, "The Writings reflect the religious pluralism and intellectual complexity of late Second Temple Judaism, inviting readers to engage with theological

33. Trible, *God and the Rhetoric of Sexuality*, 41.
34. Leiman, *Canonization of Hebrew Scripture*, 70.

reflection in multiple forms."[35] Thus I propose that the Ketuvim is best read in light of Second Temple Judaism's intellectual milieu and the way each book was used in Israelite/Jewish worship and communal life.

Ketuvim Test Case: The Lament over Jerusalem (Lam. 1)

What Is This Text About?

Lamentations 1 gives voice to Jerusalem's catastrophic fall at the hands of the Babylonians in 586 BCE. The chapter opens with the image of the once-glorious city now sitting alone "like a widow" (1:1), forsaken by her allies, deserted by her people, and judged for her transgressions. The poet speaks with vivid, wrenching imagery: the roads mourn (v. 4), her priests groan (v. 4), her children are captive (v. 5), and there is no one to comfort her (vv. 2, 9, 16, 17, 21). The city is personified as a grieving woman, left desolate and shamed under the weight of both divine judgment and the loss of her dignity.

Theologically, the chapter connects Jerusalem's suffering directly to her covenantal failures:

> Jerusalem has grievously sinned;
> therefore she has become filthy. (Lam. 1:8 AT)

Yet, this is not simply theology; it is desperate, tear-soaked poetry, and the speaker does not treat God's justice as unwarranted. Instead, Lam. 1 is filled with pleas for God to see, remember, and respond:

> Is it nothing to you, all you who pass by?
> Look and see
> if there is any sorrow like my sorrow. (Lam. 1:12)

The tension between guilt, grief, and a desperate longing for divine attention pervades the chapter.

How Does This Text Fit into This Section?

Lamentations belongs to the third major division of the Hebrew Bible, the Ketuvim. Unlike the Torah and the Nevi'im—which were canonized earlier and center on law, covenant history, and prophetic voices—the Ketuvim contains a diverse collection of theological reflection, poetry, and wisdom literature spanning a wide range of postexilic and Second Temple concerns.

35. Fishbane, *Biblical Interpretation*, 256.

Lamentations fits this category well. It is deeply reflective, highly poetic (structured as an alphabetic acrostic), and liturgical in tone.

Its placement in the Ketuvim, which was finalized by the first century CE, allows Lamentations to function not just as historical memory but as theological meditation. It is less a record of prophecy than a processing of prophetic fulfillment: Jerusalem has fallen, the temple has been destroyed, and now the question is What does faithful mourning look like?

In its canonical context, this lament is not merely historical residue. Rather, it becomes part of a community's ongoing response to trauma. As Kathleen M. O'Connor writes, "Lamentations does not explain suffering; it performs it."[36] Within the Ketuvim, this performative grief takes on a liturgical life of its own, particularly through commemorative rituals such as the annual fast day of Tisha B'Av, when Jews mourn the destruction of Jerusalem and both temples.

When Was This Section of the Canon Closed?

While the content of Lamentations likely dates to shortly after 586 BCE, the Ketuvim, the section of the Tanakh where it resides, was not finalized until the late Second Temple period, likely around the first century CE. During this time, Jewish communities under Roman occupation were grappling with questions of identity, memory, and fidelity in the absence of their own sovereign kingdom. By the time of its canonization, Lamentations no longer simply recounted Jerusalem's first destruction; it also served as a theological and liturgical script for understanding suffering across generations. The delay in canonizing the Ketuvim, in contrast to the Torah (5th cent. BCE) and Nevi'im (3rd cent. BCE), reflects the evolving concerns of a community forced to reinterpret its past and its relationship with God under new and changing imperial powers. Lamentations, therefore, became not just a lament over one specific loss but a paradigmatic text for sacred mourning and national repentance.

In What Historical Period Was This Text Written and Canonized?

Lamentations was written in the immediate aftermath of the Babylonian siege and destruction of Jerusalem in 586 BCE. Politically, Judah was shattered; socially, its population had been exiled or killed; and religiously, the loss of the temple posed a crisis of cosmic proportions. The destruction of the house of God seemed to call into question the very covenantal promise of God's presence among his people.

36. O'Connor, *Lamentations*, 23.

This poem arose out of that crucible. Its raw language and acrostic structure suggest a liturgical function even in its earliest stages. Tremper Longman posits that "the use of acrostics may suggest an attempt to bring order to chaos, to give structure to unstructured pain."[37]

By the time it was canonized within the Ketuvim, however, Lamentations functioned as more than a cry of the exiled. It became the voice of the faithful remnant, a ritualized grief that continued to frame Jewish suffering even into the Roman era. Canonization within the Ketuvim thus recontextualized its meaning across successive generations of loss.

Who Compiled This Section?

While the traditional ascription to Jeremiah persists (due to 2 Chron. 35:25 and linguistic similarities to the book of Jeremiah), modern scholarship often sees the book as a product of multiple poets or scribal disciples influenced by Jeremiah's school. These were likely exilic or postexilic scribes who preserved and shaped the poetic laments for liturgical use.

The canonizing figures who placed Lamentations in the Ketuvim, possibly the scribes associated with Ezra's lineage or later custodians of temple tradition, recognized its communal utility. They weren't just preserving history; they were embedding theological practice. As Emanuel Tov notes, "The Ketuvim were shaped not only by theological aims but also by their use in liturgical and instructional settings."[38]

What Is the Political Purpose of This Section?

Lamentations 1 does have a political dimension, but it is the politics of the theocracy rather than of earthly empires. The poem portrays Jerusalem's suffering not merely as the result of Babylonian aggression but as the outworking of divine judgment. In this sense, it critiques both Judah's misplaced political alliances and its spiritual rebellion.

The chapter does not protest foreign oppression directly but instead reframes Judah's fall as a theological consequence. It calls attention to failed political strategy (e.g., reliance on Egypt) and failed covenant fidelity:

> Her foes have become the head; . . .

not because of Babylon's might, but

37. Longman, *Jeremiah, Lamentations*, 321.
38. Tov, *Textual Criticism*, 157.

> because the Lord has afflicted her
> for the multitude of her transgressions. (Lam. 1:5)

The politics are internal; they are Judah's failure to trust in divine sovereignty over worldly power. And yet there is an undercurrent of protest:

> Look, O Lord, and see,
> for I am despised. (Lam. 1:11)

It is the cry of suffering under empire, a theological lament shaped by political displacement.

How Does This Approach Inform Our Hermeneutic of This Text?

Interpreting Lamentations through a canon-conscious lens, particularly with attention to its late placement in the Ketuvim, allows us to read the text as a deliberate theological meditation and not simply as a historical account. Its position in the Ketuvim frames it as an ongoing voice in Israel's spiritual life—not bound to one moment but relevant to many moments.

The Triple Canon approach helps modern readers see Lamentations as part of a larger biblical arc, from exile to return, from judgment to restoration. It becomes a ritual of grief that validates communal suffering while holding open the door to hope. "Lamentations is not the end of the story," writes Leslie C. Allen. "It points to the value of hope even when all seems lost."[39]

What Are the Benefits of Applying This Approach to This Text?

1. Sacred space for grief: Lamentations legitimizes lament as a spiritual act. It demonstrates that grief, mourning, and questioning are not antithetical to faith.
2. Call to repentance: The poem's reflection on sin and its consequences provides a theological framework for national and personal introspection.
3. Tension between justice and mercy: By not resolving the tension, Lamentations invites deeper engagement with God's character and the paradoxes of divine action.
4. Timeless voice: Its canonization in the Ketuvim ensures Lamentations' role as a transhistorical voice of suffering and hope, allowing each generation to reenter the pain and prayer of exilic loss.

39. Allen, *Book of Lamentations*, 8.

What Are the Potential Problems in Applying This Approach to This Text?

1. Overemphasis on retribution: There is a danger in reading the suffering solely as divine punishment, which may lead to victim-blaming or spiritual fatalism.
2. Detachment from modern contexts: The language and imagery, deeply embedded in ancient Jerusalem's destruction, might feel inaccessible to those unacquainted with its historical setting.
3. Cultural and religious exclusivity: The liturgical nature of Lamentations may limit its resonance outside Jewish tradition unless carefully contextualized.

Summary of Test Case

The canonization of Lamentations within the Ketuvim during the first century CE represents a crucial development in Jewish theological thought. Rather than occurring in a single decisive moment, the process of canonization reflected the gradual recognition of Lamentations' enduring value as a resource for communal worship, theological reflection, and identity formation. Its placement within the Ketuvim, rather than among the Nevi'im, signals its primary function as corporate liturgical poetry that provides a theological framework for understanding suffering, divine justice, and communal responsibility. This canonization established Lamentations as more than a historical document; it is a sacred memory designed to shape how future generations understand and respond to catastrophe, just as it shaped past generations. In this way, Lamentations offers a communal reflection, models theological patience, and demonstrates the legitimacy of honest lament within faith communities.

Conclusion

The Triple Canon approach presents the most widely accepted view of the Tanakh's structure and development. It asserts that the three major sections of the Hebrew Bible were each canonized during distinct historical periods and that the content, tone, and theological emphases of each section were shaped in response to the social, political, and religious realities of the canonizing time period. Far from being static or artificially segmented, this tripartite canon emerges as a dynamic, evolving narrative, reflective of Israel's journey with God through changing historical periods.

Those who adopt this perspective read the Tanakh not as a merely static sacred text but as a living testimony to centuries of transformation, from authorship to canonization period. From the oral traditions and early writings through redaction and eventual canonization, this view urges interpreters to ask essential questions of each text: What is this text's canonical placement? What is the purpose of this text within this section of the Tanakh? How did its historical moment shape its message? These questions root interpretation in the real-life challenges, hopes, and theological wrestlings of Israel across generations.

The strength of this approach lies in its ability to frame each text within the particularities of its canonical context. It sheds light on the Torah's focus on law and identity during the postexilic restoration, the Nevi'im's urgent theological reflection during times of national crisis under Hellenistic influence, and the Ketuvim's diverse meditations in a scattered and evolving religious community in the first century BCE. It honors the historical, communal, and spiritual layers of the text, making it accessible to readers who value both divine inspiration and historical awareness.

The Triple Canon approach is not without its critiques. It risks overemphasizing historical circumstances at the expense of theological depth. The layered nature of redaction may blur the lines between original intention and final form, leading to historical ambiguity. There is also the danger of projecting later concerns onto earlier texts or of fragmenting the unity of Scripture by focusing too narrowly on its formation rather than its function as a cohesive canon.

Still, the benefits are significant. The Triple Canon approach illuminates God's continuous work in history, provides narrative coherence across the Tanakh, and reinforces the missional ethic that divine election is never for privilege alone but for service to the world. It affirms that each stage of canonization did not dilute Scripture's relevance but rather enriched it by capturing the full range of Israel's experience with God, from Sinai to exile to diaspora.

In sum, the Triple Canon approach offers a historically grounded, theologically rich, and canonically sensitive framework for engaging the Tanakh. It invites readers into a conversation that spans centuries, urging them to see not only what the text says but why it was preserved in the form we now cherish.

2

Genre Author Approach

Tanakh as Literary Authorial Genres

WE LOVE TAKING OUR DAUGHTER to the local library. In the library are various signs identifying the type of literature found in each section. My daughter immediately runs to the children's board-book section and starts grabbing books to read. I usually gravitate toward the nonfiction section to look for books on ancient history or the Old Testament. My wife loves to browse the fiction section to find the latest book by one of her favorite authors. Our library is not only organized by genre but also alphabetized by author within each subcategory. Most of us have learned by experience that recognizing a book's genre and knowing something about its author prepares us to better understand the text we are reading.

This second approach to perceiving the Tanakh's structure is like our local library in that it distinguishes the three sections by genre and author. As Adele Berlin notes, "To understand biblical literature, we must know what kind of literature we are reading. . . . Genre is an interpretive aid."[1] Scholars following this approach sometimes use genre or authorship or both to help articulate the point being made by the biblical text. Hermeneutically speaking, genre and authorship are intrinsically relevant to understanding the text.

When viewed through the Genre Author approach, Torah is law that is authored/influenced by Moses, the Nevi'im contains visionary insights and prophetic teachings, and the Ketuvim contains other genres from nonprophetic

1. Berlin, *Poetics and Interpretation*, 37.

authors. The basic argument of this approach is that the three sections are organized by the predominate genre that aligns with authorial voice, and six major questions are asked of each text:

- What is the genre of this text?
- How does this genre accord with this approach to the Tanakh?
- Who is the author, and how does the authorship accord with this approach to the Tanakh?
- How does this approach inform our hermeneutic of this text?
- What are the benefits of applying this approach to this text?
- What are the potential problems in applying this approach to this text?

If the most common approach to the Tanakh is the Triple Canon approach, I'd say that the most common approach applied to the Old Testament is the Genre Author approach.[2] In fact, every hermeneutics textbook I've ever had as a primary text has focused on the questions What is the genre? and Who is the author? So let us discuss why someone would prefer this approach and what potential benefits and problems can arise from it.

Reasons for Adopting This Approach

One reason someone might desire to adopt the Genre Author approach to the Tanakh's structure is to facilitate identifying and understanding the literary form employed within a specific text.

As noted in my opening illustration, many have experience with this approach from using a library. Through this approach we can identify the text as historical narrative, poetry, prophecy, wisdom literature, or legal text. Each genre serves distinct purposes—whether instructive, reflective, or prescriptive—and understanding these genres helps contextualize the messages and themes of the texts within their respective literary conventions. After identifying the genre, we're then able to categorize the author and determine the authorial voice and intent. As Roger Beckwith notes, this allows us to assign "the oracular books to the prophets and the lyrical and sapiential books to the Hagiographa."[3] Although the authorship of many texts is debated, general authorial categorization provides insights into the organization of the Tanakh.

2. The reader will recall that I am using "Old Testament" to designate the fourfold canonical arrangement in contrast to the Tanakh's threefold structure.

3. Beckwith, *Old Testament Canon*, 200.

Proponents of This Approach

Before delving into the application of the Genre Author approach, we'll identify some notable scholars associated with this method. Adele Berlin, Robert Alter, Rolf Rendtorff, Anthony Thiselton, and Gordon Wenham all attest to genre being critical to understanding a Scripture passage. John Barton notes, "Genre is the single most important key to the meaning of any biblical passage. Without it, we misread."[4] Modern scholars such as Tremper Longman likewise continue to attest that "the genre of a biblical book provides the hermeneutical key to its interpretation."[5] In fact, H. B. Swete rightly observes that the Greek and Latin fathers arranged the books "according to their literary character or contents, or their supposed authorship."[6]

Hermann Gunkel, often credited with forming the idea of genre criticism of the Hebrew Bible, laid the foundational groundwork for this perspective. Gunkel's work emphasized the importance of identifying the *Sitz im Leben* (life setting) of various biblical texts, recognizing that different literary forms (genres) arose from specific communal contexts and served distinct functions. By categorizing psalms, sagas, and prophetic oracles according to their characteristic forms and social settings, Gunkel demonstrated that the Bible is not a monolithic text but a collection of diverse literary types. This approach inherently supports the idea that the Tanakh's sections are organized by genre, since the very act of identifying these genres necessitates a recognition of their distinct characteristics that align broadly with the divisions of Torah, Nevi'im, and Ketuvim.

Building on Gunkel's legacy, scholars such as Adele Berlin and Robert Alter further highlight the role of genre in biblical interpretation. Berlin, known for her work on biblical poetics, emphasizes literary features such as genre, shape, and meaning. Alter, a leading figure in the literary study of the Bible, meticulously demonstrates how an appreciation for the narrative and poetic conventions within different biblical books unlocks deeper layers of understanding. Their work implicitly validates the importance of genre in understanding the Tanakh and clearly articulating its distinct literary qualities.

Rolf Rendtorff and Gordon Wenham further contribute to this understanding, particularly with reference to the Torah. Rendtorff's focus on the compositional history of the Pentateuch, while complex, still implicitly recognizes the distinct legal and narrative genres present within it.[7] Wenham,

4. Barton, *Reading the Old Testament*, 31.
5. Longman, *Literary Approaches*, 87.
6. Swete in Beckwith, *Old Testament Canon*, 182.
7. Rendtorff, *Canonical Hebrew Bible*.

known for his commentaries on the Pentateuch, consistently draws attention to the literary structures and thematic coherence within the Law, underscoring the genre-specific nature of its content.[8] Their analyses, though focused on the Torah, implicitly demonstrate how its genre, while primarily legal and foundationally narrative, sets it apart from the books in the other biblical divisions.

The importance of genre is perhaps most succinctly captured by John Barton, who emphatically states that "genre shapes our expectations" of the meaning of any biblical passage.[9] This powerful assertion underscores the critical nature of genre awareness. Barton's works consistently highlight how misinterpreting the genre of a biblical text leads to fundamental misunderstandings of its message and intent. This statement directly supports the Tanakh's tripartite organization, suggesting that the very act of grouping texts into Torah, Nevi'im, and Ketuvim is an ancient recognition of their distinct generic categories, guiding the reader toward appropriate interpretive frameworks. Similarly, Anthony Thiselton emphasizes the role of genre in understanding biblical texts within a broader interpretive theory. While his work spans the entire Bible, his emphasis on the need for interpreters to be aware of the "rules of the game" for different literary forms directly applies to the Tanakh.[10] Understanding whether one is reading a historical narrative, a prophetic oracle, a psalm, or a wisdom proverb fundamentally alters the interpretive approach, aligning perfectly with the Tanakh's division by genre.

As we mentioned above, modern scholars such as Tremper Longman continue to affirm the crucial principle that the genre of a biblical book provides the hermeneutical key to its interpretation,[11] and his numerous works on biblical interpretation consistently underscore the practical necessity of identifying genre for accurate understanding. Longman demonstrates how the different genres within the Tanakh demand different reading strategies and yield different types of meaning.

The collective scholarship of Hermann Gunkel, Adele Berlin, Robert Alter, Rolf Rendtorff, Anthony Thiselton, Gordon Wenham, John Barton, and Tremper Longman provides compelling support for the idea that the Tanakh is organized by genre and, implicitly, by authorship within its three respective sections. From Gunkel's foundational work on genre criticism to the modern hermeneutical principles articulated by Longman, these scholars consistently demonstrate that recognizing the distinct literary forms and their

8. Wenham, *Book of Leviticus*; Wenham, *Genesis 1–15*; Wenham, *Genesis 16–50*.
9. Barton, *History of the Bible*, 472.
10. Thiselton, *Two Horizons*, 378.
11. Longman, *Literary Approaches*.

underlying purposes is paramount for proper biblical interpretation. The very structure of genre/authorship provides a crucial hermeneutical key for readers of the Tanakh.

Hermeneutical Realities of This Approach

When considering the structure of the Tanakh through the lens of genre, one cannot help but recognize its inherent "messiness." Unlike modern literary classifications that neatly categorize texts, the Hebrew Bible defies rigid genre divisions. This complexity presents significant hermeneutical challenges, since each section of the Tanakh seamlessly blends multiple genres. One must therefore develop a unique schema to read just one genre when the genre often shifts, even within chapters.

This genre fluidity complicates the understanding of a strict Genre Author approach. Teaching readers how to interpret a given literary form is certainly valuable, but the overlapping nature of genres in the Tanakh makes it difficult to advocate for genre being the basis of organization for the three sections of the Tanakh. While helpful, genre hermeneutics broadly applied to the Tanakh can cause a wrong theological conclusion if we misidentify the genre of a particular text. For instance, treating all of the Nevi'im as prophecy or all of the Torah as strictly law can significantly shape one's understanding of the narrative sections.

While genre awareness is an essential tool in biblical interpretation, it must also be handled with care and applied only within the appropriate portion of the Tanakh. The interconnected literary forms in the Tanakh resist simplistic classification, for the Tanakh is complex and multifaceted. To fully appreciate the Tanakh's structure, I advocate moving beyond rigid categories in order to engage with the text in its literary and theological fullness.

Correctly applying the Genre Author approach to the Tanakh highlights the authorial voice(s) that shaped distinct sections of the Tanakh. The traditional attribution of Mosaic authorship to the Torah plays a foundational role in shaping Israelite identity through laws, narratives, and theological teachings. From the voice of God to the hand of Moses on Sinai, Moses literarily establishes the covenantal relationship between God and Israel, which is why Deut. 34:10 claims that there has not been and would not be another prophet like Moses. This not only sets the stage for subsequent prophetic voices and authors but shows the primacy of the Torah as the first section of the Tanakh.

In the second section, various prophetic voices such as Isaiah, Jeremiah, and others follow in the Moses tradition and contribute significantly to the belief system of the Israelites. These texts often convey messages of divine judgment, calls for repentance, and promises of restoration tied to adherence to the Mosaic law. The prophets also spoke like Moses in the role of moral and spiritual guides, challenging societal injustices and advocating for fidelity to God's covenant amid political turmoil and social change.

Using the Genre Author approach provides clarity regarding why the Ketuvim exists. Nonprophetic authors and nonprophetic genres fill in the Ketuvim. For example, the book of Psalms offers prayers and hymns of worship, capturing the emotional and spiritual dimensions of faith. The book of Proverbs imparts wisdom for daily living, and the book of Job details Job's wrestling with the problem of suffering and divine justice. Each nonprophetic work in the Ketuvim articulates the word of God through a variety of literary forms and authors.

When considering the authors of the Tanakh, a major problem arises in determining the precise author and the author's intent for writing a certain text. The division of the Hebrew Bible into Torah, Nevi'im, and Ketuvim suggests a structural organization, but this framework does not neatly correspond to specific authorship patterns. Instead, authors of various backgrounds appear across all three sections, complicating any rigid categorization.

For example, the book of Daniel, though heavily prophetic in nature, is found in the Ketuvim rather than the Nevi'im. This placement challenges assumptions about prophetic authorship being the schema for selecting the prophetic books. Likewise, the Nevi'im contains historical books such as Joshua, Judges, Samuel, and Kings, which are more akin to the historical narratives found in the Ketuvim. The presence of historical authors within the Nevi'im indicates that the basis for the classification of books was not strictly content or authorship but broader thematic and functional considerations within the Jewish canon.

Ultimately, the mixed nature of authorship across the sections of the Tanakh highlights the complexity of understanding the Tanakh to be organized by the type of author. Rather than neatly compartmentalizing texts based on strict authorship categories, the canon reflects a dynamic interplay of various authors. The Tanakh structure seems to be a layered witness to God's work in history and across various authors' hands.

Though this approach to understanding the Tanakh is well utilized, it is fraught with potential problems. Nevertheless, let us analyze a few texts from each Tanakh section in light of the Genre Author approach and see what is unveiled and what the potential pitfalls of this approach may be. As we apply this approach to the various divisions of the Tanakh, three central questions will be posed to each text, and then three supporting questions will address each respective section of the Tanakh.

Torah: Mosaic Law

When viewing the Torah through the Genre Author lens, we encounter a text traditionally understood as *torah* (teaching or instruction) originating from the hand of Moses. This perspective regards the Torah not merely as a compilation of historical narratives and religious traditions but as a divinely given legal corpus that defines Israel's covenantal identity and forms the theological foundation of the Hebrew Bible.

The Genre Author approach places great emphasis on Moses as the central figure in the transmission of divine law. The biblical claim found in Deut. 34:10 underscores Moses's unparalleled authority as a mediator of divine revelation: "There never again arose in Israel a prophet like Moses, whom the Lord knew face to face" (AT). Brevard Childs says, "The canon understood Moses not merely as a historical figure but as the normative voice through which God's law was disclosed to the community of faith."[12] Traditional Jewish sources also maintain the centrality of Moses. The Mishnah (Avot 1.1) famously opens with "Moses received the Torah from Sinai and handed it on to Joshua," affirming the rabbinic view that Moses was not only the first recipient but also the authorized transmitter of divine instruction. Nahum Sarna writes, "The Torah is not merely a book of laws. It is a covenantal charter, and Moses is the covenant mediator par excellence."[13]

If one reads the entire Torah as law authored by Moses, then even the narrative portions serve a legal and covenantal function. As Alter says, "Biblical narrative is a prose fiction that invites us to infer the intentions of the author through literary means."[14] The genealogies, covenants, and divine encounters in Genesis are not isolated traditions but the theological and historical prologue to the laws given in Exodus, Leviticus, Numbers, and Deuteronomy. As such, "the narratives of Genesis and Exodus are not intended as mere background to the law; they are integral to its purpose. The stories provide the theological context in which the law functions as a means of covenant fidelity."[15]

A reading of the Torah as law highlights its primary function: to establish core principles, ethical mandates, and covenantal obligations that structure the identity of Israel. "The Torah is not simply law in the modern sense," writes Moshe Weinfeld. "It includes exhortation, instruction, and narrative, all working together to inspire obedience and loyalty to the covenant."[16] When

12. Childs, *Introduction to the Old Testament as Scripture*, 130.
13. Sarna, *Exploring Exodus*, 14.
14. Alter, *Art of Biblical Narrative*, 14.
15. Sailhamer, *Pentateuch as Narrative*, 19.
16. Weinfeld, *Deuteronomy*, 18.

viewed through the Moses-law paradigm, the Torah becomes the definitive theological and ethical standard for interpreting all subsequent biblical texts. The Prophets (Nevi'im) function as covenant enforcers, calling Israel back to Mosaic fidelity. "Remember the [Torah] of my servant Moses" (Mal. 4:4), declares the final prophetic voice in the Hebrew canon. Walter Brueggemann similarly notes: "The prophetic corpus does not introduce a new norm but reasserts and applies the Mosaic tradition to new situations of crisis and hope."[17] Likewise, the Writings (Ketuvim), especially the wisdom literature, reflect on how to live within the moral and theological framework established by the Torah. Michael Fishbane explains, "The sapiential texts of Proverbs, Job, and Qohelet presuppose the Torah as their theological substratum even when not citing it directly."[18]

The Genre Author approach affirms the unity and coherence of the Torah as a legal-theological document, resisting fragmentary or source-critical models that dissect it into layers (e.g., JEDP mentioned in the prior chapter). Instead, it treats the Torah as a unified, divinely orchestrated composition attributed to Moses, the covenant mediator. Rendtorff claims, "The Pentateuch must be read as a unified text shaped by authors who worked with traditions and genres to convey theological meaning."[19] The theological implications of this approach are profound: The Torah's authority is understood not merely as human tradition but as divine instruction, with Moses as God's faithful scribe.

Ultimately, reading the Torah as law authored by Moses means seeing it as the foundational document of divine instruction, a charter of Israel's election, identity, and ethical vocation. The Genre Author approach affirms the Torah as a single, unified legal narrative in which stories and statutes together shape the life of the covenant people.

Torah Test Case: The Ten Commandments (Exod. 20:1–17)

What Is This Text About?

Exodus 20:1–17 contains the Ten Commandments, the divine laws given by God to Israel at Mount Sinai. The passage begins with God declaring his identity as the one who brought Israel out of Egypt, thus establishing the covenantal context. The commandments include exclusive worship of God, prohibition of idolatry, reverence for God's name, and Sabbath observance. They also govern human relationships—commanding honor for parents and prohibiting murder, adultery, theft, false testimony, and coveting. These laws

17. Brueggemann, *Theology of the Old Testament*, 619.
18. Fishbane, *Biblical Interpretation*, 305.
19. Rendtorff, *Problem of the Process of Transmission*, 113.

serve as the moral and ethical foundation for Israel's covenant with God, shaping their identity and conduct as his chosen people.

What Is the Genre of This Text, and How Does This Genre Accord with This Approach to the Tanakh?

This text firmly rests in the genre of law. These laws (teachings) are delivered in the context of a covenant (suzerain-vassal treaty model). The laws are declarative ("You shall not . . .") and are foundational for Israel's moral, spiritual, and communal identity.

The Torah is largely composed of legal, narrative, and covenantal literature, much of which is structured around the life and ministry of Moses. Exodus 20 is a prime example of this genre and sits squarely in the Torah section, the first genre-defined division of the Tanakh. Its genre fits well within this part of the structure. Exodus 20:1–17 is legal literature and thus clearly fits within the broader narrative of the Torah. Exodus 20 is the Decalogue, which functions as a covenantal stipulation between God and Israel. As this passage is a legal law code, genre hermeneutics can easily be applied to this text. The covenantal context is crucial: These laws are given within the framework of God's covenant with Israel (Exod. 19–24). Theologically, the law code of the Torah helps to reflect God's character and expectations for his people.

Who Is the Author, and How Does the Authorship Accord with This Approach to the Tanakh?

Moses is traditionally regarded as the author or compiler of the Ten Commandments. If the Tanakh is organized by genre and author, then this text is foundational instruction for Israel's identity and covenantal relationship with God. Mosaic authorship reinforces the Torah's authority as direct divine revelation through Israel's key covenant mediator. The Ten Commandments function as law, but the presentation as God's direct speech raises questions about whether it should be read as universal moral law or covenantal stipulations specific to Israel.

How Does This Approach Inform Our Hermeneutic of This Text?

The Genre Author approach to the Tanakh profoundly shapes the hermeneutic of Exod. 20:1–17. This text, containing the Ten Commandments, is located within the Torah, the first and foundational division of the Tanakh, which is composed primarily of narrative and legal genres and is traditionally attributed to Moses as the covenant mediator. Recognizing the Ten

Commandments as legal literature within a covenantal narrative shapes its interpretation; these commands are not isolated ethical rules but stipulations embedded in the Sinai covenant between God and Israel. The genre emphasizes divine authority; the passage begins with "And God spoke all these words," highlighting its origin as direct divine revelation. The Mosaic authorship further supports this interpretation, situating Moses as the one who transmits and codifies God's covenant expectations. The Genre Author approach directs readers to see this not as abstract moral law but as a formal treaty document rooted in the suzerain-vassal model common in the ancient Near East, in which God as suzerain establishes the terms of relationship with his people. This understanding foregrounds the theological and relational dimensions of the law: God is not merely legislating but defining the identity and calling of Israel as his covenant people. The Genre Author approach highlights the Ten Commandments' role as both divine instruction (torah) and covenant stipulation, central to Israel's communal and spiritual life and foundational for later biblical ethics and theology. This approach clarifies

- God's authority and initiative in forming Israel's identity,
- the foundational ethical framework for Israelite society, and
- the relational nature of law as God's instruction rather than just legal regulation.

In essence, the genre of the Ten Commandments as part of a covenantal law clarifies that these commands are not just moral guidelines but stipulations within a divine relationship. In fact, the whole surrounding text of the Ten Commandments serves as a foundation for biblical ethics, influencing Jewish, Christian, and even secular legal traditions. Understanding both continuity and discontinuity in its application allows for distinctions between moral imperatives that remain relevant and covenantal aspects specific to Israel. This text also holds significance in Christian theology because Jesus builds on this text in the New Testament (Matt. 5:17–48).

What Are the Benefits of Applying This Approach to This Text?

1. Contextual clarity: The Genre Author approach situates the Decalogue within a covenantal narrative and Mosaic tradition, guarding against decontextualized readings.
2. Literary integrity: This approach preserves the structural unity of the Torah, allowing legal texts to be read in conversation with narrative and theological developments.

3. Covenantal theology: It strengthens the theological reading of the text by emphasizing God's role as covenant suzerain and Israel's role as covenant vassals.
4. Holistic interpretation: This approach links law with Israel's historical journey, ethical formation, and communal worship, preventing reduction of law to mere legalism.
5. Scriptural continuity: This approach provides a foundation for understanding later prophetic calls to covenant faithfulness and the wisdom literature's internalization of the law.

What Are the Potential Problems in Applying This Approach to This Text?

1. Genre oversimplification: While helpful, strict genre classifications may obscure the interweaving of narrative, law, and theology, leading to rigid interpretations.
2. Authorship debates: Modern critical scholarship disputes Mosaic authorship. Anchoring interpretation too tightly to Moses may limit engagement with literary development or redactional layers.
3. Reduction to legalism: A genre focus on "law" can tempt readers to isolate the text as a list of rules rather than part of a relational covenantal narrative.
4. Disconnection from other genres: Reading this only as "law" within "Torah" may keep readers from seeing its deep intertextuality with prophetic calls to justice or wisdom reflections on the fear of the Lord.
5. Canon-closure blind spot: Genre-authorship framing might downplay how later traditions (e.g., in the Ketuvim) reinterpret or spiritualize the commandments, thus missing the text's evolving reception history.

Summary of Test Case

Exodus 20:1–17 fits strongly within the Genre Author approach to the Tanakh as a Mosaic, covenantal legal text central to the Torah. This framework enhances theological and literary understanding, but caution must be taken not to ignore the text's layered context, canonical trajectory, and dialogue with other biblical genres and voices. In conclusion, Exod. 20:1–17 stands as a pivotal text that must be read within its covenantal, theological, and historical contexts. Recognizing its genre as legal within narrative, its Mosaic authorship, and its place within the Torah helps frame its significance.

However, issues of applicability, continuity, and interpretation remain central discussions in biblical theology.

Nevi'im: Prophetic Vision

When approaching the Nevi'im using the Genre Author approach, we encounter a body of literature fundamentally prophetic in nature, shaped not merely by literary artistry but by divinely authorized voices within Israel's history. This section of the Tanakh is not simply a collection of historical chronicles or poetic theology but a prophetic corpus, a genre of divine communication transmitted through God's chosen messengers, the prophets. It forms the critical bridge between the Torah's foundational law and the Ketuvim's reflective wisdom.

A central emphasis in this view is that the Nevi'im were not merely authors or editors, but "men of God," divinely appointed figures who served as "covenantal enforcers." Their task was not self-expression but divine communication:

> For the Lord God does nothing
> without revealing his secret
> to his servants the prophets. (Amos 3:7)

These prophetic messages are frequently marked by the formula "Thus says the Lord," underscoring their nature as revelation rather than speculation. As Gerhard von Rad explains, "The prophets are not the religious geniuses of Israel but rather recipients of a word that comes from beyond and lays claim to their lives."[20] They function as "officers of the covenant" (Meredith Kline's term), summoning Israel back to Torah faithfulness, acting in continuity with the Mosaic tradition.

Though prophetic texts vary in form, the visions, laments, oracles, and historical summaries are all unified by the prophetic function. They interpret Israel's present crises in light of the covenant, and they preach of future restoration. The prophets do not invent new laws but enforce and reiterate the Mosaic law, Torah.[21] In our English Bible structure, the Former Prophets (Joshua, Judges, Samuel, and Kings) are traditionally read as historical narratives rather than prophetic works, but we could say that they operate as prophetic historiography. These books chronicle the rise and fall of Israel's

20. Von Rad, *Old Testament Theology*, 2:36.
21. Waltke, *Old Testament Theology*, 825.

monarchy through a prophetic lens, highlighting how obedience to the Torah results in blessing and how disobedience led to the ultimate downfall of Israel and Judah. John Bright reminds us that "the biblical historians were theologians, not reporters. . . . They wrote to show that history bears out the truth of God's word."[22]

The Latter Prophets (a.k.a. the writing prophets) represent the most explicit forms of prophetic revelation, combining poetic oracles, legal exhortations, visions, laments, and symbolic actions. When one thinks of prophetic writings, these are the books that often come to mind. Prophets such as Isaiah and Ezekiel merge political critique with eschatological vision, functioning as divine prosecutors in God's covenant lawsuit with Israel (cf. Mic. 6:1–2), accusing the people of breaking the covenant. The literary genre blends legal indictment with poetic lament and visionary promise, as seen in the structure of books such as Hosea, where marriage, betrayal, and restoration mirror Israel's relationship to God. The prophets were also visionaries: Ezekiel visually acts out divine judgment (Ezek. 4), and Isaiah's throne-room vision (Isa. 6) fuses the earthly and heavenly.

The Nevi'im are deeply ethical and theological, insisting that worship without justice is an abomination. Amos condemns Israel's cultic ritualism with these words:

> I hate, I despise your feasts. . . .
> But let justice roll down like waters,
> and righteousness like an ever-flowing stream. (Amos 5:21, 24)

Likewise, Micah crystallizes the prophetic ethos this way:

> He has shown you, O man, what is good . . .
> to act justly, love mercy,
> and walk humbly with your God. (Mic. 6:8 AT)

These ethical oracles build directly on the Torah's moral code. Brueggemann emphasizes this continuity: "The prophets act as mediators of the Sinai covenant, invoking its mandates to critique and energize the life of the community."[23]

Seeing the prophets as authors in the prophetic genre affirms that their works were not literary inventions but transcriptions of divine encounters. As Isa. 8:16 instructs, "Bind up the testimony; seal the teaching among my

22. Bright, *History of Israel*, 129.
23. Brueggemann and Hankins, *Prophetic Imagination*, 59.

disciples," indicating the deliberate recording and preservation of prophetic revelation. The scribal tradition that followed often came from within prophetic circles (cf. Jeremiah's scribe, Baruch, Jer. 36), reinforcing the fact that the prophets' words were preserved because they were recognized as divinely authoritative. As Seitz explains, "The prophetic books were not merely literature about prophets, they are prophecy. Their form, content, and reception all affirm a genre of divine speech that holds Israel accountable to the covenant."[24]

By reading the Nevi'im as prophetic literature authored by prophets, we preserve the theological unity and covenantal continuity of the Tanakh. These texts do not merely recount past events or inspire through poetry; they are divine communications, enforcing the Torah and preparing the people for future restoration. The Genre Author approach reveals that every prophetic utterance is part of God's covenantal dialogue with his people, rooted in the law, motivated by justice, and energized by eschatological hope.

Nevi'im Test Case: Israel's Punishment Is Here (Hosea 9)

What Is This Text About?

Hosea 9 is a prophetic oracle of judgment against Israel, warning of impending exile due to the people's unfaithfulness to God. The text condemns Israel's misplaced joy and religious hypocrisy, highlighting how their corruption has led to divine punishment. God declares that Israel's celebrations and harvests will turn into mourning, their land will become barren, and they will be exiled to Assyria. The chapter also recalls past sins, such as those committed at Gibeah, emphasizing Israel's persistent rebellion. Ultimately, the text serves as a warning that because Israel has rejected God and his prophets, they will face devastating consequences, including loss of land, fertility, and divine favor.

What Is the Genre of This Text, and How Does This Genre Accord with This Approach to the Tanakh?

The genre of Hosea 9 is prophetic literature, specifically a judgment oracle. As a prophetic text, it requires hermeneutical attention to its poetic and figurative language, covenantal context, and historical background. Understanding the covenantal framework is essential since Israel's punishment is tied to its violation of the Mosaic covenant (Deut. 28). Additionally, recognizing symbolism and metaphors in prophetic discourse is necessary since much of the language conveys deeper spiritual realities rather than purely literal descriptions.

24. Seitz, *Prophecy and Hermeneutics*, 82.

The historical setting, the decline of the Northern Kingdom, and the looming Assyrian exile also inform interpretation, showing how the prophecy speaks to both its immediate audience and future theological themes. It contains the following:

- Woe oracles (9:1–6)
- Covenant lawsuit motifs (9:7–9)
- Judgment pronouncements grounded in divine speech (9:10–17)

According to the Genre Author approach, the Nevi'im section contains writings from divinely commissioned prophets whose main literary mode is poetry or prose oracles tied to Israel's covenant life. Hosea 9 aligns closely with this: it is poetic prophecy authored by Hosea, a recognized eighth-century prophet. Therefore, it easily accords with the Genre Author approach to the Tanakh.

Who Is the Author, and How Does the Authorship Accord with This Approach to the Tanakh?

The Nevi'im are organized around traditionally ascribed prophetic authors, and Hosea is a paradigmatic example of this. The author is Hosea, son of Beeri, a Northern Kingdom prophet during the reigns of Uzziah, Jotham, Ahaz, and Hezekiah (Hosea 1:1). His role as a covenant prosecutor for Yahweh justifies his place in the prophetic corpus. Therefore, the authorship of Hosea clearly accords with the Genre Author approach. His ministry occurred during the reign of Jeroboam II and subsequent kings, a time of political instability and moral decay. Hosea's prophecies were written to call Israel to repentance and to warn of the coming Assyrian exile. Since the book of Hosea is included in the Nevi'im section of the Tanakh, it is categorized as prophetic literature, distinct from the Torah and Ketuvim. This classification informs the hermeneutic by emphasizing divine revelation through human messengers, meaning that the text must be read as God's indictment of Israel rather than merely as Hosea's personal reflections. Additionally, the prophetic genre highlights both immediate historical consequences and eschatological themes, showing how Israel's fate serves as a warning but also anticipates later restoration.

How Does This Approach Inform Our Hermeneutic of This Text?

The Genre Author approach to the Tanakh significantly informs the hermeneutic of Hosea 9. As a prophetic text, Hosea 9 belongs to the Nevi'im, a division defined not merely by historical setting but also by its genre of divine oracle and covenantal confrontation. The prophetic genre is characterized by urgent divine speech mediated through a chosen prophet, often employing poetry, metaphor, and symbolic actions to call Israel to repentance and warn of impending judgment. Understanding Hosea 9 within this framework situates the passage as covenant enforcement, where the prophet Hosea serves as Yahweh's prosecuting voice against Israel's breach of covenant. This aligns with the traditional view of Hosea's authorship as an eighth-century prophet ministering in the Northern Kingdom of Israel before its fall. The Genre Author approach, therefore, invites a reading that emphasizes the relational and legal backdrop of the Sinai covenant, framing Hosea's harsh declarations not merely as divine wrath but as a grieving covenant partner confronting betrayal. The prophetic genre also uses metaphor-rich language, such as Hosea's imagery of barrenness, exile, and polluted feasts to dramatize the consequences of spiritual adultery. By reading Hosea 9 through this lens, the interpreter is guided to hear both the theological depth of divine justice and the tragic relational fracture between Yahweh and his people, thus preserving the ethical and emotive force intended by the prophetic author.

What Are the Benefits of Applying This Approach to This Text?

1. Historical-prophetic contextualization: This approach emphasizes Hosea's role as a prophet to the Northern Kingdom before the Assyrian exile, framing the judgment as imminent and justified.
2. Covenantal framework: It also highlights how Hosea's words stem from the Deuteronomic covenant as Israel's infidelity leads to covenant curses (e.g., barrenness, exile).
3. Theological consistency: It places Hosea within a wider prophetic tradition, reinforcing consistency in God's response to national sin across the prophets.
4. Rhetorical sensitivity: It helps readers avoid flattening prophetic poetry into didactic prose, preserving rhetorical features like irony, metaphor, and lament.

What Are the Potential Problems in Applying This Approach to This Text?

1. Reduction of literary complexity: Strict adherence to prophetic genre can obscure how Hosea 9 borrows features from other genres (lament, satire, etc.).

2. Oversimplification of authorship: While traditionally attributed to Hosea, the text may include editorial layers or redaction; the Genre Author approach tends to downplay compositional complexity.
3. Neglect of canonical reading: Focusing on author and genre may miss how Hosea 9 functions theologically across the entire Tanakh (e.g., how it is echoed or resolved in the Ketuvim or by other Latter Prophets).
4. Displacement of history: The Genre Author approach could risk treating the prophecy as static history rather than as dynamic Scripture with ongoing interpretive power.

Summary of Test Case

Hosea 9 fits naturally within the Genre Author approach to the Tanakh. It is prophetic poetry from a named prophet in the Nevi'im, offering covenantal warnings in poetic form. This interpretive approach highlights historical, theological, and rhetorical elements, but if rigidly applied, it may underappreciate literary blending and canonical theology. To mitigate these risks, readers should integrate canonical context and literary sensitivity with the Genre Author approach. In conclusion, Hosea 9 is a powerful prophetic text that warns of Israel's exile due to their unfaithfulness, using poetic and symbolic language to convey divine judgment. Understanding its genre, authorship, and place within the prophetic corpus of the Tanakh helps frame its message as both a historical indictment and a theological lesson. While interpretive challenges exist, such as distinguishing literal from figurative language and applying covenantal themes properly, this text ultimately provides important insights into divine justice, human responsibility, and the prophetic role in calling God's people back to faithfulness.

Ketuvim: Diverse Genre and Authors

When viewing the Ketuvim through the Genre Author approach, we encounter a corpus that resists narrow classification, giving rise to the generic term "Writings" for this division. Unlike the Torah, traditionally attributed to Moses and foundational as divine law, or the Nevi'im, penned by recognized prophets as vehicles of divine speech, the Ketuvim emerges as a diverse literary section. Its texts reflect a wide range of genres and authorial voices, from kings and sages to priests and anonymous scribes. In contrast to the other divisions, this section is less centralized in authority and genre and more polyphonic in nature. As James Kugel observes, "The Writings contain material that is at once canonical and yet often 'free-standing,' literature that engages with God and life without necessarily requiring a prophetic or legal framework."[25]

Unlike the Torah, which embodies divine command, or the Nevi'im, which pronounces divine judgment and hope, the Ketuvim offers a plethora of human responses to God:

- Wisdom literature (Job, Proverbs, Ecclesiastes): These texts reflect a theology of experience, not revelation. Job's anguished questions, Proverbs' practical advice, and Qohelet's existential reflections all affirm that God's truth is discernible in creation, conscience, and contemplation.
- Poetic and liturgical texts (Psalms, Lamentations, Song of Songs): These works give voice to emotion, devotion, and lament. They are liturgical responses to God rather than proclamations from him. The Psalms, for example, range from royal praise to individual lament, indicating their role in both public worship and private devotion.
- Historical and narrative works (Ruth, Esther, Daniel, Ezra-Nehemiah, Chronicles): These writings narrate events with priestly, courtly, or postexilic perspectives, often interpreting God's providence in subtle ways. Unlike the Former Prophets, they avoid explicit prophetic focus and instead highlight human agency within divine sovereignty.
- Apocalyptic literature (Daniel): Though Daniel includes visions and angelic messengers, it is markedly different from classical prophecy, relying on symbolic visions, numerical patterns, and eschatological expectations. Daniel functions more as a seer and interpreter than a covenant enforcer, signaling a post-prophetic literary shift.

A defining characteristic of the Ketuvim is the absence of explicit prophetic authority. Many of its authors are not prophets but rather kings (David, Solomon), priests (Ezra), sages (Qohelet), or anonymous compilers.[26] Their writings are theologically rich but not framed as direct oracles from God.

25. Kugel, *How to Read the Bible*, 684.

26. Although these characters are typically not regarded as prophets in Christian tradition, Jewish tradition sometimes attributes prophetic insight or divine inspiration to them (see, e.g., Berakhot 4b, Gittin 57b, and Bava Batra 14b in the Babylonian Talmud regarding David). They may have had "prophetic moments" (see Acts 2:30), but their primary role was not as prophets within the theocracy of the Israelite kingdom.

- David and Asaph (Psalms): Their prayers and songs articulate communal memory, covenant loyalty, and emotional honesty before God.
- Solomon (Proverbs, Ecclesiastes, Song of Songs): These works symbolize wisdom and royal authorship, engaging in philosophical discourse about the meaning of life rather than issuing divine commands.
- Ezra and Nehemiah: These books present postexilic reform from a priestly-administrative perspective, focusing on temple worship, Torah renewal, and social reform rather than vision or prophecy.
- Anonymous scribes (Job, Lamentations, Chronicles): These works engage with historical trauma, suffering, and divine justice, often leaving theological questions open-ended.

This shift is significant. Whereas the Torah and Nevi'im center on God's voice breaking into history, the Ketuvim illustrate how human beings live under, interpret, and respond to that divine voice. As Michael Fishbane argues, "The Writings are a commentary on Israel's lived life under the divine order. . . . They are sacred mediations rather than sacred proclamations."[27]

Because of this literary and theological variety, interpreting the Ketuvim requires a different hermeneutical posture:

- Wisdom texts urge ethical and philosophical exploration (e.g., "The fear of the Lord is the beginning of knowledge," Prov. 1:7 NIV) rather than simple obedience.
- Poetic texts draw the reader into symbolic and emotional landscapes, where lament, praise, and love reflect and shape Israel's spiritual identity.
- Historical texts function as postexilic reinterpretations of Israel's journey, providing hope, identity, and continuity.
- Apocalyptic texts introduce a genre of resistance and cosmic hope, affirming that God's purposes transcend immediate historical circumstances.

The Ketuvim serves not as the extension of prophecy but as the reception and internalization of the Torah and Prophets. It illustrates how Israel responds to God in times of silence, suffering, and exile, often without clear prophetic direction. In the absence of new law or prophets, wisdom, prayer, and memory become the modes of divine engagement. This reflects a broader theological truth: Divine revelation is not always immediate or mediated by

27. Fishbane, *Biblical Interpretation*, 434.

prophetic voice; it can also unfold through reflection, communal experience, and faithful endurance. As Ps. 1:2 suggests,

> His delight is in the law of the Lord,
> and on his law he meditates day and night.

The life of faith includes meditation, memory, and mystery.

Reading the Ketuvim employing the Genre Author approach affirms its unique role within the canon: a collection of nonprophetic but divinely inspired texts, capturing human engagement with divine truth through poetry, wisdom, and history. It shows that revelation is not exhausted by law and prophecy but continues in worship, lament, philosophical struggle, and historical resilience. The Ketuvim, then, is Israel's literary sanctuary, a space where faith survives in ambiguity, where worship flourishes in exile, and where wisdom sustains the faithful between the echoes of Sinai and the silence before the Messiah.

Ketuvim Test Case: Wisdom Personified (Prov. 4)

What Is This Text About?

Proverbs 4 is a text of wisdom literature that emphasizes the value of acquiring wisdom and living a disciplined life. The chapter is structured as a father's instruction to his son, urging him to embrace wisdom, avoid wickedness, and walk in righteousness. The text begins with an appeal to listen to a father's teaching, recounting how the speaker himself was instructed in wisdom during his youth. It then contrasts the path of the righteous, which leads to life and light, with the way of the wicked, which leads to darkness and destruction. The chapter concludes with a call to guard one's heart, control one's speech, and stay on the right path, reinforcing the idea that wisdom leads to a prosperous and morally upright life.

What Is the Genre of This Text, and How Does This Genre Accord with This Approach to the Tanakh?

Proverbs 4 is wisdom instruction, specifically a didactic poem. It resembles the form of an instructional speech from a father to a son and belongs to the genre of Hebrew wisdom literature.

According to the Genre Author approach, the Ketuvim includes wisdom texts, psalms, and reflections on life. Proverbs, including chapter 4, fits naturally into this structure because it lacks direct prophetic mediation or historical narrative and instead offers generational wisdom and ethical formation.

Who Is the Author, and How Does the Authorship Accord with This Approach to the Tanakh?

Solomon is traditionally considered the author of Proverbs (cf. Prov. 1:1), with later sections of the book displaying contributions from other sages (e.g., Agur and Lemuel). Modern scholarship recognizes the book as a collection compiled over time, with multiple voices. Solomon, renowned for his wisdom (1 Kings 3:5–14), is believed to have compiled much of Israel's wisdom literature. The reference to a father's instruction in Prov. 4 may reflect Solomon's teachings to his own sons, or it may function as a literary device to reinforce the authority of wisdom passed down through generations. If one considers a later editorial process in compiling Proverbs, the chapter could reflect a broader wisdom tradition rather than a single author's reflections. The Genre Author approach includes not only prophets but also wise scribes and royal figures (like Solomon) in the Ketuvim. Proverbs' attribution to Solomon fits the view that certain books are preserved due to their connection to key wisdom authorities in Israel's history.

How Does This Approach Inform Our Hermeneutic of This Text?

Seeing Prov. 4 within the Ketuvim and under Solomonic authorship guides the reader to approach the text not as prophecy or law but as formative instruction for living in harmony with God's created order. If the Tanakh is organized by genre and author, Proverbs falls under the Ketuvim, distinct from the Torah and Nevi'im. This classification informs how we interpret the text. Unlike the Torah's legal directives or the Nevi'im's covenantal rebukes, Proverbs provides guidance for everyday living based on human observation and divine wisdom. This suggests that the text should not be read as a prophetic declaration or a legal requirement but as wisdom instruction intended to shape character and promote ethical decision-making. It also reinforces the idea that Proverbs serves a pedagogical function, helping individuals internalize wisdom through repeated moral teachings.

The genre of wisdom literature requires specific hermeneutical rules for interpretation. Unlike historical narrative or prophetic judgment, wisdom texts often contain general principles rather than absolute promises. Proverbs, in particular, provides guidance for right living, but its statements are not always meant to be read as universal guarantees. The poetic structure also employs parallelism and metaphor, which must be understood in context to grasp the full meaning. Additionally, wisdom literature often draws on observational experience, meaning its teachings reflect common life patterns rather than legal mandates or prophetic declarations. Thus, Prov. 4 should be interpreted as guidance for developing moral character rather than as a strict formula for success.

What Are the Benefits of Applying This Approach to This Text?

1. Promotes proper genre expectations: This approach encourages reading Prov. 4 as training in virtue and perception, not as law or prophecy.
2. Validates wisdom in the canon: Wisdom is validated as part of divine revelation, even if it is mediated through human sages.
3. Acknowledges multivoice Scripture: It recognizes Solomon as a wisdom figure, not a prophet, contributing to a fuller understanding of how Israel related to God through various literary roles.
4. Facilitates liturgical and educational use: It supports the idea that this text functioned in family or community instruction, preserving Israel's values across generations.

What Are the Potential Problems in Applying This Approach to This Text?

1. Overreliance on traditional attribution: Solomon's authorship is traditional and not certain; strict adherence to that view may obscure the editorial shaping of the text.
2. Neglect of theological interconnectedness: Separating genres too sharply may keep readers from seeing how wisdom theology overlaps with covenant theology (e.g., connections between Proverbs and Deuteronomy).
3. Limits to canonical readings: This approach might restrict intertextual links between Proverbs and other genres. For example, Jesus as wisdom incarnate in the New Testament might be overlooked if wisdom is kept in an isolated genre box.
4. Underappreciation of divine voice: Without prophetic mediation, some readers may undervalue Proverbs as "merely human" unless the revelatory role of wisdom is clearly affirmed.

Summary of Test Case

Proverbs 4 aligns naturally with the Genre Author approach to the Tanakh. As wisdom literature in the Ketuvim traditionally attributed to Solomon, it fits the genre expectations of instruction passed from elder to youth. This view enhances appreciation of the text's pedagogical, ethical, and theological contributions, though care must be taken not to unduly isolate it from broader biblical theology. To rightly "fit," readers must affirm wisdom as a legitimate mode of divine communication within the Hebrew Scriptures. In conclusion, Prov. 4 is a rich wisdom text that emphasizes the value of acquiring and applying wisdom in daily life. Understanding its genre, authorship, and place within the Tanakh helps shape a responsible hermeneutic that recognizes its teachings as guiding principles rather than rigid laws or prophecies. While interpretive challenges exist, such as distinguishing general wisdom from divine guarantees, the text ultimately provides timeless instruction on character formation, moral integrity, and the pursuit of a righteous life.

Conclusion

This chapter has explored how the structure of the Tanakh can be understood through the Genre Author approach, a framework that sees the Hebrew Bible as a library organized not only by canonical sequence but by the predominant literary genre and authorial voice of each section. The Torah is understood as primarily law and narrative, traditionally linked to Moses; the Nevi'im as visionary and instructional literature authored by covenantal messengers; and the Ketuvim as a diverse collection of genres—poetry, wisdom, lament, thanksgiving—produced by nonprophetic figures. This view asks three central interpretive questions of each text: What is its genre? Who is its author (or authorial perspective)? And what is the hermeneutical impact of those two features? These questions anchor one of the most widely used hermeneutical strategies in biblical studies and teaching, as evidenced by its dominance in modern hermeneutics textbooks. For many interpreters, the Genre Author approach is not merely academic but intuitive, akin to how a library is organized by type of literature.

A primary appeal of this approach is its clarity and accessibility. It helps readers make immediate sense of a text by locating it within a recognizable literary and authorial framework. The diversity of genres in the Tanakh—legal codes, prophecy, narrative, poetry, wisdom sayings—can be intimidating without such a guide. Genre categories offer contextual clues about a text's intended function, whether it is meant to command, persuade, reflect, mourn, or praise. Moreover, connecting these genres to traditional authors or authorial schools (e.g., Mosaic lawgiver, prophetic intermediary, royal sage) grounds the interpretation in a historical and theological setting, often with devotional and practical clarity.

Yet this clarity comes with complexity. The Tanakh at times resists rigid categorization. Many texts blend genres or defy clear authorial attribution.

The "messiness" of the Tanakh's structure means that readers must employ flexibility and genre-awareness without genre-reductionism. A text's canonical placement within a genre-defined section may not fully exhaust its function, literary depth, or interpretive possibilities.

The benefits of the Genre Author approach are evident. It offers contextual clarity, situating texts such as the Decalogue (Ten Commandments) within covenantal narrative rather than isolating them as abstract moral rules. It preserves the literary integrity of large units (like the Torah), safeguards covenantal theology, promotes holistic interpretation, and allows for continuity across the canon, helping readers trace how legal codes reappear in prophetic warnings and are internalized in wisdom literature.

At the same time, this approach comes with limitations. Overemphasis on genre can result in oversimplification, ignoring the complex literary layers of the text. Anchoring too strongly to traditional authorship may lead to overlooking the editorial or redactional history of the canon. There is also the risk of reductionism, particularly with legal texts, where readers might mistake covenantal law for mere rule-following. Moreover, isolating texts by genre might obscure their intertextual relationships or their reception history within later Jewish and Christian traditions.

In the end, the Genre Author approach offers a helpful starting point—not a rigid system but a plausible set of hermeneutical lenses. It equips readers to approach the Tanakh with literary sensitivity. Yet it must be used with humility and with openness to the multilayered nature of Scripture and the ways these texts stretch beyond their initial form or attribution.

3

Theological Development Approach

Tanakh as Development in Biblical Thought

IN MANY EDUCATIONAL INSTITUTIONS across America, history is commonly divided into three broad categories: Ancient, European, and American. Each of these sections is presented as a self-contained unit, yet they build on one another in a progressive narrative. Ancient history establishes the foundational structures of civilizations; European history refines concepts such as law, governance, and nationhood; and American history emerges as a product of these developments, exploring democracy and individual rights. While each period is often studied in isolation, they are deeply interconnected.

This historical progression provides a useful analogy for understanding the threefold order of the Tanakh. The most impactful course I took during my PhD program was Old Testament theology, taught by Dr. Archie England. In that course, Dr. England guided us through the idea that the revelation of God's character and Israelite religion unfolds progressively throughout Scripture. Just as history builds upon itself, the sections of the Tanakh—Torah, the Nevi'im, and the Ketuvim—represent progressing theological eras, reflecting the evolving beliefs, practices, and understandings of the Israelite community.

This progressive theological lens urges us to examine not only individual texts but also the broader ideological and doctrinal shifts within Israelite history. Just as historical study requires an understanding of evolving political and legal systems, this view of the Tanakh demands an awareness of Israelite religion and how it unfolds across the Tanakh. As Brevard Childs notes, "The role of the author in shaping the literature according to a specific theological purpose is central to a canonical approach."[1]

By recognizing these developments, we gain a richer and more nuanced understanding of Scripture, seeing it not only as a dynamic and unfolding revelation of Israelite theology but also as a snapshot into Israelite religion at the time of the respective section's canonization.

We ask four questions that are unique to this approach to the text:

- What is the Israelite religion in this text?
- What theological themes or concepts are present in this text?
- What role does this text play in the development of Israelite/Jewish theology?
- How does this text contribute to the overall theological framework of the Tanakh?

Reasons for Adopting This Approach

One of the key benefits of this approach is that it unveils the progression of theological thought throughout the Tanakh. The texts of the Torah, Nevi'im, and Ketuvim reflect different periods in Israel's history, each contributing to the overall theological landscape. Early biblical texts often emphasize themes such as covenant and divine justice, while later writings refine, expand, or reinterpret these ideas. By analyzing this progression, scholars can discern patterns of continuity, core theological beliefs, and moments of discontinuity, where new theological beliefs emerge in response to historical circumstances. This recognition allows for a more nuanced understanding of the Hebrew Bible's composition and theological framework.

Examining the Tanakh through the lens of the Theological Development approach also enhances thematic analysis. Biblical texts engage in an ongoing conversation about foundational ideas such as divine justice, covenantal faithfulness, and the nature of prophecy. By tracing these themes across different texts and time periods, interpreters can better grasp how the biblical authors responded to theological challenges and reformulated key doctrines in light of evolving historical and cultural realities. This approach also underscores the

1. Childs, *Introduction to the Old Testament as Scripture*, 82.

interconnectedness of the biblical canon, revealing how later writings build upon, reinterpret, or challenge earlier theological perspectives.

Ultimately, approaching the Tanakh as three distinct theological snapshots allows for a richer and more comprehensive engagement with the text. Rather than reducing biblical theology to a fixed system, this approach embraces its historical situation. Understanding the theological context in which a text was written helps prevent anachronistic readings that impose later theological concepts onto earlier texts. By acknowledging the evolving nature of its theological themes, this approach permits one to read each section of the Tanakh on its own terms and see how themes are handled uniquely in each section.

Proponents of This Approach

The concept of progressing theology is one that has been held by Julius Wellhausen, Yehezkel Kaufmann, James Kugel, Walter Brueggemann, John Barton, and William M. Schniedewind—all of whom highlight different facets of the Tanakh's theological journey. Through their studies, these scholars promote the view that the tripartite Tanakh provides snapshots into the Israelite religion in the canonizing period.

Julius Wellhausen presented one of the most influential models for understanding the Pentateuch as a theological progression. He posited that the Pentateuch was a composite of four distinct sources—J, E, D, and P—each representing a different stage in the evolution of Israelite religion. From the anthropomorphic and personal God of the early Yahwist (J) and Elohist (E) sources, Wellhausen traced the development through the ethical and covenantal emphasis of the Deuteronomist (D), culminating in the rigid, cultic focus of the Priestly (P) source in the postexilic period. For Wellhausen, this arrangement was not arbitrary; it painted a picture of Israelite theology moving from a spontaneous, vibrant faith to a more institutionalized and legalistic system. Although many details of Wellhausen's view are no longer widely held, his inquiry and ideal holds great sway on the theological understanding of the Tanakh structure.

In stark contrast, Yehezkel Kaufmann championed the radical originality and antiquity of Israelite monotheism. Rather than a gradual evolution from paganism, Kaufmann argued that the core monotheistic worldview of Israel was established from the time of Moses, a distinct and unique theological innovation. For him, the Tanakh, despite its various literary layers and historical contexts, maintained a fundamental continuity centered on a singular, universal God who uniquely revealed himself to Israel. Instances of idolatry were viewed as peripheral aberrations rather than genuine attachments to polytheistic cults, underscoring his belief in the enduring and foundational nature of Israelite monotheism throughout its history. Though arguing for continuity, there is a sense in Kaufmann's work that the monotheism is "progressing" but not in the form of a progression from polytheism to henotheism and finally monotheism.

Bridging the gap between the ancient text and its subsequent interpretations, James Kugel highlights the inherent differences within the biblical narrative itself. He argues that the Tanakh reflects evolving theological ideas and practices, presenting God and human interaction with the divine in distinct ways across its various divisions. Kugel observes how earlier texts might depict a more anthropomorphic God directly involved in human affairs, while later texts present a more transcendent deity. For Kugel, these are not necessarily seamless progressions but rather "snapshots" of different periods and perspectives within Israelite religious thought. The Tanakh, in his view, is a collection of diverse voices brought together, with later processes of canonization and interpretation attempting to harmonize or reevaluate these inherent distinctions.

Coming from a more theological perspective, Walter Brueggemann views the Tanakh as a dynamic and dialogical testament to Israel's relationship with God. He perceives the various divisions as distinct "voices" or "performances" of faith that reflect a theological responsiveness to changing historical circumstances. The Torah lays down the foundational covenant, while the Nevi'im offers a crucial theological progression, challenging Israel, calling for accountability, and presenting new visions of hope. The Ketuvim, for Brueggemann, provides a diverse reflection on life under the covenant, exploring themes of wisdom, lament, and suffering. He sees the Tanakh as a continuous narrative of "creation to new creation," where theological understanding is constantly engaged and reengaged through the ongoing lived experience of faith.

John Barton emphasizes the literary and historical context of the Bible's formation, often cautioning against imposing a singular, overarching "theological progression." He views the Tanakh not as a preplanned, coherent theological treatise but as a collection of diverse writings assembled over centuries. Barton is more inclined to see the different sections as "snapshots" of specific periods and their prevailing concerns, rather than a neat linear development. He suggests that what appear to be theological "progressions" are often the result of later editorial shaping and interpretive traditions, rather than being inherently present in the original composition of each text. For

Barton, understanding *how* the Bible came to be formed and *how* it has been interpreted is paramount.[2]

Finally, William M. Schniedewind offers a sociohistorical lens, linking theological development to the evolution of literacy and textualization in ancient Israel. He argues that early Israelite religion was predominantly oral, with traditions passed down verbally. The rise of widespread literacy, particularly from the eighth century BCE onward, was crucial for the textualization of these traditions, leading to the formation of extensive literary works like the Torah. For Schniedewind, the very act of writing and canonizing these texts was a theological act, shaping and solidifying Israelite religious understanding. The progression he observes is therefore intertwined with the shift from an oral culture to a highly literate one, where the written word became central to religious authority and identity, influencing how theology was expressed, preserved, and developed over time.

In conclusion, the question of whether the Tanakh presents a theological progression or a series of historical-religious snapshots shows how many influential scholars have tried to parse the Tanakh's tripartite corpus. Harmonizing these perspectives reveals that the Tanakh is not a monolithic theological statement but a rich and complex testimony reflecting Israel's continued engagement with the divine over millennia.

Hermeneutical Realities of This Approach

Viewing the Tanakh as a developing theological order raises the question of whether later sections should be prioritized over earlier ones. Some theological frameworks suggest that later texts contain more refined or developed theological concepts, leading readers to treat them as clearer or more advanced in their insights. This notion of progressive revelation implies that as theological understanding evolved over time, later texts may provide more explicit formulations of key doctrines. Additionally, readers may naturally gravitate toward these later sections because they seem more relevant to contemporary theological discussions and challenges. By tracing the development of theological themes across the biblical canon, one may find that later texts articulate ideas with greater clarity or in response to historical experiences that shaped Israelite religious thought.

However, prioritizing later sections due to their perceived theological maturity presents certain challenges. One potential issue is the risk of anachronistic readings, where later theological concepts are projected onto earlier

2. Barton, *History of the Bible.*

texts, distorting their original meaning and context. Early biblical writings must be understood within their own historical and literary setting rather than interpreted solely through the lens of later developments. Another concern is the possible neglect of earlier texts that contain foundational theological concepts crucial for a full understanding of the biblical message. If later writings are given higher priority, key themes and doctrines found in the Torah and early prophetic literature may be overlooked or misunderstood. Furthermore, proper contextual understanding requires that each portion of the Tanakh be studied within its own historical and cultural framework. As a result, the hermeneutical risks can be abated if one values the Tanakh divisions as distinct eras rather than prioritizing one division over the others. By maintaining textual integrity and appreciating the development of ideas across time, one can gain a more nuanced and comprehensive understanding of the Tanakh as a whole.

Torah: Legal and Ethical Foundation

When examining the Torah through the lens of the Theological Development approach, we encounter the bedrock of Israelite religion. The Torah is the section of the Hebrew canon that establishes the identity and spiritual trajectory of Israel. When considering the Torah theologically, it is far more than a mere legal or historical document; it is the covenantal relationship with Yahweh. The early chapters of Genesis introduce universal theological themes such as creation, blessing, and judgment. Then the Torah narrows the scope to focus on the specific elect lineage of Abraham and his descendants. This narrowing signals a shift from a broadly human story to the particular narrative of Israel. The universal-to-particular trajectory reflects what Walter Brueggemann terms a "theological constriction," whereby "the universal claim of God's sovereignty is channeled into the concrete history of Israel."[3]

During the patriarchal period, the divine-human relationship is portrayed in vivid, personal, and often enigmatic terms, through dreams, angelic appearances, and direct dialogue. These narratives exhibit a religion that is less systematized and more experiential, consistent with a henotheistic worldview, where Yahweh is supreme but not yet confessed as the only God. As Mark S. Smith argues, "Israelite religion did not begin as monotheistic, but as a form of monolatry or henotheism in which one god is exalted without denying the existence of others."[4] The gradual movement from implicit polytheism

3. Brueggemann, *Theology of the Old Testament*, 147.
4. Smith, *Early History of God*, 32.

to explicit monotheism reflects a theological evolution that will find clearer articulation when moving from Torah into the Nevi'im.

The cultic system, particularly in Exodus through Deuteronomy, reflects both continuity and discontinuity with the surrounding ancient Near Eastern world. Sacrificial practices, ritual purity laws, and priestly mediations suggest commonality with surrounding ancient religions. Yet the Torah reconfigures these practices to being exclusive to worship of Yahweh, distinguishing Israelite religion.[5]

The giving of the Law at Sinai (Exod. 19–24) marks not merely a legal moment but a theophanic event, the climactic act of covenant ratification. The laws delivered in this context—ritual, civil, and moral—are conceived not as abstract statutes but as divine commands arising from Yahweh's redemptive relationship with his people. The unity of religion and society is so harmonious that Torah ethics is inseparable from communal identity and vocation. Gerhard von Rad states, "The Torah is not simply a legal code; it is the beginning of Israel's theological reflection on its own history and calling."[6] Viewed from the Theological Development approach to the Tanakh, the Torah provides the base upon which both the Nevi'im and the Ketuvim elaborate.

In this way, the Torah is not static but dynamically interpreted within Israel's unfolding story. The exile and postexilic periods in particular, historical crises that shake the foundations of national and cultic life, force a rearticulation and internalization of Torah. This period, as shown in texts such as Ezra-Nehemiah and Chronicles, reflects a deliberate return to Torah as the anchor of identity and renewal.

Ultimately, the Torah is "the simplest form of Israelite religion" for it is the theological ground on which the remainder of the Tanakh builds. But rather than viewing it as an elementary form of Israelite religion, maybe we should view it as the corpus that undergirds or lays the groundwork for the subsequent portions of the Tanakh.[7] The Torah represents both a beginning and an enduring point of reference; it moves humanity away from polytheism and into henotheism with Yahweh as the covenantal God.

Torah Test Case: The Call of Moses (Exod. 3)

What Is This Text About?

Exodus 3 recounts Moses's transformative encounter with God at the burning bush. While tending his father-in-law Jethro's flock near Mount Horeb,

5. Milgrom, *Leviticus*, 41.
6. Von Rad, *Old Testament Theology*, 1:205.
7. Levenson, *Sinai & Zion*, 27.

Moses observes a bush that is ablaze yet not consumed. As he approaches to investigate, God calls to him by name and commands him to remove his sandals, declaring the ground to be holy. God introduces himself as the God of Abraham, Isaac, and Jacob and expresses his intimate awareness of Israel's suffering in Egypt. He then commissions Moses to confront Pharaoh and lead Israel out of bondage and into the promised land. Moses resists the call, questioning his qualifications, but God reassures him with the promise of divine presence and reveals the divine name, "I AM WHO I AM" (YHWH; 3:14), underscoring his self-existence and eternal reliability. God also foretells Pharaoh's resistance but assures Moses of ultimate deliverance.

What Is the Israelite Religion in This Text?

In Exod. 3, Israelite religion is portrayed as a covenantal faith grounded in divine self-revelation and intervention. The episode reveals a religion rooted in historical memory and divine fidelity. The God who speaks from the burning bush is not a new deity but the God of the patriarchs, showing continuity in covenantal identity. As Brevard Childs explains, "This theophany serves not merely to authenticate Moses's call but to affirm that the divine promise given to the patriarchs continues and is now being enacted in history."[8] Thus this moment marks a shift from a familial relationship with God to a communal-national one. God's command to remove sandals on "holy ground" (v. 5) introduces a key element of ritual reverence and awareness of divine holiness, signaling that Israelite worship involves sacred time, space, and posture. Nahum Sarna comments, "The motif of sacred space is here established early in Israel's religious consciousness. The place becomes holy not due to its natural features, but solely because of the divine presence."[9] Therefore, this text is foundational for Israelite religion, representing the moment where divine calling meets national identity and worship becomes centered not only on remembrance but also on revelation and mission.

What Theological Themes or Concepts Are Present in This Text?

Several core theological themes emerge in Exod. 3:

1. Divine revelation: The self-revelation of God's name in verse 14, "I AM WHO I AM" (*ehyeh asher ehyeh*), introduces God as self-existent and eternally present.

8. Childs, *Book of Exodus*, 73.
9. Sarna, *Exodus*, 15.

2. Divine holiness: The requirement for Moses to remove his sandals points to the theme of divine holiness.
3. Divine compassion and justice: God's words in verse 7, "I have surely seen the affliction of my people . . . and have heard their cry," highlight divine empathy and justice. This signals a relational theology in which God is deeply involved in human affairs.
4. Prophetic calling: Moses's commissioning aligns him with the prophetic tradition. God's assurance "I will be with you" (v. 12) becomes a hallmark of divine calling throughout Scripture.
5. Covenant continuity: The identification of God with the patriarchs ensures theological continuity and reinforces the binding nature of God's promises to his people.

What Role Does This Text Play in the Development of Israelite/Jewish Theology?

Exodus 3 initiates the exodus narrative, Israel's defining redemptive event. The text signals that God is not only a covenant-maker but also a covenant-keeper who intervenes in history to fulfill his word. The revelation of the divine name (YHWH) in verse 15, "This is my name forever," cements a theological anchor point for Jewish worship, identity, and memory. God's memorial name links generations together through a shared covenantal consciousness. Jon Levenson adds, "This passage marks a transition from a God remembered in ancestral tradition to one whose name becomes a liturgical and communal centerpiece."[10]

This theological development is foundational for understanding God's character in the Torah and beyond, setting the stage for themes of liberation, covenant obedience, and divine presence in both the Nevi'im and the Ketuvim.

How Does This Text Contribute to the Overall Theological Framework of the Tanakh?

Exodus 3 establishes a theological grammar for the entire Tanakh. The themes of God's presence, redemptive initiative, and covenant fidelity reverberate throughout the biblical canon. The burning bush becomes emblematic of divine mystery and engagement. It portrays a God who reveals himself yet remains transcendent. The text is also foundational to biblical ethics. God's actions—seeing, hearing, remembering, and coming down—form the model

10. Levenson, *Sinai & Zion*, 31.

for Israel's social ethics, particularly in caring for the oppressed, as later codified in the Torah and echoed by the Nevi'im.

However, interpreting this text within a progressive theological framework poses challenges. One must avoid reading later theological constructs (e.g., the fully developed temple theology or messianic expectations) back into this early theophany. At the same time, it is legitimate to recognize that this moment seeds future theological reflection. Walter Moberly offers a helpful caution: "To acknowledge theological development does not diminish the original significance of a text but rather honors its generative power within the canon."[11]

So Exod. 3 is both contextually profound and canonically expansive. It defines how God is to be known—through presence, name, and action—and sets in motion the theological trajectory of redemption and covenant that echoes through the Tanakh and into later Jewish and Christian thought.

How Does This Approach Inform Our Hermeneutic of This Text?

This approach invites us to read the call of Moses and the revelation of the divine name as a theological snapshot of Israelite religion at an early stage rather than as a fully systematized doctrine of God. Exodus 3 stands within the Torah's foundational era when Yahweh reminds Abraham's descendants that he is Israel's covenant God in a henotheistic environment. As such he's the patriarchal God who redeems because he sees, hears, and comes down to deliver his people. Rather than reading later prophetic or wisdom formulations back into this scene, we allow Exod. 3 to speak on its own terms as an early articulation of covenantal identity and divine presence, a foundational layer that the Nevi'im and Ketuvim will later expand and reimagine.

What Are the Benefits of Applying This Approach to This Text?

1. Provides a snapshot of Israelite religion at this time: We see a transition from ancestral faith (God of the patriarchs) to national faith tied to covenant and deliverance.
2. Introduces theological themes: We see the origins of themes such as divine holiness, compassion and justice, and the call and mission of the people of God.
3. Marks theological development: The revelation of God's name is a milestone in Israelite religion.

11. Moberly, *Old Testament Theology*, 112.

4. Offers a theological paradigm: This text provides a paradigm for call narratives of believers and a theological anchor for others to remember.

What Are the Potential Problems in Applying This Approach to This Text?

1. Data pointing versus theology: Treating the burning bush episode primarily as an early stage in Israelite religion can reduce the text to a mere data point in a reconstructed evolution from henotheism to monotheism.
2. Overlooking theological grounding: This approach may tempt us to read the text mainly in terms of what is not yet rather than engaging the robust theology already present in the narrative. Such a focus on progression can mute the crucial theological claims of Exod. 3 that reverberate throughout the rest of the Tanakh.

Summary of Test Case

Exodus 3 presents Moses's encounter with God at the burning bush, a pivotal moment that shaped Israel's identity and informed the theological framework of the Tanakh. The themes of divine holiness, compassion, justice, covenant continuity, and prophetic calling are intrinsically connected to the "I am who I am" statement. This text plays a foundational role in Israelite theology, shifting God's relationship from the universal to the specific and familial. The result is that the declaration of Yahweh's name in this text moves the Israelites into deeper communion with the God of the cosmos, which will unfold throughout the Nevi'im, Ketuvim, and ultimately the New Testament.

Nevi'im: Consequences, Redemption, and Restoration

As the theological revelation of the Tanakh advances, the Nevi'im offers a powerful theological commentary on Israel's journey from a divine calling in the midst of henotheism to monotheism and the historical experience therein. If the Torah represents the establishment of the covenant and God's foundational blueprint for a holy nation, then the Nevi'im supplies a calling to better grasp that covenant through time. As Christopher Wright puts it, "The prophets were theologians of history . . . constantly interpreting Israel's past, present, and future in light of Yahweh's covenantal intentions."[12] The prophetic books trace the complex interplay of obedience and failure, divine

12. C. Wright, *Mission of God*, 281.

judgment and hope, articulating a vision in which theology and history are inseparably intertwined.

The core message of all the prophets revolves around consequences and the outworking of covenant obedience or disobedience as established in the Torah. The blessings and curses of Deuteronomy (chaps. 27–30) sadly come to life in the prophetic texts. In fact, Israel's failure to uphold justice, reject idolatry, and care for the vulnerable brought about the Assyrian and Babylonian exiles (Deut. 28:63). Highlighting systemic injustice as a covenant violation, the prophet Amos, for example, indicts Israel with piercing clarity:

> They sell the righteous for silver,
> and the needy for a pair of sandals. (Amos 2:6)

Walter Brueggemann explains: "The prophets act as covenantal watchdogs, reminding Israel that their public life is under the scrutiny of Yahweh's moral demands."[13]

The rise and fall of the monarchy seen in the Former Prophets reflects the deep theological tension between human governance and divine kingship. As Israel moved from henotheism to monotheism, the role of the king was called into question, for Yahweh was to be "The King." As such, the recorded history of the monarchy is written not merely to record political developments but also to evaluate the nation's covenantal fidelity in subsequent generations.

Yet judgment is not the final word in the Nevi'im. The prophets articulate a transformative view of Israel's relationship with Yahweh. Rolf Rendtorff tells us, "The prophets are not merely preachers of doom; they speak of a future shaped by God's faithfulness to the covenant, even after Israel's failure."[14] Hosea's metaphor of a broken marriage repaired through love (Hosea 2:14–23) reveals a God who disciplines to heal. Isaiah speaks of a remnant that will return (Isa. 10:20–22), and Jeremiah writes that God's plans for his people are "to prosper you and not to harm you, to give you a future and a hope" (Jer. 29:11 AT).

This development signals a deepening of covenant theology—that is, the Israelite religion. In the Torah, punishment often follows a retributive logic: blessing for obedience, curse for disobedience. In the Nevi'im, however, divine justice becomes a vehicle for moral and spiritual transformation. Exile, while devastating, becomes a catalyst for repentance, purification, and renewal. This movement toward restoration culminates in some of the most hope-filled visions in the Hebrew Bible. The prophets begin to imagine not only a return to

13. Brueggemann and Hankins, *Prophetic Imagination*, 39.
14. Rendtorff, *Canonical Hebrew Bible*, 142.

the land but a return to the heart of God. Jeremiah's prophecy of a "new covenant" (Jer. 31:31–34) written not on tablets but on human hearts redefines the relational dynamic between God and his people. It implies a future where obedience is internalized and covenant fidelity flows from transformation rather than from external compulsion. John Goldingay observes, "The prophets press forward the idea that Israel's future is not merely a reinstatement of the past, but a radical re-creation."[15] Ezekiel echoes this hope, declaring, "I will give you a new heart and put a new spirit within you" (Ezek. 36:26 AT).

Moreover, the prophetic hope reaches beyond Israel. Isaiah envisions a time when Israel will serve as "a light to the nations" (Isa. 49:6 AT), expanding the covenant's reach to a universal horizon. This is not an abandonment of Israel's identity but a fulfillment of its vocation. In this way, the Nevi'im occupies a pivotal role in the Tanakh's theological arc. The writers in this corpus mediate between the Torah's theological blueprint and the Ketuvim's theological application, serving both as covenantal prosecutors and eschatological preachers. They do not merely call Israel back to the Torah; they also rearticulate it within a broader and more theologically developed context.

Nevi'im Test Case: The Davidic Covenant (2 Sam. 7)

What Is This Text About?

Second Samuel 7 stands as a cornerstone in biblical theology, chronicling the moment when God makes a covenant with David. Having secured peace and established Jerusalem as the capital, David aspires to build a house (temple) for God. Instead, through the prophet Nathan, God reveals a greater plan: David will not build a house for God, but God will build a "house" (dynasty) for David. This covenant contains divine promises of enduring kingship, paternal favor, and unbroken loyalty, even when David's descendants sin. David's subsequent prayer is an expression of humility and awe, acknowledging God's sovereignty and faithfulness.

What Is the Israelite Religion in This Text?

Second Samuel 7 presents Israelite religion as *covenantal*, centered on divine initiative rather than human enterprise. Israel's faith is shown to be grounded in God's sovereign grace, choosing leaders and establishing his kingdom on his own terms. God's rejection of David's temple proposal highlights a theology of divine freedom and priority. The religious vision here is not temple-centric but promise-centric. God's covenantal speech, not Israel's

15. Goldingay, *Theology of the Book of Isaiah*, 143.

liturgical acts, defines the future. As a result, Robert Gordon writes, "The theology of kingship in 2 Samuel 7 displaces cultic ambition with a political theology rooted in Yahweh's choice and steadfast love."[16]

God's relationship with Israel is mediated through the Davidic dynasty, making kingship a theological institution. The emphasis shifts from sacred space to sacred person. The idea that the king is God's son (v. 14) aligns Israelite religion with a divinely sanctioned monarchy, as also seen in Ps. 2:7, "You are my Son; today I have begotten you."

What Theological Themes or Concepts Are Present in This Text?

Several theological motifs emerge clearly:

1. Divine sovereignty and initiative: God acts unilaterally in establishing the covenant.
2. Davidic covenant: The heart of the chapter is God's promise: "Your house and your kingdom shall be made sure forever before me. Your throne shall be established forever" (v. 16). This introduces the concept of an enduring royal line, which becomes the backbone of messianic theology.
3. Filial relationship: God declares, "I will be to him a father, and he shall be to me a son" (v. 14). This theology of kingship implies a covenantal bond marked by both privilege and responsibility.
4. Steadfast love (*hesed*): God's enduring commitment is emphasized: "I will not take my steadfast love from him as I took it from Saul" (v. 15 AT).

What Role Does This Text Play in the Development of Israelite/Jewish Theology?

Second Samuel 7 marks a watershed in the theological imagination of Israel. The covenant reshapes Israel's view of kingship, no longer as a pragmatic institution, but as the centerpiece of divine governance. It is here that the theological hope for a messianic king takes root. This covenantal promise becomes the lens through which Israel processes exile, suffering, and hope.

The prophetic books regularly appeal to this covenant when critiquing or encouraging Israel. Isaiah 9 and 11 envision an ideal Davidic ruler, while Jer. 23:5–6 affirms, "I will raise up for David a righteous Branch." Even amid

16. Gordon, *I & II Samuel*, 240.

national collapse, Israel's hope is anchored in the unbreakable word spoken in 2 Sam. 7.

In Jewish theology, especially during the Second Temple period, this covenant was pivotal in messianic expectations. It became part of the theological scaffolding for texts such as the Psalms of Solomon and the Dead Sea Scrolls, which anticipate a restored Davidic kingdom.

How Does This Text Contribute to the Overall Theological Framework of the Tanakh?

Second Samuel 7 links the earlier Abrahamic covenant (Gen. 12 and 15) to the emerging theology of kingship. In both covenants, divine promises of land, seed, and blessing are given unilaterally. This continuity underscores God's consistent redemptive strategy.

This text also shapes the royal psalms (e.g., Pss. 2, 72, 89, 132), which echo and expand upon the Davidic promises. Psalm 89 is especially notable; it celebrates the covenant while wrestling with its apparent failure during exile. "You have renounced the covenant with your servant" (v. 39), the psalmist laments, reflecting the theological tension between promise and historical reality.

The theological impact of 2 Sam. 7 reverberates across the Tanakh:

- In the Torah, it fulfills the leadership promises hinted at in Num. 24:17 ("A star shall come out of Jacob").
- In the Nevi'im, it becomes the basis for eschatological visions of justice and peace.
- In the Ketuvim, particularly the Psalms, it becomes a liturgical and devotional anchor.

Christopher Wright summarizes the importance of 2 Sam. 7: "This covenant introduces a messianic hope rooted not in abstract eschatology but in real, historical promises made to David, a hope that will eventually be rearticulated in the expectation of an ideal king."[17]

Although this covenantal theology is rich, it also presents interpretive tensions. First, there is the issue of conditional versus unconditional elements. The Davidic covenant in 2 Sam. 7 appears unconditional in its promise of permanence, yet later texts such as Hosea 3:4 and Ps. 89 raise questions about its endurance. Second, messianic readings create further complexity. Christian interpretations often understand the covenant in light of Jesus, though

17. C. Wright, *Mission of God*, 329.

this risks overlooking its original historical and nationalistic meaning. Jewish interpretations, on the other hand, view the covenant as future-oriented, expecting a literal Davidic king. Both traditions must grapple with what it means for the promise to be "forever." Finally, the historical evolution of kingship must be considered. Earlier texts, such as 1 Sam. 8, express ambivalence toward the monarchy, reminding interpreters to avoid constructing an overly idealized theological picture.

How Does This Approach Inform Our Hermeneutic of This Text?

Here we see Israel's religion dealing with kingship, temple, and promise in light of the earlier covenantal foundations of the Torah. Yahweh's pledge to build David a house and to adopt his descendant as son represents a fresh constriction of the divine purpose: The universal claims of Sinai are now focused through a royal line. Asking our four questions, we recognize that 2 Sam. 7 reflects an Israelite religion in which monarchy has become crucial to identity, in essence, bridging between Torah's covenant with the people and the later prophetic and wisdom reflections on failed kingship, exile, and hope for restoration.

What Are the Benefits of Applying This Approach to This Text?

1. A snapshot of Israelite religion at this time: We see the Israelite religion at this point move from the religion of Sinai nomads to being centralized around the monarchy with a dynastic/messianic future.
2. The start of theological themes: The themes of divine kingship, covenant loyalty, and God's dwelling are introduced in this text.
3. Theological development: The Davidic covenant leads to later messianic hope and reframes covenant identity as a national identity.
4. A theological paradigm: Jerusalem/Zion theology is now central as a place of worship and provision. Later writings in the Nevi'im and the Ketuvim will reinterpret it; exile will be seen as judgment, but there remains a hope of David's line being restored.

What Are the Potential Problems in Applying This Approach to This Text?

1. Reductionism: Applying this method to 2 Sam. 7 risks reducing the Davidic covenant to mere raw material for later reflectors, such as redactors with messianic hopes.

2. Political-only hermeneutic: A strong developmental lens can push us to read the chapter primarily as royal legitimation or ideological propaganda.

Summary of Test Case

Second Samuel 7 is not merely a historical report; it is a theological constitution. It defines kingship, reshapes covenant theology, and introduces hope for a future ruler who will embody God's justice and steadfast love. This text moves Israelite religion from temple-centered aspirations to promise-centered faith rooted in divine authority. While David desired to build God a house, God instead promises to build David a "house," thus changing the religious view from mere temple to something living. The God worshiped in the temple is now promised in the form of an heir of David. Though set in a particular moment, its echoes shape the structure and spirit of the Tanakh, inspiring liturgy, prophecy, and messianic longing.

Ketuvim: Personal Reflections and Wisdom

The Ketuvim represent the final movement in the theological reading of the Tanakh. Where the Torah outlines the theological foundation of covenant, and the Nevi'im wrestles with its application in national-political arenas, the Ketuvim moves toward an inward existential theology of Israel's faith. This is not to say that there is "no inward theology" in the Torah or the Nevi'im, but that the books of the Ketuvim make it the primary topic of their respective literature. In the Ketuvim, the identity of Israel is no longer merely national or prophetic; it is personal and communal. As Childs describes it, "The Writings reflect a shift from prophetic proclamation to theological meditation. The covenantal God is still present, but often veiled, and Israel's response is shaped more by reflection than by revelation."[18] The canonization of the Ketuvim, occurring last and likely after the Babylonian exile and into the Second Temple period, allowed it to absorb and integrate centuries of theological development, personal anguish, and communal liturgical practice.

Temple-Centered Faith and the Psalms

At the heart of the Ketuvim lies the Psalter, which anchors this section in the cultic life of Israel. Far from being a random selection of poems, the Psalms form a theological grammar for ancient Israelite worship. As Sigmund

18. Childs, *Introduction to the Old Testament as Scripture*, 510.

Mowinckel famously argues, many of the Psalms were originally composed for use in temple ritual, particularly for festivals and royal enthronements, and thus functioned not only as private devotions but also as actual liturgical texts within the cultus.[19] Through the Theological Development approach, one finds that the Psalms recontextualize theological themes found in the Torah and the Nevi'im—divine justice, covenant faithfulness, mercy, kingship—but now as a lived faith, where individuals or communities approach God through praise, lament, thanksgiving, and wisdom.

Festival Scrolls: The Megillot

The Megillot (Ruth, Esther, Song of Songs, Lamentations, Ecclesiastes), each tied to a major Jewish festival, anchor the theology of Israel's faith within its sacred calendar. Through the Theological Development approach, these texts are not just stories. Rather, they are lived theology via narratives, laments, songs, and philosophical reflections. The Megillot helps connect Israel's story theologically to seasons of worship and reflection. Each scroll develops a distinct theme that complements Israel's historical and liturgical identity:

- Ruth, read at Shavuot, portrays divine providence within ordinary life. Ruth's faithfulness becomes a means of covenantal inclusion and continuity.
- Esther, tied to Purim, reveals a theology of divine presence through absence. God is never named, yet God's providence shapes the entire narrative.
- Song of Songs, associated with Passover, is read as both a celebration of love and a metaphor for God's relationship with Israel.
- Lamentations, recited on Tisha B'Av, mourns the destruction of Jerusalem. It is a theologically raw response to covenant rupture.
- Ecclesiastes, linked to Sukkot, wrestles with the enigma of life's meaning in a fleeting world. Its wisdom is paradoxical and skeptical, yet profoundly God-centered.

Wisdom and Historical Reflection

In addition to the Psalms and Megillot, the Ketuvim includes wisdom literature (Proverbs, Job, Ecclesiastes) and historical reflections (Daniel, Ezra-Nehemiah, Chronicles), each contributing to Israel's theological evolution.

19. Mowinckel, *Psalms in Israel's Worship*, 15.

Proverbs theologically champions the reality of cause and effect, where wisdom leads to life, and folly to ruin. Yet Job and Ecclesiastes challenge this framework, exposing the limits of conventional wisdom. Job's protest against unjust suffering and Ecclesiastes's lament over life's futility reflect a maturing theology, one that confronts mystery and suffering without abandoning reverence. In these works, one is assured that theological questioning is common and should grow into theological wisdom (fear) of God.

The historical books (Chronicles, Ezra-Nehemiah, Daniel) reinterpret Israel's past with theological precision. Chronicles retell Israel's story with an emphasis on temple worship and Davidic legitimacy. Ezra-Nehemiah present a theology of restoration rooted in Torah observance and communal identity after exile. Daniel, though apocalyptic, also contributes to wisdom theology, offering visions of divine sovereignty amid imperial oppression.

The Final Glimpse of Israelite Religion

With the Ketuvim, the canon closes not with pronouncement but with theological reflection. The voices noted in the Chronicles are diverse—scribes, sages, poets, and priests—yet all are rooted in the memory of Israel's covenant and the hope of its future. Thus the finale of the Ketuvim is also the historical end of Israelite national religion as it was formerly practiced. With the destruction of the Second Temple in 70 CE, rabbinic Judaism arose, developing new modes of interpretation and communal life and practices. In that sense, the Ketuvim stands as "the final snapshot of Israelite theology" before the transition into Judaism as we know it.[20]

Ketuvim Test Case: The King of Glory (Ps. 24)

What Is This Text About?

Psalm 24 is a liturgical psalm that celebrates the sovereignty of God over all creation and affirms the holiness required to enter his presence. The psalm opens by declaring that the earth and everything in it belongs to the Lord, highlighting his ownership of the world. It then poses the question of who may ascend the "hill of the Lord" and stand in his holy place, answering that only those with clean hands and a pure heart, those who have not sworn deceitfully or pursued false gods, are worthy. The psalm concludes with a call to open the gates for the "King of glory," who is described as strong and mighty in battle, a reference to God as both creator and warrior. This psalm

20. Kugel, *How to Read the Bible*, 674.

may have been used in temple worship as part of the procession of the ark into Jerusalem or as an entrance liturgy into the temple itself.

What Is the Israelite Religion in This Text?

Psalm 24 reflects Israelite religion in its liturgical, covenantal, and theological dimensions, functioning as a processional hymn likely used during temple-entry rituals. It highlights Yahweh's universal kingship, the moral requirements for worshipers, and the sacredness of Zion as God's dwelling place. The psalm opens with a cosmic declaration:

> The earth is the LORD's and the fullness thereof,
> the world and those who dwell therein. (Ps. 24:1)

This affirms monotheistic belief in Yahweh as creator and sovereign over all creation, a central tenet of Israelite faith that distinguishes it from the polytheistic systems of its neighbors. The acknowledgment that God founded the world "upon the seas" and "established it upon the rivers" (v. 2) also alludes to Yahweh's dominion over chaotic forces, reinforcing his supremacy and order-bringing power. The Israelite religion in this psalm is deeply rooted in the recognition of God as the supreme sovereign of the universe and of the holiness required to approach him. It reflects the centrality of worship and purity in the life of the Israelites, emphasizing that God's dwelling place, particularly the temple, is sacred and requires holiness to enter. This calls for both external actions (clean hands) and internal purity (a pure heart) to align with God's moral and spiritual standards.

What Theological Themes or Concepts Are Present in This Text?

1. Moral and ritual conditions for entering the sanctuary (vv. 3–6): "He who has clean hands and a pure heart, who does not lift up his soul to what is false and does not swear deceitfully" (v. 4). This links external worship with internal integrity, presenting ethical monotheism as foundational to right relationship with God.
2. Connection of worship and covenant: The mention of "the generation of those who seek him, who seek the face of the God of Jacob" (v. 6) connects worship to the covenantal tradition rooted in the patriarchs. This shows that access to God is both a privilege and a responsibility of those in covenant with him.
3. God's sovereignty and holiness: Because of God's sovereignty over creation and his holiness, righteousness is required to commune with God.

4. Divine transcendence and immanence: The psalm emphasizes God's transcendence as the creator of the world. It also asserts his immanence as the one who can be approached by those who are pure and upright.
5. God as warrior (v. 8): The image of God as a warrior presents the tension between his holiness and his power to deliver and protect his people. This duality reflects the complex nature of God as both majestic and intimately involved in the life of Israel.

What Role Does This Text Play in the Development of Israelite/Jewish Theology?

Psalm 24 plays an important role in developing Israelite and Jewish theology regarding divine presence and kingship. The final section (vv. 7–10) presents a dramatic call-and-response liturgy that was likely associated with the ark entering Jerusalem or the temple:

> Lift up your heads, O gates!
> . . .
> that the King of glory may come in. (v. 7)

The identity of this "King of glory" is declared emphatically:

> The Lord, strong and mighty,
> the Lord, mighty in battle! (v. 8)

And again in verse 10 God is identified as "the Lord of hosts."

These verses combine the imagery of warrior-God with temple theology, asserting that Yahweh is both the victorious defender of Israel and the rightful ruler whose presence sanctifies the temple. This reinforces the view that God is not confined to heaven but dwells among his people in Zion, making Jerusalem a theological center in the Tanakh. This text plays an important role in the development of Israelite/Jewish theology by emphasizing the requirements for approaching God. The psalm outlines an ideal of holiness that aligns with the covenantal relationship between God and Israel. It helps to define the conditions for worship in the temple and the moral and spiritual purity expected of those who would engage with the divine. Moreover, the psalm's portrayal of God as the "King of glory" foreshadows messianic themes of a future divine ruler who will come to bring justice and establish God's rule.

How Does This Text Contribute to the Overall Theological Framework of the Tanakh?

Within the overall theological framework of the Tanakh, Ps. 24 bridges creation theology, ethical covenantal religion, and Zion theology. It builds upon the Torah's emphasis on holiness and righteousness (cf. Leviticus) while anticipating prophetic calls for sincere worship and justice (cf. Isa. 1, Amos 5). Furthermore, the depiction of Yahweh as "King of glory" ties into messianic expectations developed in texts such as Ps. 2 and Isa. 9. It prepares the theological groundwork for understanding God's kingdom not merely in abstract or cosmic terms but as personally present and dynamically active among his people. As such, Ps. 24 enriches the Tanakh's vision of God as both transcendent ruler and immanent Lord, worthy of reverent worship and ethical devotion. In the larger theological framework of the Tanakh, Ps. 24 contributes to the biblical themes of God's kingship and holiness. It connects with the broader biblical narrative of God's reign over Israel and the world, and it sets a standard for worship and relationship with God. In particular, this psalm enhances the understanding of God's temple as a holy place that must be approached with reverence, purity, and integrity, laying the foundation for the theological importance of the temple as a locus for divine presence. The psalm's vision of God's sovereignty also points toward the eschatological hope for the future coming of God's kingdom.

How Does This Approach Inform Our Hermeneutic of This Text?

Psalm 24 functions as a Ketuvim snapshot that both receives and reframes earlier theological trajectories, and thus, if the Tanakh is organized by theological development, it informs our hermeneutic by clarifying the nature of God's holiness and its relation to Israel's worship practices. Here the universal sovereignty of Yahweh ("the earth is the Lord's and everything in it") is woven together with a distinctly Zion-centered liturgical vision in which the divine King enters his sanctuary and a purified community ascends his hill. Our guiding questions reveal an Israelite religion in which temple worship, pilgrimage, and wisdom-like ethical criteria ("clean hands and a pure heart") have become central markers of covenant identity, presenting a vision of holiness consistent with earlier covenantal promises where God's presence is tied to righteousness and purity. Psalm 24 does not merely repeat the covenantal and royal themes of Torah and Nevi'im. Instead, it meditates on them poetically, interiorizing holiness and recasting kingship in cultic-liturgical terms. This shapes how we read later texts that further explore God's holiness, the qualifications for entering his presence, and the messianic expectations of God's reign, as Israel's reflection on divine kingship moves from narrative and oracle into sung communal theology.

What Are the Benefits of Applying This Approach to This Text?

1. A snapshot of Israelite religion at this time: Israelite religion is not only unified nationally but is now temple-centered worship, which extends into Israel's daily liturgical life.
2. The start of theological themes: God's sovereignty over all (not just Israel) and his presence in worship make holiness and purity essential to worship.
3. Theological development: Psalm 24 advances the concept that not only Israel but also the whole earth should worship Yahweh! The idea of universal worship exudes into Israelite life when in exile and beyond.

What Are the Potential Problems in Applying This Approach to This Text?

1. Anachronism: It is tempting to read later messianic interpretations of "the King of glory" into this psalm, potentially overlooking its immediate context in the liturgy and temple worship.
2. Risk of overlooking the psalm's immediate social and liturgical context: There is the danger of reducing the text to abstract theological principles or focusing on its eschatological future rather than on its original function within Israelite worship.

Summary of Test Case

Psalm 24 is a liturgical psalm that proclaims God's universal kingship (as foreshadowed in 2 Sam. 7) and holiness (as shown in the Torah and now via worship). Opening with the declaration that the earth belongs to Yahweh, it affirms Yahweh's sovereignty as creator over not only Israel but all creation. So not only should Yahweh be the God of Israel; he should be God over all! Specifically, Ps. 24 shapes Israelite worship again into practicing clean hands, pure heart, and covenantal faithfulness in light of all that has transpired thus far in the Tanakh and all that will happen in the future. The result of this text is the seeding of future hope for the full manifestation of God's reign both in Israel and over all creation.

Conclusion

Understanding the Tanakh as a progression of theological development provides a valuable framework for engaging its texts on their own historical and religious terms. Just as historical events unfold in layers, shaped by the unique conditions of each era, so too does Israelite theology take shape across the distinct literary and theological landscapes of the Torah, the Nevi'im, and the Ketuvim. Each section reflects not merely a new chapter in Israel's story but a fresh moment of divine-human encounter interpreted through the lenses of evolving beliefs, communal experiences, and covenantal expectations.

By asking what the Israelite religion looks like in each division, what theological ideas are present, how these ideas shape Jewish thought, and how they fit within the broader biblical canon, readers gain tools for exploring both continuity and innovation in the text. This approach resists flattening the Bible into a single theological belief system and instead highlights its dynamic theological changes. In doing so, it respects the diverse historical settings that gave rise to its various writings.

Ultimately, treating the Tanakh as a canon marked by theological development deepens our appreciation for its richness and complexity. It helps us see not only what biblical authors believed but also how they wrestled with faith amid historical upheaval, exile, restoration, and changing understandings of God. Through this lens, Scripture emerges not as a static archive of doctrine but as a living conversation that unfolds over centuries, anchored in tradition yet ever responding to the demands of the moment.

4

Spiritual Guide Approach

Tanakh as Guiding Words

According to the American Bible Society's "State of the Bible" report for 2023, the main reason Americans read their Bibles is out of a desire to be closer to God. A second important reason is to find wisdom for life decisions.[1] The Spiritual Guide approach discussed in this chapter views the Tanakh as "guiding words" and espouses the belief that one can find a rationale for the Tanakh's structure somewhere between desiring God and searching for wisdom.

As you progress in your reading through the Torah, the Nevi'im, and finally the Ketuvim, you should progress through notable topics that lead you to be closer to God and help you gain timeless wisdom. The argument of this approach is that the three divisions of the Tanakh progress through three different spiritual themes. First, the Torah lists the foundational teachings on ethics, rituals, and laws. The Nevi'im then provides moral teachings and warnings. And lastly, the Ketuvim addresses human experiences of living out the foundational teaching and prophetic application in human life and emotions while providing practical wisdom.

If the Tanakh is structured as a spiritual guide, then several questions must be asked of a particular text.

- What topic(s) does this text teach believers?
- How do these topics relate to the other sections of the Tanakh?

1. American Bible Society, "State of the Bible USA 2023," 10.

- How does this approach inform our hermeneutic of this text?
- What are the benefits of applying this approach to this text?
- What are the potential problems in applying this approach to this text?

Reasons for Adopting This Approach

The Tanakh serves as more than a historical or literary document; it functions as a profound spiritual guide. Its tripartite structure offers a layered approach to understanding divine instruction. The Torah lays the foundation by establishing laws, ethical principles, and rituals that define the covenantal relationship between God and Israel. The Nevi'im builds upon this foundation, providing moral exhortations, warnings, and calls to repentance. The Ketuvim reflects on human experiences, offering wisdom, prayers, and meditations on life's complexities. Together these divisions present a comprehensive framework for spiritual guidance. Ellen Davis clarifies how this approach differs from other ways of looking at the text: "What I am exploring here is not its prophetic function or even its moral teachings—if by that we mean a set of inflexible rules about what we should or should not do. Rather, I am looking for what the Old Testament tells us about intimate life with God."[2]

The thematic understanding of the Tanakh further reinforces its role as a guide for moral and ethical reflection. The stories of biblical figures illustrate the consequences of moral choices, while the prophetic messages challenge societies to uphold righteousness and seek divine mercy. Wisdom literature, such as Proverbs and Ecclesiastes, provides practical insight for navigating life's uncertainties. These themes remain relevant across cultures and generations, offering timeless guidance for those seeking to align their lives with divine principles.

As a spiritual guide, the Tanakh offers a multifaceted source of wisdom, instruction, and inspiration. Its structure provides a progression from foundational law to prophetic exhortation to reflective wisdom, ensuring a well-rounded approach to faith and ethics. Its themes offer moral clarity and encourage personal and communal transformation. Whether approached from a Jewish or Christian perspective, the Tanakh remains a living document that continues to shape spiritual journeys and ethical reflections.

2. Davis, *Getting Involved with God*, 2.

Proponents of This Approach

The Tanakh, the Hebrew Bible, has served as the foundational text for Jewish spiritual life for millennia, offering not merely a historical record or a collection of laws but a profound and multifaceted guide to humanity's relationship with the divine. Across diverse eras and intellectual landscapes, Jewish thinkers have found unique pathways to spiritual understanding and practice. From the rational systematization of the Geonim to the existential encounters of modern philosophy, the Tanakh has remained an enduring light, illuminating the path toward a life of meaning and connection with God.

For early medieval thinkers such as Saadia Gaon (882–942 CE), the Tanakh was the supreme source of divine revelation, a harmonious blend of revealed truth and rational wisdom. He posited that the commandments within the Torah were not arbitrary but purposeful, guiding humanity toward moral and spiritual perfection. Saadia believed that the Tanakh provided a clear and rational framework for understanding God's will, leading to true piety and a life aligned with divine wisdom. Similarly, Rashi (1040–1105 CE), the preeminent commentator, dedicated his life to making the Tanakh accessible. His meticulous commentaries, balancing the literal meaning with rich rabbinic tradition, underscored his conviction that the Tanakh was a living document, offering direct instruction for daily life and spiritual growth. Through careful study, Rashi believed, every Jew could connect with its divine message, shaping a life of integrity.

The towering figure of Maimonides (1138–1204 CE) further emphasized the rational and ethical dimensions of the Tanakh. For him, the commandments were not mere rituals but possessed profound philosophical and moral purposes aimed at refining character and establishing a just society, ultimately leading to intellectual and spiritual perfection. Maimonides saw the Tanakh as a comprehensive guide to achieving this highest form of worship, advocating for deep intellectual engagement with its wisdom. A counterpoint emerged with Nachmanides (1194–1270 CE), who, while respecting the literal, delved into the Tanakh's hidden, mystical meanings. For Nachmanides, the text contained secrets of creation and divine emanation, allowing the diligent student to connect with the divine presence itself and achieve profound mystical experiences.

The transition to modern thought brought new perspectives to the Tanakh's spiritual guidance. Martin Buber (1878–1965), with his emphasis on the "I-Thou" relationship, viewed the Tanakh as a record of humanity's ongoing dialogue with the divine. He saw the biblical narratives as invitations to a personal, reciprocal encounter with God, where the spiritual life unfolded in a dynamic exchange of address and response. This dialogical encounter, according to Buber, transformed the text from a mere historical document into a living testament to divine presence.

Mid-twentieth-century thinkers continued to explore the Tanakh's relevance in a complex world. Rabbi Joseph Soloveitchik (1903–67), bridging traditional Judaism with Western philosophy, saw the Halakha (Jewish law derived from the Torah) as the very blueprint for spiritual existence. For "the halakhic man," the Tanakh provided the framework for actively shaping one's world according to God's will, transforming chaotic existence into a sacred cosmos through disciplined adherence to its commandments. In contrast, Abraham Joshua Heschel (1907–72) highlighted the Tanakh's capacity to evoke awe and wonder, revealing God's "pathos"—his deep concern for humanity. For Heschel, the Tanakh cultivated a radical amazement at existence, fostering a life of gratitude and ethical responsiveness to God's call for justice. Even in the shadow of the Holocaust, Eliezer Berkovits (1908–92) found in the Tanakh an enduring ethical and theological foundation. He viewed it as providing the moral framework for spiritual life, emphasizing personal responsibility and a commitment to justice even when the divine presence seems hidden.

More contemporary scholars continue to enrich our understanding of the Tanakh's spiritual power. Robert Alter (1935–), through his meticulous literary analysis, demonstrates how the Tanakh's sophisticated artistry, narrative techniques, and poetic power are inseparable from its spiritual message. By unveiling the literary genius of the text, Alter reveals its capacity to shape moral imagination and a deeper appreciation for the human condition in relation to the divine. Rabbi Jonathan Sacks (1948–2020) championed the Tanakh's timeless wisdom for contemporary life, viewing it as a moral compass and a source of hope. He showed its power to foster identity, purpose, and belonging, making it a compelling guide for navigating modern challenges. Ellen Davis (1950–) draws out the Tanakh's ecological dimensions, seeing it as a profound guide for environmental stewardship and sustainable living and demonstrating how the text calls for a holistic spiritual life integrated with care for creation. Finally, Michael Fishbane (1943–) emphasizes the Tanakh as a living tradition, continually reinterpreted and re-actualized. For him, the spiritual life is intertwined with this interpretive process, where engagement with the text's rich history of meaning allows its ancient wisdom to speak to contemporary experience.

From the rational certainty of the past to the nuanced literary/existential readings of the present, these diverse thinkers underscore the Tanakh's enduring capacity to serve as a guide to spiritual life. Whether through its legal documents, its narratives, its poetry, or its philosophical wisdom, the Tanakh continues to invite readers into a transformative encounter with the divine. Its timeless wisdom ensures its place as an indispensable light for those seeking a more spiritually rich life.

Hermeneutical Realities of This Approach

Unlike purely academic approaches, which focus on historical, literary, or linguistic analysis, this perspective emphasizes the transformative potential of reading and meditating on the text. Engaging with the Tanakh in this way fosters spiritual growth, deepens one's understanding of God's character and purposes, and provides not only personal guidance but also comfort through prayerful reflection. This approach offers several key benefits that contribute to a richer hermeneutical experience. First, it integrates spiritual and moral dimensions, ensuring that the Tanakh is not studied merely for its historical value but also for its ethical and moral relevance. Readers are encouraged to bridge the gap between ancient teachings and modern life, applying its wisdom to contemporary situations.

Second, this perspective facilitates personal and communal application, prompting readers to explore how biblical principles can inform daily challenges and ethical decision-making. Third, it places significant emphasis on moral exemplars and teachings, encouraging readers to engage with figures such as Moses, David, and Esther as well as with wisdom literature such as Proverbs and Psalms and viewing the texts not only as historical narratives but also as ethical models for character formation. Lastly, this approach highlights universal themes concerning the human condition, making the Tanakh accessible across cultural and religious backgrounds. By focusing on existential questions and timeless truths, it fosters an inclusive and profound interpretation that resonates beyond academic study.

Despite its strengths, reading the Tanakh primarily as a spiritual guide introduces interpretative challenges, particularly in the realm of reader response. A hermeneutic that prioritizes personal application often leads to subjective interpretations, where meaning is shaped more by personal feelings and preferences than by textual intent. Without careful attention to historical and cultural contexts, readers risk distorting the original meaning of the text, projecting modern perspectives onto ancient writings. Additionally, the tendency to cherry-pick verses that align with personal beliefs, while disregarding those that challenge or complicate one's understanding, can result in a fragmented and imbalanced reading of the Tanakh. A lack of academic rigor in reader-response approaches may also lead to neglecting textual nuances such as genre, literary structure, and linguistic considerations, which are crucial for accurate interpretation. While it is possible to apply this method in a communal dimension, the often-individualistic reading sadly overlooks the texts that address the collective identity of Israel, covenantal obligations, and societal ethics. Furthermore, neglecting authorial intent in favor of subjective impressions can lead to misinterpretations that stray from the original purpose and message of the text. Finally, an overemphasis on reader response can contribute to theological and moral relativism, where all interpretations are treated as equally valid regardless of their coherence with broader biblical teachings. This can undermine the authoritative and normative role of the Tanakh as a guide for faith and practice.

While the Spiritual Guide approach to the Tanakh offers meaningful and enriching insights, it must be balanced with careful hermeneutical discipline. A responsible engagement with the text requires integrating both spiritual reflection and scholarly rigor, ensuring that personal application does not come at the expense of historical, cultural, and theological accuracy.

Torah: Guidance for Righteous Living

The Torah forms the theological and ethical bedrock of Jewish life and thought. It is not simply a set of laws or an ancient legal code but a divinely revealed constitution for covenantal living, offering a comprehensive vision for what it means to live righteously under God's sovereignty. As Michael Fishbane explains, "The Torah is not law alone, but instruction (torah) in the broadest sense: a teaching of divine will that embraces history, ritual, ethics, and hope."[3] For this reason, Hebrew students rarely translate "torah" as law but rather as instruction! While modern readers may be tempted to reduce the Torah to legal prescriptions, its enduring power lies in the way it interweaves law with narrative, ethics with worship, and community with divine presence. The statutes and commandments are not arbitrary or impersonal but are embedded in the vision to embody holiness in every sphere of life. As Lev. 19:2 instructs: "You shall be holy, for I the LORD your God am holy." This command stands as the ethical heartbeat of the Torah, shaping not only behavior but also internal orientation toward God and others.

The moral imperatives of the Torah, "Love your neighbor as yourself" (Lev. 19:18) and "Justice, justice you shall pursue" (Deut. 16:20 AT), reflect a covenantal ethic rooted in God's character. These are not mere rules but theological

3. Fishbane, *Biblical Interpretation*, 1.

principles intended to transform the human being. Moshe Greenberg writes: "Biblical law differs from other ancient law codes in the degree to which it is suffused with moral and theological principles. It aims not merely at justice but at holiness."[4] This concept extends to all areas of life, including ritual, economics, and care for the vulnerable. Again, the Torah is not mere law but instruction for a moral life. Sarna rightly declares, "The Torah is not content with outward conformity. It seeks to educate the conscience and transform the heart."[5] The Torah also sanctifies everyday life, from dietary practices to agricultural practices. Holiness is embedded in the ordinary. "In Judaism, law and life are inseparable. The Torah sanctifies time, space, and human behavior. It is a way of life infused with divine meaning."[6] There is no divide between sacred and secular; all of life becomes an act of covenantal worship.

These guided moral teachings are framed by story, creation, covenant, redemption, and revelation, which provide practical theological grounding. Genesis centers Israel's identity in Abraham's promises; Exodus connects ethical treatment of strangers to Israel's own experience of slavery. The Sinai revelation unites legal obligation with divine calling: "You shall be to me a kingdom of priests and a holy nation" (Exod. 19:6). According to Jon Levenson, this "covenant at Sinai is not just about legal obligation but about transforming history into a relationship with God."[7] And Umberto Cassuto concludes, "The Torah was written not merely to inform, but to form, to shape Israel into a holy nation."[8]

For over two thousand years, Torah has shaped Jewish life, thought, and worship. It is studied, debated, and cherished as a "tree of life to those who hold fast to it" (Prov. 3:18 AT). Torah is the foundation of the Jewish canon and identity, combining law and narrative to express a vision of divine justice, compassion, and holiness. Commenting on Gen. 1:1, Rashi asks "Why does the Torah begin with creation rather than with the first commandment? To declare that the whole earth belongs to God, who gave it to whom He saw fit."

Torah Test Case: Be Holy (Lev. 20:22–26)

What Is This Text About?

This text in Leviticus outlines God's command for Israel to be distinct from the nations around them by adhering to his statutes and commands.

4. Greenberg, *Understanding Exodus*, 180.
5. Sarna, *Exploring Exodus*, 15.
6. Berkovits, *God, Man and History*, 45.
7. Levenson, *Sinai & Zion*, 76.
8. Cassuto, *Book of Genesis*, 1:3.

It includes prohibitions against various immoral behaviors, such as sexual relations with close relatives, and emphasizes that these practices were part of the corrupt cultures of the Canaanites. God warns that disobedience to these commands will result in the land "vomiting" the people out, just as it did with the Canaanites. The Israelites are called to be holy and set apart for God, as he has separated them from the nations to be his own people.

What Topic(s) Does This Text Teach Believers?

1. Holiness of life: Believers are called to live holy lives, set apart from the surrounding nations and cultures.
2. Distinctiveness from pagan practices: The text emphasizes the need for Israel to reject the immoral and idolatrous practices of the Canaanites and other nations.
3. Obedience to divine law: The Israelites must follow God's laws to avoid defilement, leading to exile or loss of the land.
4. Consequences of sin: Disobedience brings serious consequences, including the land rejecting the people and loss of God's favor.

How Do These Topics Relate to Other Sections of the Tanakh?

As a text on being holy, Lev. 20 relates to the other two sections of the Tanakh by calling the believer to constantly go back to the initial call of holiness. This call of holiness echoes in the later Torah as a calling to obey divine laws for the sake of being holy and distinct. In the Nevi'im this text is echoed as a reason for expulsion. Finally, in the Ketuvim this text is at the heart of life and worship.

How Does This Approach Inform Our Hermeneutic of This Text?

If the Tanakh is seen as a spiritual guide, this text directs believers toward holiness and distinction from the world. It calls for a life lived in obedience to God's laws, focused on spiritual purity and living separate from pagan influences. The hermeneutic here emphasizes ethical behavior, the need for moral purity, and the consequences of sin.

What Are the Benefits of Applying This Approach to This Text?

1. Call to holiness: This text reinforces the importance of living a life set apart for God's purposes, which is still applicable to modern believers, who are called to live morally distinct lives.

2. Awareness of cultural influence: The text encourages believers to be cautious of cultural practices that conflict with God's commands, which is an important principle in discerning how to live faithfully in a secular world.
3. Obedience brings blessing: The idea that obedience to God's law leads to God's favor and blessing is an encouraging takeaway for those seeking to live according to his will.

What Are the Potential Problems in Applying This Approach to This Text?

1. Legalism: A strict, legalistic application of holiness can lead to an overemphasis on external behaviors while neglecting the heart and spiritual transformation that God desires.
2. Exclusion versus mission: The separation from other nations might be seen as a call to withdraw from the world, potentially discouraging engagement with nonbelievers or ministry to those outside the faith.
3. Misapplication of purity laws: Applying certain purity and holiness laws directly in modern contexts could lead to misunderstanding or misrepresenting the overall redemptive narrative of the Bible. For example, distinctions between clean and unclean may not have the same relevance in the new covenant through Christ.
4. Cultural distance: The specific laws and cultural context of ancient Israel may seem distant or irrelevant to modern believers.
5. Universal versus contextual application: While the text calls for holiness, some aspects of the ceremonial and purity laws may not seem directly applicable in a post-Christian era or in a context where the church is not a nation-state.
6. Ethical tension: Modern interpretations may struggle with applying ancient commands about physical purity or social isolation, especially when dealing with issues such as the relationship between church and culture.

Summary of Test Case

Leviticus 20:22–26 calls Israel to live as a holy and distinct people, separated from the immoral practices of the surrounding nations, particularly the Canaanites. The text emphasizes that obedience to God's laws is necessary for Israel to remain in the land, warning that disobedience will result in their expulsion, just as the Canaanites were expelled before them. In the Spiritual Guide approach, this text teaches the theme of holiness, which is echoed throughout the Torah, Nevi'im, and Ketuvim. Read as a spiritual guide, the text highlights ethical living, separation from corrupt cultural influences, and the seriousness of sin's consequences. Applying this text today, we can find valuable lessons about pursuing holiness, resisting ungodly cultural pressures, and recognizing God's blessing in obedience, but it is hard not to interpret Israel's separation as withdrawal from the world rather than faithful engagement with it.

Nevi'im: Warnings, Encouragement, and Insight

The Nevi'im captures the historical unfolding and spiritual struggles of the Israelite nation through divinely inspired dialogue. While the Torah presents the laws for guiding life, the books of the Nevi'im provide warnings, encouragement, and insight to life. These writings are not static theological statements but living words that are filled with passion, urgency, and unrelenting hope.

The prophetic message arises in times of covenant violation and national crisis, as prophets respond to moral, political, and spiritual decline. The prophets serve as both prosecutors of Israel's disobedience and messengers of divine mercy. Abraham Heschel writes, "The prophet's word is a scream in the night. While others are intoxicated with the here and now, the prophet has a vision of the end."[9] This cry echoes the breaking of covenant loyalty, as God laments through Jeremiah:

> My people have committed two sins:
> They have forsaken me,
>   the spring of living water,
> and have dug their own cisterns,
>   broken cisterns that cannot hold water. (Jer. 2:13 NIV)

Yet their indictments are not final; they are divine pleas for return, as Joel exhorts:

> Return to the Lord your God,
>   for he is gracious and compassionate,
> slow to anger and abounding in love. (Joel 2:13 NIV)

In the Spiritual Guide approach, the prophets challenge hollow religiosity, and confront the illusion that ritual alone satisfies God. Amos proclaims, "I hate, I despise your religious festivals. . . . But let justice roll on like a river,

9. Heschel, *Prophets*, 16.

righteousness like a never-failing stream!" (Amos 5:21, 24 NIV). Isaiah also rebukes superficial piety:

> This people draw near with their mouth
> and honor me with their lips,
> while their hearts are far from me. (Isa. 29:13)

Micah distills the prophetic call:

> What does the LORD require of you?
> To act justly and to love mercy
> and to walk humbly with your God. (Mic. 6:8 NIV)

Along with confronting the present, the prophets envision a future shaped by divine justice and hope. They look toward a messianic and eschatological horizon—a new covenant (Jer. 31:31–34), renewed hearts (Ezek. 36:26–27), and a suffering servant who redeems many (Isa. 53). This vision stretches from national restoration to global transformation:

> They shall beat their swords into plowshares,
> . . .
> nation shall not lift up sword against nation. (Isa. 2:4)

Walter Brueggemann writes, "The prophets anticipate a world reordered by divine justice, in which the vulnerable are lifted up and the powerful held accountable."[10]

The Nevi'im functions as Israel's moral and spiritual conscience—not as secondary to Torah but as its living extension—confronting sin, extending hope, and revealing God's heart. Prophetic literature spans history, judgment, and grace, speaking powerfully to contemporary concerns. These texts continue to be, in Jeremiah's words, "a fire shut up in [our] bones" (Jer. 20:9), a spiritual guide to a life of justice, filled with a vision of hope, and a witness to the holiness and faithfulness of God.

Nevi'im Test Case: Promise of Restoration (Jer. 29:11–13)

What Is This Text About?

In Jer. 29:11–13, God speaks through the prophet to the exiled Israelites in Babylon, offering them a message of hope and encouragement. Despite their current situation of exile and hardship, God assures them that he has a plan

10. Brueggemann, *Hopeful Imagination*, 23.

for their future, one of prosperity and peace rather than harm. He encourages them to seek him with all their heart, promising that when they do, they will find him. This text emphasizes God's faithfulness to his covenant and the assurance that, even in exile, he has not abandoned his people.

What Topic(s) Does This Text Teach Believers?

1. God's plan: Believers are reminded that God has a purposeful plan for their lives, one that aims for their ultimate well-being, even when circumstances are difficult.
2. Hope in exile: The text teaches that even in times of suffering or exile, God's plan remains good and offers hope for the future.
3. Seeking God wholeheartedly: The text stresses the importance of seeking God with sincerity and commitment, and it promises that those who earnestly seek him will find him.
4. God's faithfulness: This text highlights God's unwavering faithfulness to his covenant, even when his people are far from their homeland.

How Do These Topics Relate to Other Sections of the Tanakh?

As a spiritual guide, Jer. 29 points backward to the holy laws of the Torah and the holy covenant therein. God has not abandoned his people but indeed calls them back to the initial way of life commended to them. Jeremiah 29 furthermore points toward the Ketuvim, in which the believer will be called to lead a certain kind of life even while in exile (e.g., Daniel and Esther). We too must read this text as guiding us back into a deeper relationship with God.

How Does This Approach Inform Our Hermeneutic of This Text?

If the Tanakh is viewed as a spiritual guide, Jer. 29:11–13 directs believers toward a life of trust in God's overarching plan, especially in times of struggle or uncertainty. The text encourages believers to place their hope not in circumstances but in the unchanging goodness and faithfulness of God. In this context, the text teaches that while life may include periods of exile or hardship, God's ultimate purpose for his people is always good, and believers can trust in his promises for a future of hope and restoration.

What Are the Benefits of Applying This Approach to This Text?

1. Trust in God's sovereignty: The text reminds believers to trust that God has a good plan for their lives, even when facing adversity or uncertainty.

2. Hope for the future: In times of hardship or exile, believers can find comfort in knowing that God has not forgotten them and that he works for their good.
3. Encouragement to seek God: The text urges a wholehearted pursuit of God, assuring that those who earnestly seek him will find him.
4. Confidence in God's faithfulness: Believers are reminded of God's unwavering faithfulness, even when circumstances seem bleak. This can foster a deep sense of security and trust in God's character.

What Are the Potential Problems in Applying This Approach to This Text?

1. Misunderstanding context: Applying this text directly to every believer's situation without understanding its original context (a specific promise to the exiles) can lead to misconceptions about how God works in individual lives.
2. Mistaken expectations: Based on the promises of this text, believers may mistakenly expect a life of ease or material prosperity, ignoring the reality that God's plans for each person may involve growth through difficulty.
3. Neglecting personal responsibility: The text emphasizes that God's promises are tied to seeking him wholeheartedly. A failure to understand this conditional aspect may lead to a passive approach to faith, where people expect God to fulfill his promises without actively pursuing him or living according to his will.
4. Overspiritualizing messages: One potential issue is the tendency to overly spiritualize the text, applying it directly to personal situations without considering the historical context. While God does have plans for his people, the specific promise in Jeremiah was given to the exiled Israelites in Babylon, not directly to modern believers.
5. Misapplying promises: The text's promise of prosperity and hope could be misinterpreted as a guarantee of material wealth or immediate personal success, leading to a "prosperity gospel" mindset. This overlooks the broader context of exile and the eventual fulfillment of God's plan, which may involve trials and difficulties before restoration.
6. Ignoring the call to seek God: A focus on God's promises without emphasizing the necessity of seeking God wholeheartedly can lead to a passive approach to faith. The promise in verse 13 is conditional on actively pursuing God, which is often overlooked.

Summary of Test Case

In conclusion, Jer. 29:11–13 delivers a message of hope to the exiled Israelites in Babylon, assuring them that despite their suffering, God has not abandoned them but offers a purposeful plan for their future, a plan rooted in peace, restoration, and covenant faithfulness. The text highlights the importance of seeking God wholeheartedly, promising that those who seek God will find him, and it emphasizes trust in his sovereign care even during hardship. Read as a spiritual guide, it directs believers back to the covenant foundations of the Torah, resonates with examples from Ketuvim books such as Daniel and Esther, and underscores that exile does not negate God's presence or promises. For modern readers, the text encourages trust in God's sovereignty, hope amid adversity, and earnest pursuit of him, reminding believers of his unwavering faithfulness. Yet, care must be taken to avoid misapplication, such as interpreting it as a universal guarantee of prosperity, neglecting the conditional call to seek God, or ignoring its historical context as a promise to Israel in exile. Properly understood, the text reassures that God's plans, though sometimes unfolding through hardship, are ultimately good and lead his people toward hope and restoration.

Ketuvim: Wisdom and Comfort in Life Situations

The Ketuvim, as the final division of the Hebrew Bible, presents rich texts encompassing wisdom literature, poetry, lament, narrative history, and apocalyptic vision. Unlike the Torah, which sets forth God's laws for life; and unlike the Nevi'im, which delivers warning, encouragement, and insight; the Ketuvim gives wisdom and comfort in life's situations. These writings serve as companions in the complexity of daily existence, offering practical wisdom, deep theological reflection, and spiritual solace in times of both joy and suffering. Thus, the Ketuvim reflect a wide range of human experiences. They don't necessarily prescribe behavior but instead discuss meaning in behaviors and events.[11] This reflective quality, often centered on individual experience, makes the Ketuvim especially accessible across time and culture.

A central feature of the Ketuvim is its wisdom literature—Proverbs, Job, and Ecclesiastes—which together present a nuanced vision of life. The book of Proverbs teaches that "the fear of the Lord is the beginning of wisdom" (Prov. 9:10), reinforcing a moral order. Proverbs teaches that this morally structured life is to be universal for all, with a vision of a morally structured universe

11. Bartholomew and O'Dowd, *Old Testament Wisdom Literature*, 54.

where good behavior leads to good outcomes. Job challenges this order as a "blameless and upright" man (Job 1:1) suffers unjustly. His paradoxical faith ("Though he slay me, yet will I trust in him," Job 13:15 KJV) leads Ellen Davis to observe, "Job insists that a faithful life includes demanding answers from God, even when none are given."[12] Ecclesiastes offers a skeptical perspective ("Vanity of vanities! All is vanity," Eccles. 1:2) but concludes, "Fear God and keep his commandments" (Eccles. 12:13). So here Ketuvim wisdom is a confrontation to the limits of life and shallow faith,[13] and together these books present biblical faith as resilient, not a naive optimism.

The Psalms and Lamentations engage the emotional life of faith. They give spiritual guidance to praise ("The Lord is my shepherd; I shall not want," Ps. 23:1) and anguish ("My God, my God, why have you forsaken me?" Ps. 22:1). James Mays notes, "The Psalms show that in biblical faith, every emotion, including rage and despair, can be brought into the presence of God."[14] Mourning Jerusalem's fall, Lamentations expresses theological grief with artistic structure. Yet amid sorrow comes hope: "The steadfast love of the Lord never ceases; his mercies . . . are new every morning" (Lam. 3:22–23). As a result, "Lamentations teaches that suffering can be voiced faithfully, and that lament itself is an act of resistance against despair."[15]

Narrative books such as Ruth, Esther, and Daniel portray God's providence through human courage and fidelity. Ruth chooses loyalty ("Your people shall be my people, and your God my God," Ruth 1:16), illustrating covenantal inclusion. The book of Esther, though omitting God's name, reveals God's providence through risk: "If I perish, I perish" (Esther 4:16). Daniel's friends remain faithful in exile ("But if not, we will not serve your gods," Dan. 3:18), and Daniel himself receives apocalyptic visions that affirm divine sovereignty amid imperial oppression.

Collectively, the Ketuvim forms a theological guide for the human journey, wisdom, lament, joy, injustice, hope, and trust. These texts do not always resolve questions but walk alongside the reader in doubt, longing, and celebration. The Ketuvim complements the Torah and Nevi'im, offering images of God as Shepherd, Refuge, and Redeemer. It provides wisdom, comfort, and inspiration for navigating life with faith and integrity. As the Babylonian Talmud says, "He who has the Psalms, Job, and Proverbs has a treasury of wisdom" (Berakhot 57b). The Ketuvim remains such a treasury—timeless, textured, and attuned to the complexities of belief.

12. Davis, *Getting Involved with God*, 64.
13. Bartholomew, *Ecclesiastes*, 21.
14. Mays, *Psalms*, 13.
15. O'Connor, *Lamentations*, 78.

Ketuvim Test Case: Son, Remember My Teaching (Prov. 3)

What Is This Text About?

Proverbs 3 is a chapter that emphasizes the value of wisdom and the importance of trusting in the Lord. The chapter begins with exhortations to keep God's commands in one's heart, promising long life and peace as a result. It encourages trusting in God fully, rather than relying on one's own understanding, and assures that doing so will lead to direction and peace. The chapter also stresses the significance of honoring the Lord with one's wealth, encouraging generosity and the right use of resources. Throughout, it highlights how wisdom and understanding, when sought after and embraced, lead to a blessed and fulfilling life, filled with God's favor and protection.

What Topic(s) Does This Text Teach Believers?

1. Trusting in the Lord: The text teaches believers the importance of placing complete trust in God, rather than relying on their own understanding, especially in uncertain or challenging circumstances.
2. The value of wisdom: Wisdom is presented as a key to a well-lived life, one that leads to peace, security, and God's favor.
3. Honoring God with resources: Proverbs 3 encourages believers to honor God with their wealth, suggesting that generosity and wise use of resources are an expression of trust in him.
4. God's guidance and protection: The chapter emphasizes that God will direct those who trust in him, protecting them and leading them in the right way.

How Do These Topics Relate to Other Sections of the Tanakh?

If Torah sets forth the laws of life, and the Nevi'im calls these laws to memory, then Proverbs re-articulates the laws in a "daily sense." Proverbs relates to the first two sections of the Tanakh as the practical re-articulation of the complex. Furthermore, Proverbs calls for parents to teach the prior sections in a no-nonsense way for our children to better grasp who God is.

How Does This Approach Inform Our Hermeneutic of This Text?

Viewed as a spiritual guide, Prov. 3 serves as a practical manual for living a wise and blessed life. It directs believers to trust fully in God's guidance, promises, and wisdom, recognizing that personal understanding is limited and flawed. It serves as a reminder that wisdom, drawn from God and his

Word, leads to a life filled with peace and divine favor. From a hermeneutical perspective, this text encourages a life of active faith, one that not only trusts in God's promises but seeks his wisdom daily for decisions big and small.

What Are the Benefits of Applying This Approach to This Text?

1. Complete trust in God: One of the most important takeaways is the encouragement to trust in God with all aspects of life. This involves surrendering control, acknowledging that God's understanding surpasses our own, and leaning on his wisdom for guidance.
2. Valuing wisdom: This chapter reinforces the idea that pursuing wisdom, both in terms of understanding God's Word and practical decision-making, is essential for living a fulfilling life.
3. Generosity and stewardship: The text encourages believers to honor God with their resources, teaching that generosity is a form of trusting God and expressing gratitude for God's provision.
4. God's peace and protection: The promise that trusting God leads to peace and protection offers comfort and assurance, especially in times of uncertainty.

What Are the Potential Problems in Applying This Approach to This Text?

1. Risk of legalism: The emphasis on wisdom and following God's commands may lead some to think that a strict adherence to rules is the way to secure God's blessings. This could create a legalistic mindset that focuses on outward behavior rather than on heart transformation.
2. Unrealistic expectations: If believers misinterpret the text as a guarantee of earthly success or happiness, they may become disillusioned when their experience doesn't align with their expectations. Proverbs is not meant to promise material prosperity but is intended to promote spiritual flourishing.
3. Disregard for contextual wisdom: Another potential issue is the risk of applying the principles in Proverbs without considering the broader context of a person's life. While wisdom can guide, every situation is unique, and wisdom does not always lead to immediate or obvious results.
4. Oversimplification: The advice in Proverbs can sometimes be perceived as overly simplistic, especially in difficult or complex situations. The idea that wisdom will always lead to peace and success may not align

with real-life challenges where godly wisdom may lead to suffering or difficulty.

5. Misapplication of blessing: Proverbs 3 promises peace and prosperity to those who trust in God, but this can sometimes be misinterpreted as a guarantee of material wealth or success. The text should be understood in a broader sense of spiritual and relational flourishing, not as a prosperity gospel.
6. Assuming automatic success: A potential problem with applying the text too directly is the assumption that if one simply follows the wisdom outlined, everything will go smoothly. This can be problematic in light of the larger biblical narrative where the righteous still experience trials and suffering.

Summary of Test Case

In summary, Prov. 3 serves as a practical guide for faithful living, urging believers to trust wholly in the Lord, pursue wisdom, and honor God with their resources. The chapter promises that those who rely on God rather than on their own understanding will find peace, direction, and divine favor, while wisdom itself is portrayed as the path to a fulfilling and secure life. Related to the Torah and the Nevi'im, Proverbs rearticulates their teachings in a daily, accessible form, calling parents to pass on this wisdom to their children. Viewed as a spiritual guide, the chapter highlights that true blessing flows from trusting God's wisdom over human insight, cultivating generosity, and seeking his direction in all aspects of life. Modern application of this text offers encouragement to surrender control, value wisdom, and practice stewardship, while resting in God's peace and protection. However, careful interpretation is needed to avoid misapplications such as legalism, prosperity-gospel assumptions, or unrealistic expectations of automatic success, since Proverbs provides general principles for flourishing rather than absolute guarantees. Properly understood, the chapter encourages an active, trusting faith that leans on God's wisdom for both daily decisions and lifelong direction.

Conclusion

The Spiritual Guide approach to the Tanakh may be difficult for some to grasp. Honestly, this particular view is the hardest for me. But this approach reveals that the Tanakh can be viewed as a dynamic spiritual guide, not merely a historical or literary work. Its tripartite structure offers a layered and progressive approach to divine instruction. The Torah establishes the covenant through law, ethics, and ritual. The Nevi'im builds on this by calling for repentance, justice, and renewed faithfulness. The Ketuvim offers reflective insight through wisdom, poetry, and meditations on the human condition.

Together these sections provide a comprehensive framework for moral and spiritual formation. The narratives illustrate the consequences of ethical choices, the prophets confront societal failures, and the wisdom texts help readers navigate life's situations. This approach beautifully shows that across cultures and generations, the Tanakh's themes remain relevant, offering timeless guidance for aligning life with divine purposes.

Ultimately, the Tanakh functions as a living, multifaceted resource for instruction and transformation. Its structure moves from law to exhortation to reflection, supporting a full and complete spiritual journey for both individuals and communities.

5

Messianic Trajectory Approach

Tanakh as Testimony to Christ

I'M A HUGE *STAR WARS* FAN and love to debate which movies are part of the true canon, but many fans agree that volumes 1–6 are all about Darth Vader / Anakin Skywalker. You can watch any of the *Star Wars* movies and simply enjoy it as a stand-alone story, or you can watch them sequentially and trace the connections between concepts, themes, and characters. When I watch movies 1 through 6, I see the progression of Anakin as the hero–villain–anti-hero.

When the church was birthed and subsequent generations of believers began to canonize the New Testament, they viewed the whole structure, and specifically the shape of the Hebrew Bible, as more than a historical or literary arrangement. They saw the canon as pointing toward the expectation of a coming Messiah (not that he becomes a villain like Darth Vader). New Testament scholars often emphasize that the Old Testament should be read in light of Christ, but also Christian Old Testament canonical scholars such as Brevard Childs and John Sailhamer call the church to a deeper awareness of the messianic trajectory embedded within the structure of the Tanakh.

For Christian canonical scholars, the organization and final form of the Hebrew Scriptures are not merely a product of historical development but were intentionally shaped to direct the reader toward the Messiah. This is not a modern concept, for early Christians viewed the unity of Scripture as given by a single divine author, for a single redemptive purpose, and articulating a single unfolding story. For a reader applying the Messianic Trajectory approach, the Torah establishes the covenantal foundation and introduces the need for redemption, the Nevi'im amplifies this expectation by developing the theme of a future king/savior, and the Ketuvim reflects Israel's longing for restoration through wisdom and eschatological hope.

Most importantly, the Messianic Trajectory approach aligns with the New Testament, where Jesus is portrayed as the fulfillment of the Torah, the embodiment of prophetic hope, and the culmination of wisdom and eschatological expectation (Luke 24:44). Those who champion this approach argue that the messianic trajectory of the Hebrew Bible is not a view they are imposing on the text but is an inherent feature of its canonical shape.

For John Sailhamer, the three parts of the Tanakh are "stitched together" at specific intersections flowing from a thematic end of the section into the next canonical section.[1]

Torah → Nevi'im: The Torah ends (Deut. 34) with Moses's death and a note that no prophet like Moses has yet risen. As such, this seam anticipates a future prophet and sets up the Nevi'im division as the search for "the prophet like Moses" who will lead Israel faithfully. The result of the search within the Nevi'im is the continued search for the great messianic prophet yet to come.

Nevi'im → Ketuvim: The Nevi'im ends with hope for restoration (Mal. 4), a coming Davidic figure, and a return to God's instruction. The seam points forward to a future act of God that has not yet arrived, creating expectation that the answer lies ahead in the Ketuvim. Thus the Psalms begin with the Davidic work and point toward a wise coming Messiah.

Ketuvim → Canon-level closure: The Ketuvim concludes with the hope of a renewed kingdom (2 Chron. 36:22–23) and an open-ended invitation to return and rebuild. This seam does not resolve the story but instead directs the reader back to the Torah's promises and forward toward the awaited prophet, king, and ultimate act of God in Christ.

By applying this approach to the Tanakh, one gains an expectation for a coming Messiah-King who is rooted in Torah, confirmed in the Nevi'im, and longed for in the Ketuvim. The Messianic Trajectory approach requires three unique hermeneutical questions. We will also ask the same three takeaway questions used with the other approaches:

1. Sailhamer, *Meaning of the Pentateuch*, 48–49.

- What messianic topic(s) does this text teach believers?
- How do these topics relate to other sections of the Tanakh and ultimately to Christ?
- How does this approach inform our hermeneutic of this text?
- What potential problems arise from the above question?
- What are the benefits of applying this approach to this text?
- What are the potential problems of applying this approach to this text?

Reasons for Adopting This Approach

Adopting this approach allows one to view the Tanakh not merely as a collection of ancient texts but as a divinely orchestrated narrative moving toward fulfillment in Christ in the New Testament. Furthermore, this is not just a progressive revelation of Messiah but highlights that Messiah has always been the plan from the fall of Adam onward. The Torah serves as the foundation, establishing the covenant between God and Israel, laying out divine law, and foreshadowing the need for ultimate redemption. The Nevi'im then expands this narrative by cultivating a longing for a future king and savior and emphasizing Israel's failures, God's continued faithfulness, and the promise of a restored kingdom. Finally, the Ketuvim reflects on trials, wisdom, and messianic hope, reinforcing the expectation of a future Anointed One who will bring about the restoration of God's people and the fulfillment of divine promises.

While one may view the Messianic Trajectory approach as a Christian concept, this approach actually aligns with Jewish interpretive traditions. Most notably in the Second Temple period, there was a messianic expectation with apocalyptic and royal dimensions. The belief that history was moving toward a climactic intervention by God, via a Messiah, permeated Jewish thought during this period and influenced both Jewish interpretations and early Christian readings of the Tanakh. One of the most notable Jewish sources for this approach is from the Essenes of Qumran, the area where the Dead Sea Scrolls were discovered. In their "Book of Order," known as the Damascus Document (CD), they discuss their hope in and for the "teacher of righteousness."[2]

Viewing the Tanakh through this lens highlights its theological continuity and purpose, demonstrating that its redemptive arc is not incidental but

2. Taylor, *Essenes, the Scrolls, and the Dead Sea*; Moriarty, "Habakkuk Scroll and a Controversy."

intentional. It allows readers to see the Scriptures not merely as a record of Israel's past but as a living testament to God's unfolding plan of salvation. By adopting this approach, one finds company with both Christian and early Jewish reading methods.

Proponents of This Approach

From the Essenes and early church fathers to modern theologians, many believers have consistently argued that the Tanakh points forward with increasing clarity to the person and work of a messianic figure, and for Christians this person is Jesus of Nazareth. Notable scholars holding this view include Justin Martyr, Irenaeus, Augustine, Thomas Aquinas, Martin Luther, Franz Delitzsch, Alfred Edersheim, David Baron, Brevard Childs, Arnold Fruchtenbaum, John Sailhamer, Stephen Dempster, and Michael Brown. They have all articulated and expanded on this foundational messianic understanding of the Tanakh.[3] The church father Augustine of Hippo provided perhaps the most concise and lasting articulation of this view: "In the Old Testament, the New lies hid; in the New Testament, the Old is exposed," or more poetically, "The New is in the Old concealed; the Old is in the New revealed."[4] This statement laid the grounding thought for subsequent Christian readings of the Tanakh. Augustine argued that the Old Testament, though veiled in typology and prophecy, contains the essential truths later made explicit in the New Testament through Christ. Conversely, the New Testament illuminates and unpacks the hidden meanings of the Old, revealing Christ as its central theme and ultimate fulfillment. For Augustine, Christ is the key that unlocks the entirety of Scripture.

The Protestant Reformation brought renewed emphasis on the centrality of Christ in all of Scripture. Martin Luther's words have been appropriately summarized: "Everywhere that God speaks in the Old Testament, Christ speaks."[5] For Luther, the Old Testament was centered around Christ. He saw the narratives, laws, and prophetic pronouncements as all testifying to Christ's presence, his ongoing work, and his ultimate redemptive mission. This reading has become a hallmark of Protestant hermeneutics and ties in well with the Messianic Trajectory approach to reading the Tanakh.

3. Although they all highlight Christ as the message of the Old Testament, not all of the scholars listed use the threefold Tanakh structure. Those holding the Tanakh order will be noted in a later discussion.

4. Augustine, *Quaestiones in Heptateuchum* 7.2.73.

5. Riley, "How Luther Pointed Me to Christ in the Old Testament."

In the nineteenth century, Franz Delitzsch continued to build on this tradition and specifically emphasized the progressive nature of messianic revelation within the Tanakh. Delitzsch saw in the Old Testament a trajectory leading directly to Christ, noting that "according to the prophecy concerning Shiloh, the kingdom of God from Judah, through the Messiah, will overcome all the kingdoms of this world."[6] Likewise, Alfred Edersheim, another prominent nineteenth-century scholar, reinforced this idea by meticulously tracing Jewish customs and prophecies to their ultimate fulfillment in Jesus.[7] His extensive works demonstrate how deeply interwoven the Old Testament expectations were with the person of Christ. Brevard Childs advocates for reading the Bible as a unified witness to God's work, emphasizing the continuity between the Testaments. His view that "to understand the Bible as scripture means to reflect on the witnesses of the text transmitted through the testimony of the prophets and apostles"[8] underscores the idea that both Old and New Testaments contribute to a single, overarching narrative of God's redemptive plan, culminating in Christ.

Contemporary scholars such as Arnold Fruchtenbaum bring a specific focus on the fulfillment of covenants through the Messiah. John Sailhamer, known for his work on the Pentateuch, views the earliest books of the Tanakh as already pointing toward a future king and a "new covenant." His interpretation that in the last days (eschatological trajectory) a new covenant will be implemented with the reign of a future king shows how the messianic thread is woven even into the foundational narratives of Israel and demonstrates a deep anticipatory element for Christ from the very beginning. Likewise, Stephen Dempster powerfully articulates that the New Testament, with its revelation of Christ, is the culmination of a long and deliberate divine plan laid out in the Tanakh. Finally, Michael Brown, a contemporary advocate for messianic Judaism, succinctly summarizes this entire perspective: "It's all about the Messiah."[9] This declaration encapsulates the profound conviction that the Tanakh in its entirety is centered on and finds its ultimate meaning in Jesus Christ.

In conclusion, the scholarly tradition, stretching from the early church fathers to modern theologians, consistently views the Tanakh as a progressing revelation of the Messiah. Collectively, these scholars demonstrate a profound conviction that the Tanakh is not a separate religious text but an indispensable

6. Delitzsch, *Messianic Prophecies in Historical Succession*, 57.
7. Edersheim, *Bible History, Old Testament.*
8. Childs, *Struggle to Understand Isaiah*, 321.
9. Brown, "It's All About the Messiah."

part of God's unfolding story, culminating in the person and work of Jesus Christ, the promised Messiah.

Hermeneutical Realities of This Approach

Of the approaches presented in this book, the Messianic Trajectory approach is most antithetical to critical hermeneutics. Many modern critical approaches view the Tanakh as a collection of disparate texts with evolving theological viewpoints. By contrast, the Messianic Trajectory approach sees the Tanakh as a progressive unfolding of divine intention that reveals an overarching metanarrative. The structure of the Tanakh is not merely a historical sequence but a theological journey that moves from covenantal foundations to prophetic anticipation and finally to wisdom reflecting an eschatological hope. Like some of the other approaches presented thus far, this view connects seemingly isolated texts into a grander overarching redemptive-historical arc instead of treating the texts as independent theological traditions.

Traditional historical-critical methods often reduce texts to their immediate historical context, which can limit their theological depth and future orientation. The Messianic Trajectory approach acknowledges the historical settings of these texts but also recognizes how biblical authors and redactors intentionally shaped the canon to espouse a messianic expectation. Prophetic oracles, such as Isaiah's Servant Songs, were not just politically contextual but had long-term fulfillment trajectories, as seen in Second Temple Jewish interpretations. Even postexilic books such as Chronicles and Daniel were shaped with a forward-looking messianic hope rather than simply reflecting on past restoration. This approach honors historical settings while also engaging the Tanakh's theological trajectory toward redemption and future hope.

Studying the Tanakh through a Messianic Trajectory approach means interpreting texts in light of their contribution to the unfolding messianic expectation and divine redemptive plan. Specific hermeneutical questions are therefore necessary to determine how each text relates to the messianic future. These key questions include the following:

How does this text relate to God's covenants: Abrahamic, Mosaic, Davidic, or New?

Does it reveal a need for redemption from human failure, sin, or exile or a promise of restoration?

How does this text advance or challenge God's covenantal faithfulness?

Another important hermeneutical inquiry involves typology:

Does the text contain types, symbols, or figures that anticipate the Messiah?
Are there repeated patterns such as righteous suffering, kingly figures, or priestly mediators that later texts develop messianically?
How does an event or character serve as a prototype of future fulfillment?

Similarly, prophetic expectation plays a crucial role:

Does the text contain direct messianic prophecy (such as Isa. 9:6–7) or indirect foreshadowing of a future ruler, priest, or redeemer?
How does it contribute to Israel's hope for deliverance, a renewed kingdom, or the coming of an anointed figure?

It is essential to examine a text in relation to thematic development across the canon:

Where else in the Tanakh does this theme resurface and develop?
How does the text relate to the larger literary and theological trajectory of the Tanakh?
Does it find culmination or reinterpretation in later biblical texts?

A related concern is eschatology and final restoration:

Does the text point toward a future renewal, a final redemption, or an idealized kingdom?
How does it contribute to Israel's longing for an eschatological deliverer?

While the Messianic Trajectory approach highlights theological unity and prophetic fulfillment, it can also misread texts by imposing later theological constructs, neglecting historical settings, or disregarding the diversity of voices within the Tanakh. Focusing on the messianic trajectory of the Tanakh often tempts the reader to overlook original context and intent. If one overlooks the immediate implication for the original hearers, one overlooks how God was faithfully caring for and speaking to every generation, not just via the final Messiah. By overlooking the original context, readers may force later meanings onto texts that were written for immediate historical concerns. For example, Isa. 7:14's reference to a virgin conceiving had an immediate historical fulfillment in a child born in the time of Ahaz that is independent of any future messianic implications. Reading only through a messianic lens may sideline the original audience and intent, reducing the text to a coded prediction rather than a dynamic engagement with Israel's history and its future in the Messiah.

Overlooking the immediate historical fulfillment is not the only potential danger of the Messianic Trajectory approach. It may also superimpose later theological concepts onto texts where they were not originally present. For example, Ps. 22 is often read exclusively as messianic even though it was originally a personal lament by the historical figure David. Overuse of typology can blur the boundaries between literary symbolism and explicit prophecy, treating every righteous figure as a Christ-figure, even when the text does not justify it.

Furthermore, the Tanakh contains multiple theological voices, some of which do not directly fit into a linear messianic framework. The wisdom literature, for example, rarely speaks of an anointed king or of eschatological deliverance, and reading them exclusively through a messianic lens can flatten their theological depth. However, by acknowledging both the strengths and potential weaknesses of a Messianic Trajectory approach, interpreters can engage the Tanakh in a way that honors its theological depth, historical context, and eschatological hope while maintaining hermeneutical integrity.[10]

Torah: Messiah as Torah's Fulfillment

In the Messianic Trajectory approach, the Torah is not just a mere law code but a theological narrative pointing toward a future redemptive figure, the Messiah. The Torah serves as the foundation, establishing the covenant between God and Israel and foreshadowing the need for ultimate redemption. Let's consider a few of the messianic texts/themes cited most often.

First, John Sailhamer argues that this trajectory begins in Gen. 3:15, where God declares to the serpent,

> I will put enmity between you and the woman,
>   and between your seed and her seed;
> he shall bruise your head,
>   and you shall bruise his heel. (RSV)

Sailhamer sees this as the first messianic prophecy, writing: "This verse marks the beginning of the Messianic hope in the Pentateuch. . . . The text

10. The Messianic Trajectory approach can be used by advocates of either the threefold Tanakh order or the traditional fourfold order. However, the approach espoused by modern canonicalists and defended in this chapter calls for the Messiah to be seen in the three specific ways laid out by Sailhamer at the beginning of this chapter.

anticipates a future 'seed' who will ultimately defeat the serpent. The rest of the Pentateuch unfolds as a search for that promised seed."[11] According to this approach, the Torah is not merely a historical narrative but a narrative of hopeful anticipation. In the Messianic Trajectory approach, the Torah sets into motion a theological arc that culminates in a redeemer who will overcome sin, death, and chaos.

Second, let's consider the Abrahamic covenant, which is a messianic blessing to the nations and the next major development in the messianic trajectory. God promises Abraham, "In you all the families of the earth shall be blessed" (Gen. 12:3). This is not only about land and descendants but also about universal restoration. Genesis 22:18 clarifies: "And in your offspring shall all the nations of the earth be blessed." As Sailhamer explains, "The term 'seed' (זֶרַע) in Genesis becomes a key term in tracing the messianic line. . . . The Torah presents this blessing through Abraham's 'seed' as a singular hope culminating in a specific individual."[12]

Later, Gen. 49:10 adds a royal dimension to this hope:

> The scepter will not depart from Judah,
> Nor the ruler's staff from between his feet,
> Until Shiloh comes,
> And to him shall be the obedience of the peoples. (NASB)

Brevard Childs observes that this oracle "introduces a dynastic expectation within the Pentateuch itself. . . . Israel's future hopes are tied to a royal figure from Judah."[13] This prophetic blessing anticipates a kingly Messiah, narrowing the lineage of the promised seed and aligning it with the tribe of Judah—a theme later taken up in the Davidic covenant and solidified in messianic expectation.

In Deut. 18:15 the Torah also anticipates a future prophet-redeemer: "The Lord your God will raise up for you a prophet like me from among you, from your brothers—it is to him you shall listen." As Sailhamer notes, this is more than a prediction of a future prophet: "Deuteronomy's prophecy is forward-looking, leaving the reader in a posture of expectation. The Torah ends with the statement that 'no prophet has arisen like Moses,' thus keeping the reader looking ahead for such a prophet."[14] Indeed, Deut. 34:10 concludes: "And there has not arisen a prophet since in Israel like Moses, whom the Lord

11. Sailhamer, *Pentateuch as Narrative*, 98.
12. Sailhamer, *Meaning of the Pentateuch*, 415.
13. Childs, *Introduction to the Old Testament as Scripture*, 146.
14. Sailhamer, *Pentateuch as Narrative*, 475.

knew face to face." Christopher Wright remarks, "This unfulfilled prophecy left an interpretive gap that later generations would fill with messianic hope, awaiting the prophet who would both represent and reveal God fully."[15] This figure, like Moses, would mediate God's word, intercede for the people, and initiate covenantal renewal—roles ultimately fulfilled in messianic typology.

The Torah also introduces priestly and kingly motifs of the future Messiah. In Gen. 14, Melchizedek, king of Salem and "priest of God Most High," blesses Abram. Though a brief mention, this mysterious figure becomes a prototype of a future priest-king. As Ps. 110:4 later proclaims: "You are a priest forever after the order of Melchizedek." Childs notes, "The Melchizedek episode offers a glimpse of a non-Levitical priesthood that becomes essential to messianic theology."[16] This priest-king figure anticipates the Messiah's dual role as intercessor and ruler, a theme especially developed in Hebrews. In Num. 24:17, the prophet Balaam speaks of a royal deliverer:

> I see him, but not now;
>   I behold him, but not near:
> a star shall come out of Jacob,
>   and a scepter shall rise out of Israel.

Jewish and Christian interpreters alike have recognized this as a messianic oracle. Jacob Milgrom writes: "The star and scepter are ancient symbols of kingship, and their appearance in this oracle underscores the expectation of a future ruler who will establish dominion and judgment."[17]

Although the Torah never names the Messiah, it builds the foundation for the messianic identity as serpent-crusher, royal son, prophetic revealer, and priestly intercessor. These anticipatory motifs remain open-ended and even conclude with Deut. 34 inviting further development in the Nevi'im. In essence, the Torah functions as a messianic prologue, its covenantal promises, prophetic oracles, and narrative structures all contributing to a longing for the one who will finally fulfill God's plan of redemption.

Torah Test Case: Enmity Between the Serpent and the Woman (Gen. 3:15)

What Is This Text About?

Genesis 3:15 introduces what is commonly called the protevangelium, or "first gospel." This verse sets the foundation for messianic expectation in

15. C. Wright, *Knowing Jesus Through the Old Testament*, 88.
16. Childs, *Biblical Theology*, 110.
17. Milgrom, *Numbers*, 202.

the biblical narrative by portraying a future conflict between the "seed of the woman" and the "seed of the serpent."

What Messianic Topic(s) Does This Text Teach Believers?

The key messianic themes present include the enduring conflict between good and evil, the promise of a redeemer who would deliver a fatal blow to the serpent, and the suffering and triumph of this deliverer. The text foreshadows a personal, victorious agent who will crush the head of the serpent, widely interpreted as a reference to Christ's defeat of Satan. Graeme Goldsworthy captures this well, stating, "Genesis 3:15 is the first glimmer of the gospel, setting the stage for the coming of one who would undo the curse and defeat the serpent."[18] This verse thus introduces a redemptive trajectory that shapes the rest of Scripture, signaling that redemption is already in motion even at the point of humanity's fall.

How Do These Topics Relate to Other Sections of the Tanakh and Ultimately to Christ?

The messianic promise in Gen. 3:15 unfolds progressively throughout the Tanakh. The concept of the "seed" develops through the promises to Abraham (Gen. 12:7; 22:18), narrowing further in the Davidic covenant (2 Sam. 7), and is echoed in prophetic visions of a coming ruler (Isa. 9, Mic. 5). In these texts, the "seed" is linked with both kingship and deliverance. For example, Isaiah's suffering servant (Isa. 52–53) absorbs the language of injury and victory, as the servant is "bruised for our iniquities," a thematic link to the "bruised heel" in Genesis. This messianic seed ultimately finds its fulfillment in Jesus Christ. The apostle Paul explicitly connects the promise to Christ in Gal. 3:16: "Now the promises were made to Abraham and to his offspring, . . . who is Christ." Furthermore, in Rom. 16:20 Paul echoes Gen. 3:15 with the affirmation, "The God of peace will soon crush Satan under your feet." T. Desmond Alexander observes, "The promise in Genesis 3:15 sets the trajectory for all biblical prophecy and eschatology. From Eve to Abraham to David, and ultimately to Christ, the expectation builds that God will send a deliverer who will vanquish evil."[19] Thus, Gen. 3:15 not only initiates messianic hope but serves as a theological seedbed for understanding the entire biblical narrative as culminating in Christ.

18. Goldsworthy, *According to Plan*, 135.
19. Alexander, *From Paradise to the Promised Land*, 102.

How Does This Approach Inform Our Hermeneutic of This Text?

Viewing the messianic trajectory of the Tanakh dramatically influences how one interprets Gen. 3:15. It prompts a canonical and typological hermeneutic, one that reads the text not in isolation but as an integral part of the unfolding drama of redemption. A canonical approach recognizes the unity and progression of Scripture, allowing earlier texts to be interpreted in light of later revelation. Typology helps interpret the figures and motifs in Gen. 3:15 (such as the "seed" and the serpent) as anticipations of a messianic figure. This "messianic trajectory invites us to see Genesis 3:15 not as an isolated promise but as the headwaters of a biblical river flowing toward Christ."[20] Such a trajectory-aware hermeneutic enables readers to see how early seeds of promise develop organically into full messianic prophecy, particularly within the structure of Torah–Nevi'im–Ketuvim. This approach also honors the progressive nature of revelation, acknowledging that fuller meaning is disclosed as Scripture unfolds.

What Potential Problems Arise from the Above Question?

While the Messianic Trajectory approach has rich theological value, it also presents interpretive challenges. Chief among them is the risk of eisegesis—reading New Testament theology into Old Testament texts in a way that ignores their original historical and literary contexts. This may distort the meaning intended for the ancient audience. Additionally, this approach may inadvertently neglect the multilayered nature of prophecy, where a text such as Gen. 3:15 may have immediate, ongoing, and ultimate fulfillments. "The challenge is to avoid collapsing the text into its fulfillment without appreciating the progressive nature of revelation."[21] Moreover, applying a messianic lens too early or broadly risks minimizing Jewish readings of the text, which tend to see Gen. 3:15 as symbolic of human struggle against evil rather than a direct messianic prophecy. Thus careful balance is needed to avoid theological overreach while appreciating the canonical significance of the text.

What Are the Benefits of Applying This Approach to This Text?

1. Unity of Scripture: This approach portrays the Bible not as a disconnected set of writings but as a cohesive narrative of redemption.
2. Instilling hope: It demonstrates that even amid judgment, God's grace and plan for salvation were already in motion. This hope is rooted in a divine promise that evil will not prevail forever.

20. Dempster, *Dominion and Dynasty*, 67.
21. Gentry and Wellum, *Kingdom Through Covenant*, 132.

3. Christological depth: This approach shows how the earliest biblical chapters set the stage for the work of Christ.
4. Deeper appreciation: Seeing the typology and patterns that the Holy Spirit embedded in Scripture enhances both theological study and devotional reading.

What Are the Potential Problems in Applying This Approach to This Text?

1. Over-allegorization: Symbols and types may be emphasized at the expense of the historical and grammatical sense of the text, leading interpreters to find messianic references where none are intended.
2. Neglect of the immediate context: We must remember that Gen. 3:15 is situated in a narrative of divine judgment and curse, with its primary referent being the enmity between humanity and evil in general.
3. Excluding Jewish interpretive traditions: Many see the "seed" as humanity at large or Israel specifically rather than as a single messianic figure. John Walton warns, "We must tread carefully to avoid making Gen. 3:15 a direct prophecy of Jesus in a way that disregards its complex literary and covenantal dimensions."[22] So although a messianic reading can enrich our understanding of Scripture, this approach must be balanced with sensitivity to genre, audience, and the broader theological witness of Scripture.

Summary of Test Case

Read canonically, this verse becomes the beginning of the redemptive storyline that runs through Abraham, David, and the prophets and ultimately finds its fulfillment in Christ's victory. This approach highlights the unity of Scripture, shows that hope and grace are present even at the moment of the fall, and deepens christological reading by tracing how early patterns and images grow into full messianic expectation. At the same time, it requires careful handling so that we do not override the text's original context or ignore humanity's ongoing struggle with evil by focusing on a single messianic figure.

Nevi'im: Messiah as Prophetic Hope

Moving from the Torah's foreshadowing of a law-fulfilling Messiah, the books of the Nevi'im serve as both interpreters and developers of the messianic

22. Walton, *Lost World of Adam and Eve*, 84.

promises established in the Torah. The prophets expand the Tanakh's messianic trajectory by refining and deepening expectations of the coming redeemer, who will fulfill the role of prophet as Deut. 34 alludes. While the Torah lays the covenantal foundation for Israel's future hope, the Nevi'im provides clarity, correction, and expansion in light of Israel's failures and exile. In the Nevi'im we find a reaffirmation and reinterpretation of messianic promises, emphasizing the need for a better covenant and a messianic king who will establish eternal justice and eternal rule.

The Former Prophets (Joshua–Kings) recount the rise and fall of human kingship, demonstrating Israel's inability to uphold the covenant. This failure establishes the theological necessity of an ideal Davidic king, who will not only rule with righteousness but also restore the broken covenant between God and his people. The themes of exile and return dominate the historical and prophetic narratives. These stories point to a better leader and hero, reinforcing the need for a Messiah whose intervention transcends mere political restoration, a redeemer who will bring true spiritual renewal.

The Latter Prophets (Isaiah, Jeremiah, Ezekiel, and the Twelve) take up the messianic expectation and hope that has been reframed in the wake of exile. These themes are often emphasized by newness, such as a new covenant, a new heart, a new creation. Their visions extend beyond national security to global salvation, and beyond royal imagery to suffering, atonement, and inner renewal.

Texts such as Isa. 9:6–7 envision a child-king whose reign brings justice, peace, and eternal stability.

> For to us a child is born, . . .
> and the government shall be upon his shoulder. . . .
> Of the increase of his government and of peace
>   there will be no end,
> on the throne of David . . .
> with justice and with righteousness
>   . . . forevermore.

Walter Kaiser asserts: "Isaiah's prophecy is not a vague spiritual promise but a concrete expectation of a Davidic king whose rule will be both political and moral, embodying divine attributes."[23] Jeremiah 23:5–6 echoes this hope, speaking of a righteous Branch from David's line who will "reign as king and deal wisely, . . . and this is the name by which he will be called: 'The Lord is our righteousness.'"

23. Kaiser, *Messiah in the Old Testament*, 158.

Perhaps the most dramatic transformation of messianic expectation occurs in Isa. 52:13–53:12, where the servant of the Lord is portrayed not as a triumphant warrior, but as a suffering, rejected, and sacrificial figure:

> He was pierced for our transgressions;
> he was crushed for our iniquities; . . .
> and with his wounds we are healed. (Isa. 53:5)

Alec Motyer writes: "The Servant's suffering is not merely exemplary, it is substitutionary. The Messiah here is cast as priest and sacrifice in one, accomplishing redemption by bearing the sin of others."[24] This vision of the Messiah introduces a redemptive function far surpassing political kingship, laying the groundwork for the New Testament's understanding of Christ's atoning work.

Crucially, Jer. 31:31–34 introduces the new covenant, a paradigm shift from external law to internal transformation: "I will put my law within them, and I will write it on their hearts, . . . for they shall all know me, . . . for I will forgive their iniquity." According to Gerhard Hasel: "This new covenant is not a break with the past but its fulfillment. The promises to Abraham and David find their true realization in a covenant of forgiveness, intimacy, and universal knowledge of God."[25] Again, as in the Torah, the Messiah is not named but is the implied mediator of this new relationship, aligning closely with the servant and shepherd imagery found throughout the prophetic books.

The vision of messianic restoration is not confined to Israel alone. In Ezek. 37, the uniting of the two sticks (Israel and Judah) and the promise of "one shepherd" to rule them anticipates a reunified, restored people under a Davidic king. "My servant David shall be king over them, and they shall all have one shepherd, . . . and David my servant shall be their prince forever" (Ezek. 37:24–25). Zechariah 12–14 expands this hope to the nations, foreseeing a global acknowledgment of Israel's king and the mourning of the pierced one (Zech. 12:10), blending royal, priestly, and sacrificial motifs. As John Goldingay notes: "The prophetic vision does not restrict itself to one model. It fuses kingly and suffering motifs, locating hope in a figure who will simultaneously rule, restore, and reconcile."[26]

In light of all this, the Nevi'im serves as a theological bridge, linking the covenantal promises of the Torah to the eschatological fulfillment awaited in later texts. They expand the identity and mission of the Messiah from a

24. Motyer, *Prophecy of Isaiah*, 429.
25. Hasel, *Old Testament Theology*, 169.
26. Goldingay, *Theology of the Book of Isaiah*, 207.

prophet like Moses to a suffering servant, from a national deliverer to a cosmic redeemer. Brevard Childs concludes: "The prophetic literature performs a dual task; it renders judgment on the past and projects hope into the future. The hope is focused in a coming figure whose identity merges king, prophet, and priest into a redemptive whole."[27] The culmination of the Nevi'im (Mal. 4:5) is the hope of a Messiah who is like David but better than the kings of Israel/Judah. In doing so, the Nevi'im sustains and transforms Israel's expectation, ensuring that the messianic trajectory remains central to the unfolding narrative of redemption—one that continues to point beyond exile and judgment to renewal, justice, and peace through God's appointed one.

Nevi'im Test Case: A New Covenant (Jer. 31:31–34)

What Is This Text About?

Jeremiah 31:31–34 is one of the most explicitly messianic texts in the Tanakh, centered on the promise of a new covenant. This covenant, unlike the one made at Sinai, will be internal, transformative, and permanent, involving the forgiveness of sins and an intimate knowledge of God.

What Messianic Topic(s) Does This Text Teach Believers?

The messianic topics here include covenantal renewal, internalization of God's law, and complete forgiveness, all of which are fulfilled in the person and work of Jesus Christ. The text sets up a framework for understanding the Messiah as the mediator of a new relationship between God and his people. This internalization of Torah signals a shift from institutional religion to a deeply personal encounter with the divine, making it a cornerstone of messianic expectation.

How Do These Topics Relate to Other Sections of the Tanakh and Ultimately to Christ?

The themes of Jer. 31:31–34 find echoes and developments throughout the Tanakh and culminate in the New Testament portrayal of Jesus. The idea of a new heart and spirit resonates with promises in Ezek. 36:26–27, where God pledges to give his people a new heart and put his Spirit within them. Similarly, Isa. 53 anticipates the forgiveness of sins through the suffering servant, linking the new covenant with a redemptive act. These covenantal themes converge in the person of Christ, who explicitly invokes Jeremiah's prophecy

27. Childs, *Biblical Theology*, 378.

at the Last Supper: "This cup that is poured out for you is the new covenant in my blood" (Luke 22:20). The author of Hebrews cites Jer. 31 at length (Heb. 8:8–12; 10:16–17), emphasizing that Christ has inaugurated this better covenant, marked by an internal transformation and true forgiveness. "The new covenant in Jeremiah is not merely a renewed Mosaic covenant but a qualitatively new covenant, which finds its realization in Christ's priestly mediation."[28] Thus Jer. 31 bridges the promises of the Tanakh with the fulfillment in the Messiah, affirming the unity of God's redemptive plan.

How Does This Approach Inform Our Hermeneutic of This Text?

Interpreting Jer. 31:31–34 through the Messianic Trajectory approach allows us to see this promise not in isolation, but as part of the forward-moving storyline of redemptive history. If the Tanakh is viewed as progressing toward the coming of the Messiah, then Jeremiah's new-covenant prophecy becomes a major turning point in that trajectory. This hermeneutic recognizes the continuity and escalation of God's covenantal dealings with his people, from the Abrahamic, Mosaic, and Davidic covenants to their ultimate fulfillment in Christ. Kaiser argues, "Jeremiah 31 functions as a prophetic anticipation of the complete and final covenantal arrangement God will establish with His people through the Messiah."[29] A trajectory-informed reading helps us grasp the typological fulfillment: Israel's repeated covenant failure leads to the need for a new kind of covenant, one grounded not in external law but in inward regeneration, something only the Messiah can secure. This enriches our theological reading while maintaining coherence across the biblical canon.

What Potential Problems Arise from the Above Question?

While the Messianic Trajectory approach enhances our understanding of Jer. 31, it is not without interpretive challenges. One key issue is the potential over-Christianization of a Hebrew prophetic text. Some scholars argue that applying this text too directly to Christ may obscure its original audience and intent—namely, a postexilic hope for Israel's restoration. Furthermore, Christian readers may bypass the fact that Jeremiah's audience would have understood the "new covenant" as a national renewal for Israel, not a universal covenant through Jesus. Jewish scholar Jon Levenson asserts, "To interpret Jeremiah's new covenant as solely a Christian reality is to misappropriate the eschatological hope it held for ancient Israel."[30] Additionally, this hermeneutic

28. Beale, *New Testament Biblical Theology*, 730.
29. Kaiser, *Messiah in the Old Testament*, 208.
30. Levenson, *Sinai & Zion*, 94.

raises questions about continuity and discontinuity: How does this "new" covenant relate to the "old"? Does it abrogate, fulfill, or transform it? These tensions require thoughtful engagement to avoid theological reductionism or supersessionist readings that ignore the Jewish roots of the promise.

What Are the Benefits of Applying This Approach to This Text?

1. Consistency of God's plan: Seeing the consistency of God's redemptive plan shows that the New Testament is not a theological detour but the anticipated climax of Israel's story.
2. Centrality of the Messiah: As the agent of covenantal renewal, Jesus does not discard Israel's covenants but fulfills and transforms them.
3. Depth of spiritual transformation: The gospel promises the law written on hearts, personal knowledge of God, and complete forgiveness of sin.
4. Theological coherence: Believers can read both Testaments as one continuous narrative of grace, covenant, and salvation.

What Are the Potential Problems in Applying This Approach to This Text?

1. Neglect of Israel's national identity: If the text is read only through a Christocentric lens, the promises to "the house of Israel and the house of Judah" (v. 31) may be spiritualized to the point of erasure.
2. Misunderstanding covenant continuity: Readers might incorrectly assume that the Mosaic covenant is nullified rather than fulfilled and transformed, leading to theological confusion about the role of law, grace, and obedience.
3. Overlooking the already/not-yet tension: Though the new covenant is inaugurated through Christ, its full realization (universal knowledge of God, sinlessness, etc.) remains eschatological, requiring that this approach be applied with care, theological nuance, and sensitivity to the original prophetic context.

Summary of Test Case

The prophets expose the failure of Israel's kings and covenants and instead project hope toward an ideal Davidic ruler and a new covenant, which comes with inward transformation and intimate knowledge of God. Jeremiah's promise of the Torah being written on the heart aligns with Isaiah, Ezekiel, and the Book of the Twelve, where the Messiah appears as king, servant, shepherd, and priest who restores not only Israel but ultimately the nations. Read alongside other prophets, Jer. 31 stands as a pivotal turning point that bridges the older covenants of Abraham, Moses, and David with their fulfillment in Christ's covenant. But readers of Jer. 31 must also wrestle with the text's original horizon of postexilic restoration and Israel's ongoing hope before jumping to the christological fulfillment.

Ketuvim: Messiah Longed For

The Torah provides the covenantal foundations, and the Nevi'im reinterprets Israel's story in light of exile and future hope. The Ketuvim then engages the messianic expectation through liturgical poetry, wisdom reflection, and apocalyptic vision. These texts do not always present messianic visions explicitly, but they sustain the hope of a coming David-like redeemer as prophesied in Mal. 4:5. In the Ketuvim this redeemer is one who will bring cosmic justice, divine wisdom, and everlasting peace.

The Psalms form the liturgical heart of the Ketuvim. In the poetry of the Psalms, we find messianic promises often built explicitly around the Davidic monarchy as the centerpiece of God's plan for justice and peace. John Sailhamer emphasizes that the Psalms are not merely devotional reflections but "messianic commentaries on the Pentateuch" particularly highlighting God's covenant with David: "The placement and shaping of the Psalms point to a messianic hope, a future king in the line of David who will reign with God's authority and fulfill the promises of Genesis and 2 Samuel."[31] Psalm 110, cited frequently in the New Testament, links messianic kingship with priesthood:

> The LORD says to my Lord:
> "Sit at my right hand
> until I make your enemies your footstool." (Ps. 110:1)
>
> "You are a priest forever
> after the order of Melchizedek." (Ps. 110:4)

This fusion of king and priest becomes a foundational messianic theme. Bruce Waltke observes: "Psalm 110 anticipates a messiah who will both reign and intercede, a priest-king who unites the roles of David and Melchizedek."[32]

31. Sailhamer, *Meaning of the Pentateuch*, 472.
32. Waltke, *Old Testament Theology*, 880.

The book of Daniel, a prophetic work though categorized among the Ketuvim, provides messianic apocalyptic symbolism. In Dan. 7:13–14, we find a heavenly messianic figure, "one like a Son of Man," coming with the clouds and receiving everlasting dominion:

> And to him was given dominion
> and glory and a kingdom,
> that all peoples . . .
> should serve him. (Dan. 7:14)

John J. Collins observes, "The 'Son of Man' is not just a symbol of the saints but an exalted figure who stands as an agent of divine rule, perhaps the most explicit pre-Christian messianic figure in the Hebrew canon."[33] Daniel 9:24–27 expounds the expectation of a redemptive intervention, "to finish the transgression, to put an end to sin, and to atone for iniquity, to bring in everlasting righteousness" (v. 24). These visions shape a hope that transcends earthly monarchy, pointing to a divine-human ruler whose kingdom will never be destroyed.

Regarding the messianic trajectory in the Wisdom Books (Proverbs, Job, Ecclesiastes), they deeply reflect on the moral and existential longing for a future redeemer. In Job 19:25, the suffering patriarch exclaims:

> For I know that my Redeemer lives,
> and at the last he will stand upon the earth.

This statement has long been interpreted in messianic terms. Tremper Longman writes: "While Job likely speaks from a personal, existential hope, his words resonate with the broader biblical expectation of a vindicating, redemptive figure who will set all things right."[34]

In Ecclesiastes, the cry "Vanity of vanities! All is vanity" (Eccles. 1:2) ends with a cryptic call to judgment: "*God will bring every deed into judgment*" (12:14, emphasis added). This divine justice points forward to a coming day of reckoning and restoration at the hands of a Messiah. Proverbs 8 introduces Wisdom as a preexistent figure, sometimes associated in later tradition with the Logos or the Messiah: "The Lord possessed me at the beginning of his work; . . . then I was beside him, like a master workman" (vv. 22, 30). Michael Fox observes, "While Wisdom is not identified with the Messiah, the depiction of Wisdom as divine, eternal, and creative lays the conceptual groundwork for later messianic interpretations."[35]

33. Collins, *Daniel*, 299.
34. Longman, *Job*, 229.
35. Fox, *Proverbs 1–9*, 296.

Finally, the historical logbooks of the Ketuvim reconsider Israel's history in light of the Davidic lineage. Though many find the genealogies to be dry lists, the genealogies are acts of theological memory, reaffirming God's covenantal promises after the exile. Sara Japhet writes: "The Chronicler constructs a historical bridge between the past Davidic kingdom and a hoped-for future fulfillment, keeping the messianic promise alive in postexilic theology."[36] By ending with Cyrus's decree (2 Chron. 36:23), Chronicles closes on a hopeful note: the way is open for return, for temple rebuilding, and for the reign of a future Davidic king. John Sailhamer summarizes the trajectory of this conclusion:

> In the version of the Tanak that ends with Chronicles, the next biblical events are to be the coming of the Messiah (Dan. 9:25), the death of the Messiah (Dan. 9:26) and the destruction of the temple (Dan. 9:26b). These events, all taken from Daniel 9, are projected onto the screen of the future by 2 Chronicles 36 at the close of the Tanak. . . . The ending of the OT is fixed by its reference to Daniel 9, the last great prophetic word recorded in the Tanak. . . .
>
> The countdown begins with "the issuing of a decree to restore and rebuild Jerusalem" (Dan. 9:25). It is that decree of Cyrus that brings the OT to its proper conclusion. At the same time, that conclusion also signals an important new beginning. It is the beginning of the countdown to the coming of the biblical Messiah. . . .
>
> By marking the effective end of the Tanak with Daniel 9, the framers of the OT canon were making a statement that the next great event in Israel's history was the advent of the Messiah (Dan. 9:25). There was little left to do but wait for that event. All else, biblically as well as historically, was put on hold.[37]

In conclusion, the Ketuvim offers a liturgy of messianic longings. While these books do not present a systematic messianology, they speak of God's promises (like the Nevi'im) and Israel's lived reality (like the Torah laws). In Psalms, the cry for justice finds its answer in a Messiah. In Wisdom, the brokenness of the world cries out for a Messiah. In Daniel, the fall of empires gives way to the vision of a glorious Messiah. And in Chronicles, genealogy becomes a signpost pointing toward the return of God's Messiah. As Brevard Childs concludes, "The Writings complete the Tanakh not by offering closure, but by preserving the unresolved questions, the silence of God, the problem of suffering, the hope of deliverance, which find their answer only in the coming of the Messiah."[38]

36. Japhet, *I and II Chronicles*, 29.
37. Sailhamer, *Meaning of the Pentateuch*, 214–15.
38. Childs, *Biblical Theology*, 645.

Ketuvim Test Case: The Divine Priest-King (Ps. 110)

What Is This Text About?

Psalm 110 is one of the clearest messianic passages in the entire Tanakh, presenting a divine king who is also a priest.

What Messianic Topic(s) Does This Text Teach Believers?

The two dominant messianic themes are the eternal kingship and priesthood of the Messiah. Verse 1 introduces the exaltation of the Lord's chosen king: "The Lord says to my Lord: 'Sit at my right hand, until I make your enemies your footstool.'" This establishes the Messiah's divine authority and enthronement. Verse 4 introduces a unique priesthood: "You are a priest forever after the order of Melchizedek." This coupling of royal and priestly roles is highly unusual in the Tanakh, and it lays the foundation for the New Testament's portrait of Jesus. Derek Kidner observes, "This psalm is so compact and yet so rich in implications that it becomes a cornerstone for New Testament Christology."[39] The psalm envisions a ruler who is both divine and priestly, expanding the messianic hope beyond the Davidic monarchy to include an eternal priest-king.

How Do These Topics Relate to Other Sections of the Tanakh and Ultimately to Christ?

The themes of Ps. 110 build upon earlier biblical concepts while pointing forward to their fulfillment in Christ. The idea of the Messiah as king continues the promises to David in 2 Sam. 7, but the reference to Melchizedek reaches further back, to Gen. 14:18–20, where Melchizedek appears as both king and priest. This priestly role is outside the Levitical line, signaling a new and superior priesthood. The New Testament takes up this theme, especially in Heb. 5–7, where Jesus is identified as the high priest "in the order of Melchizedek." The psalm's declaration that the Messiah sits at God's right hand is applied by Jesus himself in Matt. 22:41–45 to affirm his divine authority, and it becomes a central verse in early Christian preaching (Acts 2:34–36). As N. T. Wright summarizes, "Psalm 110 presents a royal figure whose authority transcends David's line and merges royal and priestly power in a way only fully realized in Jesus."[40] Thus Ps. 110 serves as a critical link between the Hebrew Bible's hope and the New Testament's fulfillment.

39. Kidner, *Psalms 73–150*, 393.
40. N. T. Wright, *Jesus and the Victory of God*, 652.

How Does This Approach Inform Our Hermeneutic of This Text?

Reading Ps. 110 with the Messianic Trajectory approach illuminates how the psalm participates in the progressive revelation of God's redemptive plan. The psalm does not stand alone but reflects a culmination of themes: divine kingship, Davidic promise, and priestly mediation. A trajectory reading encourages us to see Ps. 110 not merely as a royal psalm for an earthly king but also as an inspired prophecy pointing to a greater figure who combines kingly and priestly roles forever. This approach justifies the New Testament's interpretive use of the psalm as messianic and eschatological. Goldsworthy explains, "Psalm 110, through typological and prophetic means, projects the Davidic king's role into an eschatological future, culminating in Christ, the enthroned Son and eternal priest."[41] This kind of hermeneutic views the psalm as a theological bridge, rooted in Israel's monarchy yet pointing toward the Messiah's cosmic reign.

What Potential Problems Arise from the Above Question?

Using a Messianic Trajectory approach can invite certain interpretive tensions. First, it risks overlooking the historical setting of the psalm. Psalm 110 likely originated as a royal enthronement psalm, possibly composed for a Davidic king's coronation. Some scholars argue that reading it exclusively as messianic projects later theological meanings onto the text, thereby diminishing its original liturgical or national context. Additionally, the identity of "my Lord" in verse 1 has been contested; Jewish interpreters often understand this as referring to David or another human ruler, not a divine Messiah. As James Kugel warns, "Interpreters who leap too quickly to Christian messianism from these texts may miss the subtle and multilayered nature of biblical poetry."[42] Finally, this trajectory-based reading raises the question of canon development: If later texts reshape earlier ones, how do we discern original meaning from eschatological fulfillment without collapsing one into the other?

What Are the Benefits of Applying This Approach to This Text?

1. Unity of Scripture: This approach shows how seemingly disparate threads—royal enthronement, Melchizedek's priesthood, and divine authority—coalesce in the Messiah.
2. Divine nature of the Messiah: This person is invited to sit at God's right hand, a position of supreme honor and rule.

41. Goldsworthy, *According to Plan*, 203.
42. Kugel, *How to Read the Bible*, 256.

3. Dual role of Christ: This approach affirms Christ's unique role as both high priest and reigning king, reinforcing key doctrines such as his intercession (Heb. 7:25) and sovereignty (Eph. 1:20–22). These insights fuel Christian worship, theology, and eschatological hope by rooting them in the promises and poetry of the Hebrew Scriptures.

What Are the Potential Problems in Applying This Approach to This Text?

1. Anachronism: Reading New Testament ideas back into an ancient Israelite context without regard for original meaning or audience can result in a flattening of the text's historical and poetic dimensions.
2. Assuming uniform messianic expectation: Messianic ideas were diverse across the Hebrew Bible and often implicit.
3. Supersessionism: Christian interpretations of Ps. 110 may suggest that the original Jewish meaning has been fully replaced rather than fulfilled.
4. Over-systematizing poetic texts: This approach may unintentionally turn metaphor and exalted language into rigid doctrinal propositions. The Messianic Trajectory approach must be balanced by attention to genre, context, and the gradual unfolding of revelation.

Summary of Test Case

Within the messianic trajectory of the Tanakh, Ps. 110 stands at the center of the Ketuvim as a clear statement of messianic hope. Here the Davidic promise is intensified into a vision of a priest-king who is enthroned at God's right hand and given universal rule: "Sit at my right hand, until I make your enemies your footstool." The psalm fuses royal and priestly imagery—"You are a priest forever after the order of Melchizedek"—so that the coming figure not only reigns but also mediates between God and his people. Read along this trajectory, Ps. 110 functions as a liturgical articulation of Israel's longing for a Davidic ruler whose authority is divine, whose priesthood is eternal, and whose victory finally secures the justice and peace anticipated throughout the rest of the Writings.

Conclusion

When read through the lens of a messianic trajectory, the Tanakh reveals a drama of anticipation. From Genesis to Chronicles, the Hebrew Scriptures do not merely present historical records or religious laws; they also narrate a deepening expectation for a messianic figure who will bring the texts of the Tanakh to fulfillment. The Torah, as the theological prologue, lays the structural and thematic groundwork that the Messiah fulfills—the serpent-crusher of Eden, the royal heir of Abraham and Judah, the prophet like Moses, and the priestly figure seen in Melchizedek and in Levitical patterns. These motifs are not fulfilled within the Torah but left deliberately open, creating a hope that moves readers forward.

The Nevi'im furthers the Torah's themes and hopes by giving voice to the covenant of God and revealing more deeply the future messianic hope of Deut. 34. They take the raw materials of Torah expectation and mold them into a portrait of a coming one who will both judge and heal, who suffers and reigns. In prophetic literature, we find that the Messiah is the axis upon which Israel's story and hope turns—from exile to return, from corruption to righteousness, from despair to hope.

Finally, the Ketuvim gathers Israel's prayers, laments, reflections, and memories into a liturgy of longing for a David-like Messiah. These books do not fulfill the messianic prophecy but move the messianic trajectory into an emotional, corporate messianic message as hoped for in Mal. 4:5. Through praise and pain, through wisdom and waiting, the Ketuvim sustains the unresolved cry for God's deliverance. Daniel envisions a divine Son of Man who will receive eternal dominion, and Chronicles re-centers the reader's gaze on the Davidic line as the enduring hope of Israel. In this way, the Ketuvim concludes the Tanakh not with certainty but with sacred anticipation.

Torah, Nevi'im, and Ketuvim together offer a unified yet unfinished messianic hope. They converge in an expectation for a redemptive figure who embodies the ideal prophet, priest, and king, a Messiah whose identity will resolve the tensions and fulfill the promises scattered throughout Israel's sacred texts. The Tanakh ends not with an answer but with a question still echoing: When will the promised one come? For adherents of the Messianic Trajectory approach, Christ is the Yes and Amen of the Hebrew Bible. The hermeneutic is Christocentric, and as such the Tanakh gestures to the New Testament, inviting readers to look beyond its pages for the completion of the hope it so richly nourishes.

6

Sacred Structure Approach

Tanakh as Parallel to the Temple Structure

IN GRADUATE SCHOOL, I learned of the practice called the "memory palace." The memory palace involves mentally placing information you want to remember within a familiar physical space, such as your home or a route you walk often. As you imagine walking through this space, each location along the path becomes a container or a mental image tied to a specific piece of information. This practice traces back to the ancient Greek poet Simonides of Ceos, who reportedly created it after a banquet hall collapsed. He alone survived the tragedy and was able to identify the victims by mentally visualizing where each person had been seated prior to the collapse. From this, he realized that spatial memory can help organize and recall information with remarkable accuracy. Today the memory palace remains a cornerstone of memory training and is used by everyone from students to memory champions, including the Sherlock Holmes character played by Benedict Cumberbatch.

The memory-palace method ties closely with my favorite way of grasping the structure of the Tanakh. In the museum of the Karaite synagogue and yeshiva in Jerusalem, one can find a small plaque that presents our last view of the Tanakh. It reads as follows:

> The Pentateuch (Torah), Prophets (Nevi'im) and Hagiography (Ketuvim) [. . .] are equated to the arrangement in the Holy of Holies, the Holy and the Courtyard in the "Tent of Meeting," namely Torah–Holy of Holies, Nevi'im (Prophets)–Holy,

> Ketuvim (Hagiography)–Courtyard. The Bible and the Temple are parallel on various levels, expressed throughout their spatial sequence and the hierarchy of sanctity of their ordering.

After the fall of the Jerusalem temple in 70 CE, diaspora Jews formulated a concept of the Bible as a reflection of, and substitute for, the temple. In fact, many Middle Eastern communities named Scripture *Miqdashyah* (Yahweh's Temple). This chapter draws intriguing parallels between biblical narratives and ancient temple practices. It uncovers symbolic connections, rituals, and spiritual motifs within the text, revealing a deeper layer of significance and resonance with the sacred spaces of antiquity. In the tenth century the Masoretes brought the Tanakh into its final form discussed in this book. One notable Karaite Masorete named Aaron ben Asher summarized the analogy this way: "The Torah, *Nevi'im* and *Ketuvim* [. . .] are as the Holy of Holies, the Holy and the Courtyard of the Tent of Meeting."[1] The three-court concept offers another hermeneutical approach and a refreshed means of grasping the threefold text. By using the three-court analogy, readers should know God's invitation (Ketuvim), God's word (Nevi'im), and God's presence (Torah).

Reasons for Adopting This Approach

The Sacred Structure approach to the Tanakh's organization holds a significant place in biblical studies, particularly because it is the oldest known structural interpretation, having been espoused by the Masoretes, who meticulously preserved the Hebrew text. This approach provides a unique lens through which the Tanakh can be understood, not merely as a historical or literary collection but as a sacred composition deeply interwoven with the symbolic framework of the Jewish temple. Naftali Wieder explains how the text and temple are connected:

> The Sanctuary is the most sacred place; the Torah the most sacred book. The former is the abode of the Divine Glory; the latter the depository of the divine message. God reveals Himself in the Sanctuary; the Torah is a record of the divine revelation. If the divine voice is heard in the former, God speaks from the pages of the latter. The Sanctuary is the unifying center, the Torah the unifying bond, of the nation.[2]

1. Ben Asher, *Sefer Diqduqei ha-Te'amim*, 3–4.
2. Wieder, "'Sanctuary' as a Metaphor for Scripture," 166.

By examining the Tanakh through this lens, one can uncover intricate connections between biblical narratives and the rituals, practices, and spatial divisions of the ancient temple structure.

At the heart of this approach is the recognition that the Tanakh is not simply a text of laws, prophecies, and writings; it reflects the sacred rhythms and theological depth of temple worship. The narratives, laws, and prophecies within the Tanakh often align with the structure and functions of the temple, suggesting a deliberate organization that mirrors the sacred space of Israelite worship. The temple was more than a physical location; it was the epicenter of divine presence, a place of encounter between God and his people. Similarly, the Tanakh can be seen as a textual temple in which the reader moves through various degrees of sanctity and revelation.

One of the primary objectives of this interpretative approach is to explore the sacred symbolism embedded within the text. By uncovering parallels between biblical accounts and temple practices, the Sacred Structure approach illuminates how the structure of the Tanakh itself mirrors the organization of worship in ancient Israel. This perspective does not merely identify symbolic similarities but seeks to demonstrate how the form and function of the Tanakh as a whole contribute to its deeper spiritual significance. In this approach, the threefold division of the Tanakh aligns with the tripartite structure of the temple courts, each division corresponding with a distinct aspect of worship and divine encounter.

The interpretative key to this approach is the three-court analogy, which offers a hermeneutical framework for understanding the canon's structure and purpose. The Ketuvim corresponds to the outer court, where worshipers first enter and engage with the broader expressions of faith. This division includes wisdom literature, poetic reflections, and historical accounts, which invite the reader into contemplation and response to God's works. The Nevi'im aligns with the inner court, where the priests minister and the divine word is proclaimed. The prophetic books contain the revelations, warnings, and calls to covenant faithfulness that function as God's direct communication to his people. Finally, the Torah represents the holy of holies, the sacred center of divine presence. Just as the ark of the covenant, containing God's law, resided in the innermost sanctuary, the Torah is the foundation of divine instruction, the heart of the covenant, and the ultimate expression of God's presence among his people.

This structured view of the Tanakh allows for a more profound appreciation of its sacred coherence. Each text within its respective division can be understood in relation to the function and symbolism of its corresponding temple court. The narratives of the Ketuvim reflect humanity's response to divine invitation, the messages of the Nevi'im convey the authoritative word of God, and the Torah encapsulates the very presence of God as revealed through his law and covenant. Through this approach, the Tanakh is not only read but experienced as a spiritual journey that mirrors the progression from common space to sacred space, ultimately leading to an encounter with the divine.

By adopting the Sacred Structure approach, readers gain a renewed means of grasping the significance of the Tanakh's organization. Rather than viewing the threefold division as merely historical or functional, this approach reveals its theological and liturgical depth. It underscores the continuity between the sacred text and the sacred space, showing that the Tanakh is not just a collection of writings but a structured theological construct meant to guide worshipers into deeper communion with God. In this way, the Sacred Structure view not only enriches biblical interpretation but also enhances the spiritual engagement of those who seek to understand the Tanakh in light of its sacred heritage.

Proponents of This Approach

The destruction of the Jerusalem temple in 70 CE precipitated a profound theological crisis within Judaism that was met with remarkable creative resilience. In the absence of a physical center for sacrificial worship and divine communion, the focus of religious life shifted to prayer, righteous deeds, and, most significantly, the sacred text. Out of this shift arose a powerful and elegant concept: the Tanakh, the Hebrew Bible itself, came to be seen as a spiritual sanctuary, a textual temple meticulously structured to mirror the sanctity and architecture of its lost physical counterpart. This idea, encapsulated in the term *Miqdashyah* (Yahweh's Temple), was not the invention of a single mind but a concept that evolved over centuries, articulated with varying degrees of explicitness by Talmudic sages, Masoretic scribes, Jewish philosophers, and mystics who sought to preserve the experience of sacred space within the pages of a holy book.[3]

The conceptual groundwork for viewing the Tanakh as a structured edifice was laid out in the Babylonian Talmud. The famous passage in Bava Batra (14b–15a), which delineates the order of the prophetic and historical books, reveals a conscious effort by the Sages to organize the sacred canon. While this text does not draw a direct analogy to the temple, its act of ordering is paramount. By establishing a received sequence for the Nevi'im and Ketuvim

3. Wieder, "'Sanctuary' as a Metaphor for Scripture."

to follow the Torah, the Sages treated the biblical corpus not as a random assortment of scrolls but as a cohesive, intentionally designed whole. This fundamental step was crucial because a building, unlike a heap of stones, is defined by its structure. The Talmudic ordering thus imbued the Tanakh with architectural integrity, paving the way for its later interpretation as a spiritual sanctuary.

This architectural vision found its most explicit and influential expression in the work of the Masoretic scholars, the meticulous scribes who preserved the biblical text. Aaron ben Asher, a leading Masorete of the tenth century, moved beyond mere organization to articulate a direct correspondence. In his grammatical work *Sefer Diqduqei ha-Teʿamim*, Ben Asher posited that the three sections of the Tanakh were analogous to the three distinct domains of the temple's sanctity.[4] The Torah, as the direct word of God, corresponded to the holy of holies, the innermost sanctum. The Nevi'im, the words of divine messengers, mirrored the holy place, the chamber accessible to the priests. Finally, the Ketuvim, a more diverse collection of inspired writings, paralleled the *azarah*, the outer courtyard. This framework transformed the act of reading into a form of spiritual pilgrimage, allowing the student to progress through levels of sanctity and draw near to the divine presence through engagement with the text. This concept was not confined to scholarly treatises but permeated the broader religious culture, particularly in Sephardic Jewry. The fourteenth-century philosopher Profiat Duran (the "Efodi") championed the idea that in the era of exile, Bible study had become the truest form of divine worship. During his time, entire Bibles were sometimes referred to as *Miqdashyah*, explicitly naming the book as a "sanctuary of the Lord." This nomenclature was often visually reinforced in the magnificent illuminated manuscripts of the age, whose decorated pages and architectural frontispieces transformed the physical book into a symbolic representation of the temple, a sacred space one could enter with the turning of a page.

While the Masoretes provided the explicit architectural blueprint, earlier thinkers had laid the philosophical foundations for such a view. Philo of Alexandria, writing while the Second Temple still stood, employed allegorical interpretation to uncover the universal truths hidden within the biblical text. For Philo, the Torah was a map of the soul's journey toward God. While he did not draw the specific tripartite analogy, his treatment of Scripture as a multilayered symbolic edifice, a repository of ultimate divine wisdom, implicitly positioned it as a spiritual structure that served the same function as the temple: a locus for encountering the divine.

4. Ben Asher, *Sefer Diqduqei ha-Teʿamim*, 3–4.

This understanding of the Tanakh as a deeply structured and sacred space was further enriched by later exegetical and mystical traditions. The sixteenth-century Italian commentator Obadiah Sforno suggested that the physical tabernacle was a concession to human weakness after the sin of the golden calf. In its absence, the structured guidance of the Tanakh, its laws, prophecies, and wisdom, serves as the primary means for humanity to approach God. Later, the eighteenth-century kabbalist Moshe Chaim Luzzatto, in his detailed mystical analysis of the temple, *Mishkanei Elyon*, described the sanctuary as a physical manifestation of profound spiritual realities designed to channel divine influx. This mystical lens, which sees divine purpose in every detail of the temple's design, is easily transposed onto the Tanakh, which kabbalah likewise views as a divinely encoded text where every letter and word holds immense spiritual power.

By harmonizing these perspectives—from the rabbinic ordering of the canon to the explicit analogy of the Masoretes and the philosophical depth of Philo—a cohesive vision emerges. The concept of *Miqdashyah* is more than a mere metaphor; it is a testament to the enduring Jewish belief in the power of text to create sacred space. It represents a theological innovation that allowed Judaism to thrive after its geographical and ritualistic center was destroyed. The Tanakh, structured with the sanctity and intentionality of the temple, became a portable homeland and an eternal sanctuary, ensuring that the encounter with the divine was not lost in the ashes of Jerusalem but rediscovered in the enduring words of Scripture.

Hermeneutic Realities of This Approach

The Sacred Structure approach to the Tanakh provides my favorite framework for interpreting the text in alignment with the sacred spatial divisions of the Israelite temple. Hermeneutically, each section corresponds to a specific court of the temple structure, thereby shaping the way texts are read and understood. However, there are no known full articulations of creators of this model explaining how to fully flesh out the approach with a particular text. So while the approach offers a compelling way to engage with the text, it also raises important hermeneutical questions and leaves other methodological ones unanswered.

As noted, the central concern in applying this structure to biblical interpretation is determining how each section of the Tanakh relates to its respective temple court. The Torah, often identified with the holy of holies, is viewed as the ultimate revelation of God's presence, containing his law and covenant instructions. The books of the Nevi'im, aligned with the inner court, serve as the mediators of divine communication, much like the priests who operated within the temple to convey God's will to the people. Finally, the Ketuvim books, corresponding to the outer court, provide wisdom, reflections, and historical accounts that invite worshipers into engagement with God from a more communal and experiential perspective. Each text, then, should be considered in light of how it aligns with the role and function of its respective court.

We may pose some significant interpretive questions to this approach. If each text functions within the Tanakh as its respective court would within the temple, what does this mean for texts that do not fit neatly within a temple-centered worldview? For instance, prophetic texts such as Jonah, Nahum, and Obadiah that are directed to the nations seem to challenge the notion that the Nevi'im functions strictly as an inner-court revelation since these books address audiences outside Israel's covenantal worship system. If the inner court is meant to mediate God's word to his people, how do prophetic books that engage foreign nations fit within the temple-structure model? Do they represent an outward-facing role of the inner court, or do they complicate the analogy altogether?

Another challenge arises when considering the prominence of the Psalms in revealing God's character and presence. If the Torah is equated with the holy of holies, the most sacred space where God's presence dwelled, why does the book of Psalms, which belongs to the Ketuvim, seem to offer some of the most profound expressions of divine revelation? The Psalms articulate God's attributes, his kingship, his justice, and his mercy in ways that are deeply personal and theological, often surpassing the explicit theological reflections found in the Torah. Does this suggest that the Ketuvim, particularly Psalms, serves a role beyond what the outer-court analogy allows? Or does it indicate that divine revelation is not confined strictly to the most sacred space but is accessible through worship and communal expressions of faith as well?

Moreover, a fundamental critique of the Sacred Structure approach is that it assumes a level of familiarity with the temple system that many modern readers may not possess. The intricacies of temple worship, the spatial dynamics of the courts, and the roles of priests and worshipers are concepts that require background knowledge, which may not be readily available to all interpreters. If understanding the Tanakh through this framework necessitates temple knowledge, does that limit its accessibility, or does it rather invite a more profound study of the historical and liturgical context of the text?

Embracing the Sacred Structure approach to the Tanakh offers a unique and enriching way to engage with the Hebrew Scriptures by integrating sacred imagery into biblical interpretation. The temple was not merely a physical structure but a theological blueprint of God's relationship with his people. By applying this paradigm to the organization of the Tanakh, readers can gain a heightened appreciation for the text's spiritual depth. Just as the temple's courts progressively led worshipers into deeper encounters with God, the Tanakh's structure can be seen as a literary temple, guiding the reader through increasing levels of divine revelation and engagement. This perspective enhances one's ability to see the text not just as a historical compilation but also as a sacred journey through which one moves from invitation (Ketuvim) to divine proclamation (Nevi'im) to the presence of God himself (Torah).

One means of applying this approach is to consider the imagery that connects the temple courts and the Tanakh. Each section of the temple was filled with symbolic elements such as lampstands, incense, veils, and altars that represented various aspects of divine truth. These images appear throughout the Tanakh in ways that correspond with their temple functions. For example, the menorah, which provided light in the temple, mirrors the way the Psalms and wisdom literature illuminate the human experience with divine guidance. The altar of incense, representing the prayers of the people, finds its literary counterpart in the prophetic texts, which often convey Israel's cries to God and his responses. The ark of the covenant, residing in the holy of holies, holds the tablets of the law, much like how the Torah serves as the central foundation of divine instruction. Seeing these connections allows readers to appreciate the Tanakh as more than a collection of writings; it is a constructed space of divine revelation, where each section plays a role in drawing the reader nearer to God's presence.

Furthermore, this perspective offers a cohesive interpretive framework that unifies the diverse genres and themes within the Tanakh. The Sacred Structure approach highlights the intentionality behind the organization of the Hebrew canon, demonstrating how its divisions reflect an overarching theological purpose. This challenges modern tendencies to read the Tanakh merely as a historical or literary artifact and instead encourages a reading strategy that recognizes its sacred architecture. By viewing the text through the lens of temple imagery, readers can engage with the Scriptures in a way that reflects Israel's worship experience, approaching the text not just for knowledge but as an act of devotion.

Additionally, this model fosters a greater appreciation for the interplay between space, revelation, and worship. The temple was a space where human action met divine presence, and the Tanakh, structured accordingly, reflects this dynamic. The Ketuvim invites participation and reflection, the Nevi'im proclaims divine truth, and the Torah establishes the very foundation of God's covenantal relationship with his people. Applying this approach allows one to see the text as more than words on a page; it becomes a living structure where the reader, like an Israelite worshiper, progresses through different levels of spiritual engagement. By adopting this perspective, we not only study the Tanakh but also experience it as a theological journey into the presence of God.

To apply the approach, I propose that we consider the characteristics of each court, the actions that happen within that court, and the articles appearing in that court. The following five questions will help us in applying the Sacred Structure approach.

1. How does this canonical division relate to this temple court?
2. What does this text espouse as this temple court would?
3. How does this approach inform our hermeneutic of this text?
4. What are the benefits of applying this approach to this text?
5. What are the potential problems with applying this approach to this text?

Torah: The Holy of Holies

The Torah parallels the holy of holies in the tent of meeting as the place to know God's presence. Its narratives and laws are not just historical or ethical texts but revelations of God's intent to dwell among his people. Michael Fishbane writes, "The Torah is not only a record of God's will; it is the place where divine presence and human obedience meet."[5] As Exod. 25:8 states, "Let them make me a sanctuary, that I may dwell in their midst." Nahum Sarna affirms, "The Tabernacle is the visible symbol of the presence of God in the midst of Israel. . . . Its detailed instructions mirror the gravity of that presence."[6] So from the narrative of creation (Gen. 1–2) to covenant (Gen. 12; Exod. 19) to the sanctuary (Exod. 25–40), there is a movement toward divine intimacy culminating in "the glory of the Lord filled the tabernacle" (Exod. 40:34). In the temple paradigm the Torah takes centrality. Abraham Joshua Heschel writes, "The Torah is the soul of the sanctuary . . . a living dialogue between God and His people."[7] Stephen Dempster adds, "Just as the Holy of Holies was restricted and sacred, so the Torah forms the restricted, revered center of Israel's Scriptures."[8]

5. Fishbane, *Biblical Interpretation*, 351.
6. Sarna, *Exodus*, 156.
7. Heschel, *God in Search of Man*, 274.
8. Dempster, *Dominion and Dynasty*, 36.

Just as only the high priest could enter the holy of holies once annually (Lev. 16:2), so the Torah is approached with deep reverence. Barry Holtz writes, "Handling the Torah is itself a liturgy."[9] The Torah is lifted, kissed, read ritually, and guarded like the sanctuary. The Torah is the most sacred object in modern Judaism "because it contains the living words of the God of Israel," declares Moshe Halbertal.[10]

The Torah represents the holy of holies, the sacred center of divine presence. Just as the ark of the covenant, containing God's law, resided in the innermost sanctuary, the Torah is the foundation of divine instruction, the heart of the covenant, and the ultimate expression of God's presence among his people. The parallels between the holy of holies and the Torah reinforce the idea that, within Judaism, the Torah is not merely a set of teachings but the very manifestation of God's will and presence. It is the textual holy of holies where the divine and human meet, where covenant is affirmed, and where the sacred truths of Yahweh are revealed to his people.

Actions

Within the temple motif, one needs to understand not only the characteristics of the court but also the actions performed there and what each court contained. The most sacred action that happened in the holy of holies was the ritual of atonement performed by the high priest. This action on Yom Kippur stands as the most sacred event in Israel's religious calendar, encapsulating themes of intercession, forgiveness, and covenant restoration. As Lev. 16 describes in careful detail, this was not an ordinary priestly function; it was an annual moment of national renewal, where one man stood as mediator between the people and the divine presence. In the same way that the holy of holies was the site of the most sacred act of reconciliation between God and Israel, the Torah functions as the textual equivalent, where divine justice, mercy, and the means of atonement are most clearly articulated. Baruch Levine asserts, "The Day of Atonement represents the most profound expression of divine mercy in the ritual calendar of ancient Israel. It is where the pollution of sin is not only confronted but removed through sacred drama."[11] Likewise, as the theological center of the Tanakh, the Torah is the sourcebook for understanding God's provision for sin and his desire for restored relationship. It not only outlines the mechanics of sacrifice but also reveals the divine heart behind the ritual. As Lev. 17:11 declares, "For the life of the flesh is in

9. Holtz, *Back to the Sources*, 141.
10. Halbertal, *People of the Book*, 3.
11. Levine, *Leviticus*, 103.

the blood, and I have given it to you on the altar to make atonement for your souls, for it is the blood that makes atonement by the life."

The Torah is more than a legal text; it is the narrative and instructional environment in which atonement becomes possible. As Michael Fishbane puts it, "The Torah embodies the covenantal drama of sin, purification, and divine closeness. Its texts are structured to draw the worshiper into God's redemptive rhythm."[12] Leviticus 16:21 highlights this verbal priestly act: "[He] shall . . . confess over it all the iniquities of the people of Israel, and all their transgressions, all their sins." This confession, spoken within the veil, gave voice to national guilt and trust in divine mercy. It mirrored the covenantal promises of texts such as Exod. 34:6–7, where God reveals himself as "the LORD, the LORD, a God merciful and gracious, slow to anger, and abounding in steadfast love and faithfulness."

As the literary holy of holies, the Torah preserves and proclaims this very confession. As the high priest stood interceding before the *kapporet* (mercy seat), so the Torah speaks into the life of every generation, calling Israel to confession, obedience, and hope. Walter Brueggemann writes: "The Torah is not merely prescriptive but dialogical, it initiates a conversation between God and His people about sin, restoration, and fidelity."[13] Like the high priest entering the sacred chamber, the reader of Torah enters into a space where divine mercy is encountered through God's revealed word. The psalmist expresses this dynamic clearly: "I have hidden your word in my heart that I might not sin against you" (Ps. 119:11 NIV). Or "Your word is very pure; therefore your servant loves it" (Ps. 119:140 AT).

Seen through the lens of temple structure, the Tanakh moves progressively inward, from invitation (Ketuvim), to proclamation (Nevi'im), to presence (Torah). The high priest's path on Yom Kippur, through the outer courts, past the altar, and behind the veil becomes a metaphor for the reader's movement through Scripture. The Torah stands at the literary holy of holies, the locus where sin is addressed, God is encountered, and reconciliation begins. Grant Osborne captures this dynamic powerfully: Torah was not merely Israel's constitution, it was the revelatory center of their relationship with Yahweh, where law, grace, and presence intertwined.[14]

To read the Torah, then, is to approach the divine. It is to enter into the sacred drama of intercession and redemption. Just as the high priest risked his life to seek mercy, the Torah reader approaches with awe, knowing that within its words dwell both the justice and compassion of God.

12. Fishbane, *Biblical Interpretation*, 361.
13. Brueggemann, *Theology of the Old Testament*, 202.
14. Osborne, "Testing God's Son," 372–73.

Articles

Like the actions in the holy of holies, the contents of the court aids in the hermeneutic of reading the Torah. Let us consider two articles: the ark of the covenant and the cherubim.

Situated in the innermost part of the tabernacle was the ark of the covenant with the cherubim stationed above the mercy seat on top of the ark. Exodus 25:22 affirms, "There I will meet with you, and from above the mercy seat, from between the two cherubim, . . . I will speak with you." Thus we see that the ark, guarded by golden cherubim with outstretched wings (Exod. 25:18–22), was more than a container; it was the footstool of the divine king (1 Chron. 28:2), the throne from which God's covenantal voice resounded. As we consider the cherubim first, we must ask if they have a deeper meaning that can parallel with the Torah. Gordon Wenham observes, "The cherubim are not ornamental; they represent the very glory-presence of God enthroned in holiness."[15] In the same way, the Torah operates as the communication platform of God's enthroned glory, mirroring the cherubim's role in highlighting divine kingship and covenantal authority.

Just as the ark anchored the physical temple, the Torah centers Israel's communal and liturgical life. Jacob Milgrom explains, "The entire structure of the Temple was oriented toward the Ark, . . . the heart of Israel's encounter with God."[16] Nahum Sarna adds, "The Torah is not only the path to holiness, but also the enduring medium through which God's will is revealed."[17]

Since the ark contained the covenant tablets, Exod. 25:21–22 underscores that it was the center of divine-human communion: "There . . . I will meet with you." T. Desmond Alexander emphasizes, "The Ark enshrines not only the tablets, but also the very memory of covenantal encounter at Sinai."[18] The Torah itself becomes a kind of "literary ark." Hebrews 9:4 recalls that the ark held "the gold jar of manna, Aaron's staff, . . . and the stone tablets." Each of these items corresponds to key theological dimensions within the Torah and Tanakh:

1. The tablets: Covenant and law. The stone tablets (Deut. 10:1–5) represented the foundational moral covenant between God and Israel. John Sailhamer comments, "The Torah is more than a collection of laws; it is the narrative and legal articulation of God's purpose in forming a

15. Wenham, *Book of Leviticus*, 239.
16. Milgrom, *Leviticus 1–16*, 1015.
17. Sarna, *Exploring Exodus*, 142.
18. Alexander, *From Paradise to the Promised Land*, 169.

covenant people for Himself."[19] This purpose is celebrated in Ps. 19:7: "The law of the LORD is perfect, reviving the soul."

2. The jar of manna: Divine provision. As a testimony to Yahweh's faithfulness, the manna (Exod. 16:32–34) symbolized God's provision of sustenance in the wilderness. Psalm 78:24–25 recalls: "He rained down manna for the people to eat, he gave them the grain of heaven. Human beings ate the bread of angels" (NIV). An unidentified rabbinic commentary links manna to Torah: "As the manna was daily and sufficient, so too is Torah, given fresh each day." Similarly, Mekilta de Rabbi Ishmael states, "Your fathers, who studied Torah, see how they were fed. You, too, if you study Torah, the Holy One Blessed be He will feed you of this" (Vayassa 6).
3. Aaron's staff: Divine authority. The budding staff (Num. 17:8) authenticated the Levitical priesthood and quelled rebellion. Desmond Alexander writes, "The budding staff is a divine endorsement of authority, much like the prophets' words are authenticated by the Lord's commissioning voice."[20] Like Aaron's staff, the Nevi'im represents divine authority calling Israel to covenant fidelity.

Thus the Torah not only holds the commandments but also bears witness to God's provision and authority. John Walton affirms, "The Torah contains not merely laws, but the very acts by which God made Himself known to Israel."[21] The parallel between temple and text culminates in the understanding of the Torah as the *textual* holy of holies. Abraham Joshua Heschel beautifully writes, "The Torah is a sanctuary in words."[22] So the Tanakh, like the temple, leads its readers on a journey from the outer courts of history and poetry into the sacred core of Torah, where the covenant and presence of God dwell.

The ark's mobility also highlights a key parallel of the Torah. The ark moved through the wilderness (Josh. 3:6; 6:6–7), signaling God's ongoing presence. The Torah too is never static. Deuteronomy 6:6–9 commands its integration into daily life, from teaching children to writing on doorposts. Moshe Halbertal insists, "The Torah is not simply read, it is lived. It is not a relic to be guarded, but a covenant to be enacted."[23]

In the end, both ark and Torah converge as sacred vessels of divine encounter. The following summary captures this vision with clarity: The Scriptures

19. Sailhamer, *Meaning of the Pentateuch*, 25.
20. Alexander, *From Paradise to the Promised Land*, 169.
21. Walton, *Old Testament Theology for Christians*, 42.
22. Heschel, *God in Search of Man*, 273.
23. Halbertal, *People of the Book*, 29.

are architectonic.[24] The Tanakh is not simply a collection but a sanctuary in words, designed to bring worshipers step-by-step toward the presence of God. Both the holy of holies and the Torah serve as sacred spaces where God speaks, provides, chooses, and forgives. This understanding reframes the Tanakh not as a mere "holy book" but as a literary temple progressively drawing the reader ever closer to communion with the God of Israel.

Torah Test Case: The Passover (Exod. 12:1–20)

What Is This Text About?

Exodus 12:1–20 details the instructions given to the Israelites regarding the first Passover. God commands the Israelites to select a lamb, slaughter it, and apply its blood to the doorposts of their homes as a sign of protection from the upcoming plague of the death of the firstborn. The lamb must be roasted and eaten with unleavened bread and bitter herbs. This ritual is to be observed annually as a lasting ordinance. The text emphasizes the significance of the blood for salvation and deliverance and the importance of following God's instructions exactly.

How Does This Canonical Division Relate to This Temple Court?

In considering the temple and its courts, we can draw parallels between the rituals in Exod. 12 and the actions performed in the temple. While not directly linked in the text, the Passover could foreshadow the ultimate sacrifice of the Lamb (John 1:29), pointing toward the presence of God and ultimate atonement. The lamb's blood is the protective agent, much like the sacrificial system in the temple.

What Does This Text Espouse as This Temple Court Would?

The Passover, like the temple ritual, is a means of drawing near to God's presence.

1. Access to God's presence: The Passover ritual can be seen as giving access to God's protection and favor. The blood of the lamb allows the Israelites to be saved from destruction, much like the high priest's sacrifice allowed him to approach the presence of God in the holy of holies.
2. Purity and separation: Only those who follow the instructions correctly are allowed to partake in the benefits (safety, deliverance). The ritual

24. That is, they are architectural in their design.

purity of the lamb, the unleavened bread, and the bitter herbs correspond to the purification processes in temple worship.

How Does This Approach Inform Our Hermeneutic of This Text?

Approaching the Tanakh as structured like the temple courts influences our reading by framing the sacred text in terms of divine proximity:

1. Outer court (universal access): Exodus 12's message of deliverance can be seen as universally accessible in principle. God offers protection to the entire community, similar to the outer court where non-Israelites could enter, symbolizing God's broader reach.
2. Closer to the divine (intimacy): The deeper into the courts one goes, the closer to the divine presence. Reading Exod. 12 in this light suggests that the text invites believers into deeper covenant with God, akin to temple worship, where rituals bring one nearer to God.

What Are the Benefits of Applying This Approach to This Text?

1. Holistic understanding of salvation: Viewing the Passover through the lens of temple courts helps to emphasize that salvation and access to God require purity, sacrifice, and obedience—themes deeply embedded in the later temple rituals.
2. Holistic covenant relationship: The view highlights the personal and communal nature of covenant. Just as access to the temple depends on one's standing within the community, the Passover requires the active participation of individuals and families within the broader community of Israel.

What Are the Potential Problems in Applying This Approach to This Text?

1. Anachronistic assumptions: It could impose later temple structures onto a much earlier and different context. The Passover in Exodus was not initially designed as a ritual to fit into a temple setting, and using temple symbolism might obscure its original focus as a communal act of deliverance.
2. Overemphasis on structure: Focusing too much on the temple courts could overshadow the redemptive and relational elements of the Passover, which centers on God's deliverance rather than a ritualized approach to God's presence.

3. Inconsistent application: If this model were applied to all passages of the Torah, it might force unnatural connections between unrelated themes or rituals, potentially distorting their original meaning and purpose.

Summary of Test Case

In summary, Exod. 12:1–20 records God's instructions for the first Passover, commanding Israel to select a lamb, apply its blood to their doorposts, and eat it with unleavened bread and bitter herbs as a sign of deliverance from the plague of the firstborn, a ritual to be observed annually. When read through the framework of the temple courts, the text resonates with themes of sacrifice, purity, and access to God's presence. The lamb's blood functions as protection much like the later sacrificial system, while the strict obedience required reflects the purity demanded in temple worship. This view highlights holistic aspects of salvation and covenant, showing both personal and communal participation in God's deliverance. Such an approach can enrich understanding of the text, but it needs to be balanced with awareness of historical context and purpose.

Nevi'im: The Court of the Jews

The Nevi'im occupies the central space of the Tanakh, which corresponds symbolically to the court of the priests in the temple. This court goes by numerous names throughout biblical history: "the holy place" (1 Kings 8:8–10), "the greater house" (2 Chron. 3:5), "the inner court" (1 Kings 6:36), and "the temple" (1 Kings 6:17). As the second court, the Nevi'im reminds believers to be obedient to the presence of God via the word of God. It was in the court of the priests (2 Chron. 4:9) that Scripture was read, interpreted, taught, and debated. In 1 Kings 8:10–11, we read that when the priests exited the holy place, the cloud filled the house of the Lord, showing that this inner space served as another place of divine interaction. "These are the prophets who spoke from the mouth of God, and the priests and judges who acted in accordance with the Torah."[25] Much like the priests speaking in the holy place, the prophets called the wayward people to revive covenant fidelity, even in the social realm.[26] The court contained a number of sacred ritual objects useful to parallel the prophets. The seven-branched lampstand (1 Kings 7:49) parallels the call for the people to be a light to the world like Yahweh. The altar of incense calls

25. Wieder, "'Sanctuary' as a Metaphor for Scripture," 168.
26. Brueggemann and Hankins, *Prophetic Imagination*, 21–23.

for believers to lift up prayers to Yahweh. Finally, the table of the showbread reminds believers to come to the Lord as the place of provision. In the porch stood the two pillars Jachin (he establishes) and Boaz (in strength; 1 Kings 7:21; 2 Kings 11:14; 23:3). The two pillars boldly proclaim to the court of all that, if you enter, Yahweh will establish you in strength.

The Nevi'im echo and amplify God's word, interpreting the Torah amid Israel's historical crises. Considering the Nevi'im in light of the temple moves the prophetic texts far from mere predictors into being covenantal prosecutors. As Gerhard von Rad states, "The prophets constantly return to the Sinai tradition. Their preaching is full of reminiscences of it; their accusations are made in the name of the covenant."[27] Their messages often begin with "Thus says the Lord," signaling their role as divine spokesmen, just as priests read Torah in the court of Israel and call for repentance. A great passage that captures this parallel is Isa. 1:18:

> Come now, let us reason together, says the Lord:
> though your sins are like scarlet,
> they shall be as white as snow.

As Bruce Waltke notes, "The prophets were not innovators. Their authority was not their own but derived from the Torah, and their message called people to return to it."[28]

We see four main ways in which the messages of the prophets paralleled the Jewish court system:

1. Moral and ethical guidance: The Nevi'im contains many ethical and moral teachings that are relevant to the lives of the Jewish people. These teachings can be seen as indirectly influencing the behavior and decisions made within the Jewish community and its court system. The prophetic writings often call for justice, compassion, and adherence to the laws and commandments of the Torah.
2. Historical context: The historical narratives in the Nevi'im provide insights into the political and social contexts of ancient Israel. Understanding these historical contexts can shed light on the challenges and issues that the Jewish courts may have faced during those times. For example, the books of Samuel and Kings provide accounts of the leadership and governance of Israel, which can be relevant to discussions about leadership and justice in a court setting.

27. Von Rad, *Old Testament Theology*, 2:75.
28. Waltke, *Old Testament Theology*, 825.

3. Prophetic critique: The prophets in the Nevi'im often delivered messages of critique and admonishment to the leaders and people of Israel when they strayed from the path of righteousness and justice. This can be seen as a form of accountability, which is also a function of a court system. The prophets called for repentance and a return to moral and ethical behavior, much as a court may seek to correct wrongdoing and administer justice.
4. Legal implications: While the books of the Nevi'im do not contain legal codes like the Torah, they do touch on legal matters and issues of justice. The books of the prophets may contain references to disputes, legal judgments, and the consequences of legal and moral transgressions. These narratives and teachings can indirectly inform the Jewish legal tradition and the principles applied in Jewish courts.

The Former Prophets—Joshua through Kings—offer theological history. Their narratives link national success to covenant faithfulness and use phrases such as "He did what was right" or "He did evil" to assess leadership through a Torah lens. The message preached not only for Israel to return to Torah and covenant faithfulness but also to share the covenant to the nations. As Christopher Wright says, "The mission of God in the Old Testament is fundamentally universal. The prophetic writings never let Israel forget that their calling is tied to the nations."[29] Much like the priests in the holy place, the prophets often operate as a covenantal courtroom. They offer charges, warnings, and restoration promises—seen clearly in Mic. 6:1–2: "Arise, plead your case before the mountains. . . . For the LORD has a controversy with his people" (AT).

Like the court of the priests, the Nevi'im books are not ends in themselves but point the people back to Torah obedience and forward to God's eschatological promises. They hold up the mirror of covenant accountability and offer the means for national and personal renewal. To read the Nevi'im is to step into God's holy court, where truth, justice, mercy, and repentance meet under the watchful gaze of divine instruction.

Actions

As we consider the actions in the court of the priests, there are many rituals to consider for Tanakh parallels. These rituals include sacrifices, prayers, Torah readings, and music. While these acts were central to worship, the Nevi'im continually calls Israel to refresh these worship elements

29. C. Wright, *Mission of God*, 319.

toward covenant faithfulness. The prophets often rebuke empty ritual that is divorced from ethical and covenantal faithfulness. As Isaiah declares, "Bring no more vain offerings. . . . Wash yourselves, . . . seek justice, correct oppression" (Isa. 1:11–17). Amos echoes this sentiment: "I hate, I despise your feasts. . . . But let justice roll down like waters" (Amos 5:21–24). "The prophets act as the conscience of the Temple system. They remind Israel that worship divorced from ethical obligation is offensive to Yahweh."[30] Though sacrifices addressed sin, communal prayers expressed Israel's longing for favor. The Priestly Blessing (Num. 6:24–26) aligns with Jer. 29:11–13: "You will seek me and find me, when you seek me with all your heart." Thus Jon Levenson states, "The prophetic literature does not reject ritual but calls for its integration with a life of covenant loyalty."[31] Pilgrimage festivals to the temple would culminate in worship and Torah readings (Deut. 31:10–13). So Hosea 6:6 echoes the priestly court when he declares, "For I desire steadfast love and not sacrifice." Prophets condemned neglect and defilement. Malachi warns, "When you offer blind animals, . . . is that not evil?" (Mal. 1:8). Like the priests in the courtyard of the temple, "the prophets were not critics of ritual, but of ritualism, acts performed with the hands but not the heart."[32]

Incense, symbolizing prayer (Ps. 141:2), finds prophetic parallels in intercession. Like the priests who interceded for Israel in the holy of holies, the prophets interceded between the divine and the covenant people. Jeremiah reminds God, "I stood before you to speak good for them" (Jer. 18:20). Music, played in the court as vital to temple worship (1 Chron. 25:1), permeates prophetic language. Isaiah 26:1 and Hab. 3:19 close with songs of triumph. Thus Amos condemns hypocritical singing (Amos 6:5), while Zephaniah envisions God singing over his people (Zeph. 3:17). Ultimately, the prophets don't reject temple worship but elevate it. A way to understand Mic. 6 or Amos 5, for instance, may be that ritual must lead to righteousness, and worship must inspire justice. As the temple courts hosted offering and instruction, the Nevi'im function as literary courts, summoning Israel to covenant loyalty with both mercy and warning.

Articles

Within the holy place of the temple are sacred articles that symbolize Yahweh's covenant with Israel. These visible signs of spiritual truths are echoed

30. Brueggemann and Hankins, *Prophetic Imagination*, 41.
31. Levenson, *Sinai & Zion*, 137.
32. Heschel, *Prophets*, 46.

in the Nevi'im. Let's consider the menorah, altar of incense, table of showbread, and the pillars.

The golden menorah (Exod. 25:31–40; 1 Kings 7:48) symbolizes divine light and Israel's calling. Its continuous flame reflects God's presence and Israel's mission:

> You are my servant,
> Israel, in whom I will be glorified. (Isa. 49:3)

> I will make you as a light for the nations. (Isa. 49:6)

Connecting light to glory also connects the light to the message of Torah! Micah 4:2 affirms, "For out of Zion shall go forth the law." The prophetic call to justice and holiness is itself an extension of the temple's light; for it seeks to radiate God's purity beyond the veil and into the world.

The altar of incense (Exod. 30:1–10) stood before the veil, symbolizing prayer: "Let my prayer be counted as incense before you" (Ps. 141:2). Isaiah 56:7 affirms, "My house shall be called a house of prayer for all peoples." Yet prophets condemn insincere incense/prayer: "Bring no more vain offerings; incense is an abomination to me" (Isa. 1:13); "What use to me is frankincense? . . . Your burnt offerings are not acceptable" (Jer. 6:20). These rebukes connect the prophetic message with the call to right prayer and worship.

The table of showbread (Lev. 24:5–9), with twelve loaves for the tribes, symbolizes God's provision and fellowship. Isaiah 55:2 speaks of the misguided spending of the people of God: "Why do you spend your money for that which is not bread? . . . Eat what is good." Amos 8:11 warns that poor worship will result in a spiritual famine "of hearing the words of the LORD." Where the table of showbread was to be a message of spiritual food for the nation, the prophets give this message and at times show that the food is drying up due to lack of proper covenant fidelity. Prophetic hunger is a call not just to eat but also to listen and be fed by righteousness.

The bronze pillars Jachin and Boaz (1 Kings 7:21) symbolize covenant strength and stability. Jeremiah's call echoes the pillar/wall imagery: "I make you . . . an iron pillar, and bronze walls" (Jer. 1:18–19). Isaiah ties strength to trust: "In returning and rest you shall be saved; . . . in trust shall be your strength" (Isa. 30:15). In contrast, Ezek. 13:14 warns, "I will break down the wall . . . so that its foundation will be laid bare." Prophetic rhetoric repeatedly dismantles false security in favor of the solid rock of covenant obedience.

In summary, while the books of the Nevi'im do not parallel the court of the Jews in a direct or prescriptive manner, they provide important moral, ethical, historical, and prophetic insights that can influence the behavior and decisions of the Jewish community and its legal institutions. The Nevi'im books contribute to the broader ethical and religious framework within which Jewish law and jurisprudence operates. The temple furnishings, when viewed through prophetic lenses, are not static symbols but theological anchors, calling Israel to light-bearing mission, sincere worship, spiritual nourishment, and covenantal strength. Each item in the holy place does not merely represent an ancient ritual; it reverberates with theological meaning that the Nevi'im harnesses to call Israel back to its sacred identity. The menorah illuminates the moral path, the incense altar elevates true prayer, the showbread testifies to God's sustaining word, and the pillars declare his enduring covenant. These elements, once confined to the temple, are animated in prophetic oracles that extend their significance to every generation.

Nevi'im Test Case: The Promised Royal Child (Isa. 9)

What Is This Text About?

Isaiah 9 is a prophecy about the future messianic reign and the coming of a child who will bring light and hope to a dark world. The passage opens by declaring that those in darkness will see a great light. It describes the birth of a child who will be called Wonderful Counselor, Mighty God, Everlasting Father, Prince of Peace. This child is expected to bring justice and peace to Israel, and his government will be everlasting. The passage ends with a declaration of the coming judgment on Israel's unfaithfulness, which will culminate in destruction, but the hope of the messianic king remains central.

How Does This Canonical Division Relate to This Temple Court?

In the context of the temple and its courts, Isa. 9 can be connected to the anticipated transformation of worship and access to God. The court of Israel, where those closest to God could enter, can symbolize the expected intimate relationship that Israel would have with God under the messianic reign. The Prince of Peace will restore justice and purity, as the priests were intended to interpret and bring about. As the priestly and kingly system began to fail theologically, this passage placed in the court of Israel gives a harmony between the two offices and a theological hope for the Messiah to come.

What Does This Text Espouse as This Temple Court Would?

The messianic prophecy of Isa. 9 emphasizes divine justice, peace, and closeness to God's presence.

1. Access to God's presence: The child in Isa. 9 is a divine figure who brings the peace and justice of God's kingdom. As the "Prince of Peace," he will usher in a reign where the barriers to divine presence, whether through sin or distance, will be overcome.
2. Purity and restoration: The messianic figure will rule with justice, ensuring that Israel (and ultimately the world) will be able to approach God with righteousness, much like the cleansing rituals in the temple that prepared the faithful to stand in God's presence.

How Does This Approach Inform Our Hermeneutic of This Text?

Applying the temple-court model to the structure of Isa. 9 could inform the interpretation of this prophecy.

1. Outer court (universal access): The message of light and salvation is not limited to Israel but extends to the gentiles. This aligns with the outer court, where all nations had some degree of access to the divine presence.
2. Deeper into divine presence: As the prophecy speaks of peace and justice brought by the Messiah, we understand that the closer one gets to the divine presence, the more justice and righteousness are necessary, which the Messiah brings to fulfillment.
3. Access to God: Though not the holy of holies, the Messiah, as the prince of peace, brings the final access to God, purifying the people and ensuring that those who come to God can do so with peace, reconciliation, and justice.

What Are the Benefits of Applying This Approach to This Text?

1. Universal reach of salvation: By using the temple-court analogy, we can understand that the Messiah's reign will have a universal impact, drawing all nations to God's presence, much like the temple courts invited outsiders to participate in the blessings of God.
2. Messiah as bridge to divine presence: Just as the high priest had access to the holy of holies, the Messiah acts as the intermediary who makes the very presence of God accessible to all. His justice and peace prepare the way for this intimacy with God.
3. Holistic justice and peace: The messianic reign is not just about spiritual deliverance but also about societal restoration. The analogy can help us understand that God's justice is not only about individual atonement

but also about societal transformation, akin to temple practices that restored order and purity.

What Are the Potential Problems in Applying This Approach to This Text?

1. Overspiritualizing the message: The prophetic message of Isa. 9 is not purely about spiritual worship and access to God in a temple sense; it's about peace and justice in the world. The temple-court model may overly spiritualize the message of political and social restoration.
2. Messiah's reign not yet fully realized: The analogy might obscure the reality that the full reign of the Messiah, including the peace described in Isa. 9, is still awaited. Applying a completed sacred structure could mislead us into thinking that this reign has already been fully realized in the present.
3. Contextual disconnect: While the temple-court analogy can enrich the understanding of the text, it risks imposing later temple-based practices on a prophecy that had a distinct historical and social context. The message of Isa. 9 may lose its prophetic edge if overlaid too heavily with temple imagery.

Summary of Test Case

In conclusion, Isa. 9 proclaims the coming of a messianic child who will bring light, peace, and justice to a people dwelling in darkness, described with titles such as Wonderful Counselor, Mighty God, Everlasting Father, and Prince of Peace. Interpreted through the framework of the temple courts, the prophecy reflects both intimacy with God and the hope of restored access to his presence, as the Messiah unites priestly and kingly roles that had failed in Israel's history. This lens highlights themes of universal salvation, messianic mediation, and holistic peace that extend beyond individual deliverance to societal renewal. By applying the temple-court analogy to Isa. 9, we gain a deeper understanding of the Messiah's role in restoring access to God, but we must be cautious not to let this lens overshadow the broader political, social, and eschatological dimensions of the prophecy.

Ketuvim: The Court of All

As the final division of the Hebrew Bible, the Ketuvim functions as both culmination and invitation, a symbolic "outer court" of the temple accessible to all, including gentiles, where divine wisdom and human longing meet. This outermost court surrounded the whole temple. As 2 Chron. 4:9 describes, "He made the court of the priests and the great court . . . and overlaid their doors with bronze," evoking openness and shared worship. This diverse collection of poetry, wisdom, lament, history, and apocalyptic texts, extends a broad welcome. "The Writings are the most inclusive section of the canon," writes Stephen Dempster, "inviting the individual to reflect, question, and respond in worship."[33] Many of the books within this section concern gentiles and hardly use the name Yahweh. These books benefit from a hermeneutic of evangelism to grasp their often-obscure theological implications. In the outer court, one can find the altar of burnt offering (2 Chron. 15:8), where sacrifices for sin were offered. Likewise, the Ketuvim proclaims to all that there is a means of forgiveness and justification for sin. Also in the courtyard were the brazen sea (4:2–5, 10) and ten lavers (1 Kings 7:38–39), which were used to purify worshipers. The Ketuvim parallels the outer court by also showing how both Jew and gentile can be purified and welcomed into the religiously obedient people of God.

1. Inclusiveness and access: The court of the gentiles was a space within the Second Temple precincts where non-Jews could access and experience the sacred environment of the temple, even though they couldn't enter the inner courts reserved for Jews. Similarly, the Ketuvim is a division of the Hebrew Bible containing texts accessible to both Jews and non-Jews. It is not limited to the religious elite or specific groups within Judaism, making it more inclusive.
2. Cultural and spiritual diversity: The court of the gentiles was a place where people from various backgrounds and cultures could gather and interact, as it attracted visitors from different parts of the world. The Ketuvim, likewise, consists of diverse texts that cover a wide range of topics, including poetry, philosophy, history, and theology. It reflects the multifaceted nature of Jewish religious and cultural expression.
3. Reflecting on universal themes: The court of the gentiles allowed non-Jewish visitors to engage with aspects of the Jewish faith and rituals, even if they were not part of the Jewish community. Similarly, the Ketuvim contains texts that explore universal themes and moral principles that can resonate with people of various faiths and backgrounds. For example, the book of Psalms contains prayers and expressions of human emotions that can be relatable to people of different religious traditions.

33. Dempster, *Dominion and Dynasty*, 210.

4. Bridging gaps: The court of the gentiles served as a bridge between the Jewish and non-Jewish worlds, allowing for dialogue and interaction. The Ketuvim, in its inclusiveness and diversity, can also serve as a bridge between different cultures and religious communities by offering insights into Jewish thought and wisdom.

The comparison between the Ketuvim and the court of the gentiles is symbolic and metaphorical, highlighting their inclusive and universal aspects rather than suggesting a direct correspondence. While the court of the gentiles was a physical space in the temple, the Ketuvim is a literary and religious collection, but both share the idea of reaching out to a broader audience and fostering understanding among different groups of people.

The two primary wisdom texts of the Ketuvim, Proverbs and Ecclesiastes, speak universal truths (understandable to all, not just Israelites). Thus Prov. 1:7 affirms, "The fear of the Lord is the beginning of knowledge," while Eccles. 3:11 declares, "He has set eternity in the human heart" (NIV). So the innate desire to gain wisdom is God given and pulls both the Israelite and gentile to a relationship with Yahweh. "Wisdom literature stands at the crossroads of revelation and reason . . . not only special revelation."[34]

Narratives in this division are a great parallel to the court of the gentiles, for in them we see many gentiles involved with Israelites and adopted into the people of God. Ruth's confession, "Your people shall be my people, and your God my God" (Ruth 1:16), is one of adoption and inclusion into the people of God just as the court of all welcomes the gentile to join fellowship. Nebuchadnezzar's praise in Dan. 4:34, "His dominion is an eternal dominion," highlights the divine evangelism / outreach in the Ketuvim. As Seitz notes, "The inclusion of Ruth and Daniel . . . signals a shift: salvation history . . . spills over into Gentile soil."[35]

Moving to the worship text of the Ketuvim, Psalms acts as a spiritual altar: "Let my prayer be counted as incense" (Ps. 141:2), opening worship to all. Psalms is indeed the hymn book of Israel, but also songs for all! Brueggemann writes, "Psalms democratizes the Temple . . . into the hands of all who seek God."[36] Thus we rightly see that all nations are called into the court to praise. "Praise the Lord, all nations!" (Ps. 117:1).

Exilic books such as Daniel and Ezra-Nehemiah redefine holiness beyond the land. Daniel prays faithfully under threat (Dan. 6:10). According to N. T. Wright, "The exile forced Israel to rethink holiness . . . as fidelity in all

34. Walton and Hill, *Old Testament Today*, 278.
35. Seitz, *Character of Christian Scripture*, 93.
36. Brueggemann, *Message of the Psalms*, 19.

places."[37] As such, the Ketuvim again highlights the need for public reading, as seen in Neh. 8:8, "They gave the sense, so that the people understood." The declaration to know Scripture and obey it now moves beyond just Israel![38]

In sum, the Ketuvim acts as a theological outer court, welcoming all people, Jew and gentile alike, to approach the sacred through wisdom, worship, and reflection. It is here that seekers are purified, not by sacrifice but by confession, not by ritual but by honest engagement with divine truth. As a temple court, the Ketuvim extends an invitation: come near, listen, lament, and learn. Waltke sums it up: "If Torah is God's voice and the Prophets His messengers, the Writings are God's embrace, gathering every human ache and aspiration into His presence."[39]

Actions

The outermost court of the temple functioned as a space between the sacred and the secular, inviting yet limited. Within this court, we find several actions that parallel the Tanakh: worship, commerce, teaching, and preparation. Each of these highlights the court and the Ketuvim as space for all people to engage with God's wisdom and presence, even if not fully immersed in covenant life.

Interestingly, there was commerce and money-changing in this court. These two actions enabled worshipers from afar to participate in sacrificial rituals. The court was a place "where all may come, but none may enter further without preparation," notes Rabbi Akiva (m. Middot 2.1). Chrysostom observes, "The merchants . . . polluted the sacred precincts, yet the Lord's zeal cleansed the house; . . . outer appearances must be matched by inner purity" (*Homilies on John*, homily 13). So as we parallel the Ketuvim with the court, we find that those journeying toward God must make the right conversion for worship. Calvin comments, "True worship is not given with hands, but with a heart sanctified by grace, offering the proper 'currency' of faith and obedience" (*Institutes* 1.6.4). The outer court welcomes the visitor to bring what they have and exchange it for what God takes pleasure in.

While one often thinks of the middle court as the place of teaching, it also occurred in the outer court. Rabbis debated Scripture there, Solomon taught his wisdom books there, and Jesus taught there (Mark 12:35–37). Likewise, the Ketuvim offers accessible wisdom. Proverbs and Ecclesiastes speak beyond cultural borders. "The words of the wise are like goads" (b. Eruvin 54a). Rabbi

37. N. T. Wright, *New Testament and the People of God*, 268.
38. Hamilton, *God's Glory in Salvation*, 222.
39. Waltke, *Old Testament Theology*, 922.

Hillel likens public learning to planting in the field (m. Avot 1.4). So as we consider the teaching parallel, the Ketuvim has no lack of wise teachings for both Israel and gentiles, for the Yahweh worshiper and the curious. In addition to the teaching of wisdom, the Ketuvim offers an invitation to handle honest life struggles through the book of Job and the Psalms. A non-Israelite, Job deals with the struggles of death, loss, and grief, which those who visited the outer court would also have faced. Psalms, filled with pilgrim songs, also offers comfort for the soul who is journeying ever closer to the presence of God.

The outer court allowed gentiles to worship from afar: "The outer court was made for Gentiles to bring offerings" (m. Middot 2.4). In the New Testament, Paul offers a similar parallel: "You who once were far off have been brought near" (Eph. 2:13). These books show that Yahweh "stands as a pillar of faith for all nations" (b. Megillah 14b).

The outer court was not only a place to exchange funds for proper sacrifice purchases; it was also a place of preparation for the sacrifices. Likewise, the psalmist prayed, "Prepare my heart, O God" (Ps. 119:32 AT). Psalms and Proverbs guide inner readiness. Augustine notes that the psalms can articulate the soul's spiritual sacrifice (*Confessions* 9.1). The limitation of the outer court allowed outsiders to observe rituals but not to participate in them: "From the outer court one could see the rituals but not partake fully" (m. Middot 2.2). Similarly, the Ketuvim introduces theological themes that are distant depictions of deeper theology held within the Nevi'im and Torah.[40]

Finally, the court was also a gathering place where all peoples mingled. The Ketuvim captures this diversity better than any other section. In the Ketuvim we find Ruth a Moabitess, Job a Canaanite, Esther a princess of Persia, and Daniel a prophet in a foreign court. These books testify to the gentile inclusion via primary characters being either gentile or heavily involved with other gentiles.

In sum, both the court of the gentiles and the Ketuvim are threshold spaces, welcoming and preparatory. Through commerce, teaching, prayer, and observation, they invite seekers into deeper relationship with God and serve as gateways into the sacred heart of Scripture.

Articles

As previously noted, the outer courtyard of the temple was a place of preparation, purification, and sacrifice. These actions required sacred articles to facilitate worship and obedience to God's commandments. These physical

40. Salkin, *Righteous Gentiles in the Hebrew Bible*.

articles played a crucial role in mediating the relationship between God and his people, ensuring that both the worshipers and the priests approached him in the appropriate manner. Just as the articles of the outer court made worship possible, the Ketuvim offers instruction, guidance, and a pathway for spiritual purification.

At the center of the outer court stood the bronze altar, also known as the altar of burnt offering. This was the primary location for animal sacrifices, where atonement for sin was made and worshipers expressed their devotion to God (2 Chron. 15:8–15). The act of sacrifice was central to Israelite worship, signifying both the cost of sin and the means of reconciliation with God. In the Ketuvim, particularly in books such as Psalms and Job, there are messages on the nature of suffering, repentance, and restoration. The psalmist's cry echoes the sacrificial system of the outer court:

> Have mercy on me, O God,
> according to your steadfast love;
> according to your abundant mercy
> blot out my transgressions. (Ps. 51:1)

Job's wrestling with suffering and divine justice further illuminates the spiritual reality behind sacrifice, whether in the form of offerings at the altar or the surrender of one's heart in faith and obedience. Just as the bronze altar was the meeting place between human sin and divine mercy, the Ketuvim invites all people—Jew and gentile alike—to understand the possibility of forgiveness and reconciliation with God. Rabbi Jonathan Sacks notes that sacrifice was never about blood for its own sake but about turning the heart toward God in true repentance.[41]

Adjacent to the altar stood the bronze sea, a massive basin supported by twelve oxen, used by the priests for ritual washings (2 Chron. 4:2–5, 10). This purification was necessary before entering the more sacred spaces of the temple, which emphasized the importance of holiness in approaching God. The Mishnah teaches, "No one may enter the inner sanctum without first purifying himself" (m. Yoma 3.1), highlighting the need of not only sacrifice but also spiritual cleansing. Similarly, the Ketuvim functions not only as a call to sacrifice but also as a place of cleansing to prepare the heart for deeper engagement with God's covenant. Through their prayers and praises, the Psalms purify the heart, teaching worshipers how to approach God with sincerity and humility. As the psalmist declares,

41. Sacks, *Genesis*, 343–44.

> Create in me a clean heart, O God,
> and renew a right spirit within me. (Ps. 51:10)

Just as the bronze sea cleansed the priests before their service, the Ketuvim offers spiritual cleansing, equipping its readers with the knowledge and devotion necessary for faithful living. Where the Torah offers laws of life, the Ketuvim offers means of life.

Like the bronze sea, the outer court also had ten basins used for washing the utensils and instruments of worship (1 Kings 7:38–39). These basins ensured that every tool used in the sacrificial system remained clean and holy, reinforcing the idea that even the smallest details of worship required purification. This parallels the role of the Ketuvim in refining not only grand theological concepts but also the daily aspects of human life. Books such as Ecclesiastes, Song of Songs, and Proverbs deal with the ordinary yet profound experiences of life, work, love, pleasure, and mortality, demonstrating that every part of human existence can be brought into alignment with divine wisdom. Just as the basins ensured that every vessel used in worship was clean, the Ketuvim provides insight and guidance to purify the thoughts, actions, and desires of those who want a right relationship with God. Even in the New Testament, the apostle Paul urges, "Let us cleanse ourselves from every defilement of body and spirit, bringing holiness to completion in the fear of God" (2 Cor. 7:1).

In light of the Tanakh as a temple structure, the sacred articles of the outer court and the books of the Ketuvim find many parallels. Both offer preparation, purification, and accessibility for those seeking to have a relationship with God. The bronze altar reflects the call to repentance and sacrifice, the bronze sea and basins symbolize purification and readiness, and the basins purify utensils necessary for worship and service. Similarly, the Ketuvim prepares the heart through wisdom, cleanses the soul through poetry and prayer, and provides the practical means for engaging with God's ways. Together, these elements emphasize that while the outer court may be only the first step in the journey toward God, it is vital in welcoming all people into the path of worship, obedience, and relationship with God. I think this may be what James was thinking as he stated, "Draw near to God, and he will draw near to you" (James 4:8).

Ketuvim Test Case: Redemption of Naomi and Ruth (Ruth 4)

What Is This Text About?

This final chapter of the book of Ruth focuses on the legal and redemptive processes that secure Ruth's future and Naomi's restoration. Boaz, a relative of Naomi's deceased husband, acts as the kinsman-redeemer by redeeming the land that belonged to Naomi's family and marrying Ruth, thereby preserving the family line. The chapter also highlights a legal transaction where Boaz takes on the responsibilities of the redeemer in front of the town elders and witnesses. As a result, Ruth and Boaz marry, and they have a son, Obed, who becomes the grandfather of King David. This chapter concludes with the genealogy of David, emphasizing the role of Ruth in the lineage of Israel's greatest king.

How Does This Canonical Division Relate to This Temple Court?

In applying the Sacred Structure approach to Ruth 4, we can explore the relational dynamics and the sacred acts involved: Ruth, a Moabite woman, is initially an outsider, representing a gentile who has come to embrace the God of Israel. The legal transaction involving Boaz and the elders can be seen as the outer court's approach to welcoming outsiders into the blessings of Israel. Ruth's participation in this process symbolizes the broader scope of God's grace and inclusion. Ruth's status as a foreign widow could be connected to the court of women, where women had access to the temple but were restricted from closer proximity to God's presence. Her redemption through Boaz's act of kindness and justice reflects God's favor and acceptance, allowing her to fully partake in the blessings of the covenant people.

What Does This Text Espouse as This Temple Court Would?

In this text, the redemption process reflects the broader theme of God's faithfulness and the restoration of his people, symbolizing the approach to God's presence:

1. Access to God's presence: Boaz's role as the kinsman-redeemer reflects the concept of salvation in the temple with restoration and cleansing. As Ruth and Naomi are redeemed, they are brought into the community and receive God's blessing, paralleling the way the temple's rituals restore individuals and families to divine favor.
2. Purity and restoration: Just as the temple rituals ensure purification and restoration, Boaz's actions restore the family lineage and social standing of Naomi and Ruth. His legal and familial actions provide them with security and hope for the future.

How Does This Approach Inform Our Hermeneutic of This Text?

By applying the Sacred Structure approach to the story of Ruth 4, we can interpret the text with a lens of access to divine favor and justice:

1. Outer court (universal access): Ruth's inclusion into the community of Israel through her redemption is akin to the access given to those in the outer court. She is a gentile brought into the fold of Israel through Boaz's kindness, symbolizing the wider reach of God's grace to all nations.
2. Court of women: Ruth's transition from widowhood and foreign status to a married, redeemed woman reflects a movement toward fuller participation in Israel's community life, similar to the role women could take in the temple, especially as they participated in public worship and rituals.

What Are the Benefits of Applying This Approach to This Text?

1. God's inclusive grace: By viewing Ruth's redemption through the temple-court lens, we see how God's grace extends to outsiders. Ruth's acceptance into the family of Israel reflects God's broader plan to bring all nations into his covenant, as symbolized by the inclusion of gentiles in the outer court.
2. Restoration and justice: Boaz's role as the kinsman-redeemer demonstrates God's justice and care for the marginalized, akin to the temple's role in maintaining justice and restoring purity. The text shows that divine justice is not only about temple rites but about real-world actions that restore people to community and to God.
3. Covenantal faithfulness: Boaz's fulfillment of the kinsman-redeemer role mirrors God's faithfulness to his covenant. Just as the temple courts ensured the right relationship with God, Boaz ensures the right relationship within the family, reflecting God's ongoing care for his people.

What Are the Potential Problems in Applying This Approach to This Text?

1. Overspiritualization: Focusing too much on temple structure might overemphasize the religious aspect of Ruth's redemption, potentially overshadowing the personal and relational elements of the story, which are grounded in social justice, kindness, and covenant faithfulness.
2. Loss of historical context: The kinsman-redeemer practice in Ruth 4 is deeply tied to Israel's legal and social structures rather than its temple practices. Using the temple-court analogy might blur the story's

focus on familial duty and legal obligations, which were central to the narrative.

3. Misapplication of temple symbolism: The temple-court analogy may lead to reading ritual purity and access to the divine too heavily into a story where the primary concern is social redemption and justice, not ritual acts of worship.

Summary of Test Case

In summary, Ruth 4 narrates the redemption of Naomi and Ruth through Boaz, who fulfills the role of kinsman-redeemer by legally reclaiming Naomi's land and marrying Ruth, ensuring the continuation of a family line that ultimately becomes the genealogy of King David. When read using the Sacred Structure approach, this story reflects themes of access, inclusion, and restoration: Ruth, a foreigner, parallels those welcomed into the outer courts, while her redemption mirrors the temple's role in restoring purity and favor before God. The text underscores God's inclusive grace, covenantal faithfulness, and justice through real-world acts of kindness and legal responsibility, not just ritual. While the temple-court model can offer insights into Ruth 4, especially regarding God's justice and grace, it is crucial to balance this with the story's historical and social context, which emphasizes personal redemption and community restoration. When held in balance, the temple perspective enriches Ruth 4 by highlighting how divine grace extends to outsiders and how redemption restores both individuals and community to wholeness.

Conclusion

In conclusion, viewing the Tanakh through the lens of the temple's architectural and ritual structure offers a rich framework for understanding its three major divisions, progressively drawing readers closer to God's presence. Together, these three divisions embody a spiritual progression: from the Torah's direct encounter with divine law and atonement, through the Nevi'im's challenging call to obedience and justice, to the Ketuvim's open invitation to reflection, worship, and wisdom. The temple structure emphasizes that the Tanakh is not merely a collection of disparate writings but a sacred literary space that mirrors the physical temple's movement from outer courts to the holy of holies. As the temple's physical elements facilitated worship, purification, and mediation, so too do the Tanakh's texts provide the theological and spiritual instruments necessary for entering into covenantal relationship with God. Possibly this is what Ben Asher was proposing—Tanakh as an invitation for readers into the presence of God. Understanding the Tanakh in this way deepens appreciation for its enduring power as both sacred Scripture and a living pathway toward God's presence, mercy, and guidance. Wieder describes this view as "a fine poetic comparison, a metaphor embodying a grand concept."[42]

42. Wieder, "'Sanctuary' as a Metaphor for Scripture," 166.

7

Combined Testing of Approaches

IN THIS FINAL CHAPTER, I present a sample designed to explore the rich complexity of the interpretive frameworks introduced throughout this work. Each approach to the Tanakh will be applied to the same biblical text—one from the Torah, one from the Nevi'im, and one from the Ketuvim—to demonstrate how the different approaches can yield contrasting yet complementary insights.

We begin by interpreting the Tanakh according to the historical periods during which each of its sections was canonized—Torah in the fifth century BCE, Nevi'im in the third century BCE, and Ketuvim in the first century CE—highlighting how historical context shaped theological emphasis. Next, we consider traditional divisions based on genre and authorship, analyzing the text as it fits within the legal, prophetic, or poetic/wisdom traditions of ancient Israel. Third, we examine the Tanakh as a collection that reflects the evolving theological beliefs and religious practices of the Israelite community, with attention to how those beliefs are embedded in the structure and content of the text. Fourth, we explore the Tanakh as a spiritual guide: the Torah as God's law for life, the Nevi'im as voices of divine warning and encouragement, and the Ketuvim as a source of wisdom, comfort, and reflection for navigating life's complexities. Fifth, we assess the Tanakh's messianic trajectory, reading the Torah as anticipating the Messiah through its legal and covenantal foundations, the Nevi'im as proclaiming messianic hope, and the Ketuvim as expressing the deep longing for final redemption. Finally, we apply the sacred-structure analogy: the Torah as the temple's inner court representing God's holy presence, the Nevi'im as the inner sanctuary where God's word confronts and calls Israel to covenant faithfulness, and the Ketuvim as the outer court, an open space where all peoples are invited to draw near through worship, wisdom, and reflection.

By comparing how each approach interprets the same text, this chapter will show the interpretive depth of the various approaches to the Tanakh. Each approach offers unique insights, and together they reveal that the Scriptures are dynamic, layered, and profoundly relevant across time, genre, theology, and spiritual experience.

Torah: Shema (Deut. 6:4–9)

What Is This Text About?

Deuteronomy 6:4–9 contains the Shema (v. 4), a central declaration of faith in Israel: "Hear, O Israel: Yahweh is our God, and Yahweh alone [or "is one"]" (AT). This famous passage proceeds to emphasize loving the Lord with all one's heart, soul, and strength (v. 5). The text then instructs the Israelites to keep these words in their hearts, to teach them diligently to their children, and to talk of them at home, when traveling, and while lying down or rising up (vv. 6–9). As a whole, this passage introduces theology proper, practical life application, and generational preservation of the faith.

Triple Canon Approach

How Does This Text Fit into This Section?

This text is situated in the book of Deuteronomy, the last book of the Torah, whose legal and narrative content provides a final restatement of the law (the word *Deuteronomy* means "second law"). It provides crucial instructions for Israel's covenantal identity, emphasizing the necessity of wholehearted devotion to God as the people prepare to enter the promised land, and it sets the tone for the covenant renewal and the laws that will guide the nation.

When Was This Section of the Canon Closed?

The final form of Deuteronomy, including this text, is generally believed to have been completed during or shortly after the Babylonian exile (6th cent. BCE). However, its content originates from earlier periods—especially from the seventh century BCE, during the reign of King Josiah, when reforms took place to centralize worship and strengthen adherence to the covenant.

In What Historical Period Was This Text Written and Canonized?

The final form of Deuteronomy was likely canonized during the postexilic period, after 539 BCE, when the Jewish community returned from Babylonian exile. Politically, this was a time of rebuilding and reestablishing religious identity; socially, it was a period of reconstruction after the trauma of exile; and religiously, the focus was on reaffirming covenantal commitments. The reforms of King Josiah (ca. 621 BCE) were also significant in the shaping of this material, aiming to restore the nation's devotion to God.

Who Compiled This Section?

The text of Deuteronomy, like much of the Torah, is traditionally attributed to Moses. However, scholars often argue that it was compiled and edited by later scribes, particularly during the reign of Josiah and later during the postexilic period. The Priestly writers and Deuteronomistic historians may have had a role in shaping the final form of the book.

What Is the Political Purpose of This Section?

By emphasizing loyalty to Yahweh and the observance of his commandments, Deut. 6:4–9 is also about strengthening the religious and political identity of the nation of Israel. It calls for the people to maintain a distinct identity, which will help them resist political and cultural pressures from surrounding nations. The instruction to teach the law diligently to children could also serve as a form of social and political consolidation.

How Does This Approach Inform Our Hermeneutic of This Text?

The canonical arrangement of the Tanakh—Torah, Nevi'im, and Ketuvim—forms a framework that sees the historical narrative of Israel as culminating in the covenant established in Deuteronomy. This informs our hermeneutic by grounding the text in the context of Israel's covenant with God, both as a theological and political concept. It suggests that the Shema and the commandments are not just important religiously but are also central to national identity, guiding the community's life in both spiritual and political terms.

What Are the Benefits of Applying This Approach to This Text?

1. Strengthening of covenant identity: The text reminds the people of Israel of their unique relationship with God and encourages them to continually renew this relationship.

2. Committing completely to God: It teaches that devotion to God is all-encompassing, not just ceremonial but a way of life that shapes every aspect of daily living.
3. Passing faith to future generations: The emphasis on teaching the commandments to children highlights the importance of preserving and transmitting the faith to future generations, ensuring the survival of Israel's identity.

What Are the Potential Problems in Applying This Approach to This Text?

1. Risk of over-politicization: Viewing the text mainly as a political tool could overshadow its religious and spiritual significance, reducing the focus on loving God for his own sake.
2. Historical reconstruction issues: If we view the text as a product of postexilic canonization, it could lead to a disconnection between the original context and the text's use in later periods. This may make it more difficult to understand its relevance to earlier generations of Israelites.
3. Cultural alienation: The emphasis on constant devotion and teaching could be difficult to apply directly in a modern context without understanding the cultural differences between ancient Israel and contemporary life.

Summary of Test Case

Through the Triple Canon approach, Deut. 6:4–9 provides a foundational statement of faith and commitment to God, emphasizing that religious devotion should shape every aspect of life. While it serves both religious and political purposes in its historical context, its primary message remains one of deep, ongoing covenant loyalty.

Genre Author Approach

What Is the Genre of This Text, and How Does This Genre Accord with This Approach to the Tanakh?

1. Genre: This text belongs to the genre of legal instruction and covenantal declaration. It is a combination of exhortation and law, with a strong theological focus on the nature of God (monotheism) and the command to love God with all one's heart, soul, and strength. This type of text also

has an element of wisdom literature since it gives practical instructions on how to live according to God's commands.

2. Hermeneutical Rules:
   a. Historical-grammatical method: This text must be understood in light of its historical context, Israel's relationship with God in the covenant context, and the legal/social life it dictates.
   b. Contextual reading: This text should be read as part of the larger book of Deuteronomy, which serves as Moses's final instructions to Israel before entering the promised land. It is not isolated but part of a larger narrative of covenant renewal.
   c. Theological interpretation: Since it is a religious and covenantal text, theological rules should be applied, understanding the Shema (v. 4) as a declaration of the uniqueness and unity of God and viewing the commandments (vv. 5–9) as guidelines for living in relationship with God.

Who Is the Author, and How Does the Authorship Accord with This Approach to the Tanakh?

The author is traditionally understood to be Moses, the leader and prophet of Israel, who is believed to have received these instructions from God. Modern scholarship, however, recognizes that the text was likely compiled and edited by later writers or redactors, particularly during the time of the Deuteronomistic historians in the seventh–sixth centuries BCE (during the reign of King Josiah or the exile).

How Does This Approach Inform the Hermeneutic of This Text?

If we view the Tanakh as organized by genre and author, this text falls under the legal and covenantal genre (specifically within the Torah, the first five books) and is traditionally attributed to Moses. This would inform our hermeneutic in the following ways:

1. Understanding that this text is part of a legal framework in which the people of Israel are being called to live by the stipulations of God's covenant.
2. Recognizing the text as authoritative within the covenant context, laying out what is required for Israel to live faithfully as the people of God.
3. Taking into account the Mosaic authorship and how it would shape the interpretation of God's commands, possibly giving weight to the view that these laws are eternal and unchanging given their divine origin.

What Are the Benefits of Applying This Approach to This Text?

1. Theological consistency: Understanding the text through the lens of Mosaic authorship (whether or not we affirm traditional authorship) helps maintain theological continuity. The command to love God with everything reinforces the centrality of God's commands in shaping Israel's life.
2. Covenant emphasis: This interpretation emphasizes the binding covenant between God and Israel, which is foundational for understanding the entire book of Deuteronomy. It directs the reader's focus toward Israel's role as a distinct people called to live in accordance with God's will.
3. Comprehensive commitment to God: The genre's focus on law provides a reminder that loving God is not just an internal or private act but also something that should affect every aspect of one's life—daily actions, thoughts, relationships, and identity. It encourages a holistic approach to spirituality.

What Are the Potential Problems in Applying This Approach to This Text?

1. Overlooking later redaction: If we strictly follow the traditional understanding of Mosaic authorship, we risk ignoring the later editorial work that reflects a postexilic or Josianic context. This might lead to a misreading of the text in light of its historical development.
2. Literalism in law: By emphasizing the text as part of the legal tradition, there might be a tendency to interpret the command as purely legalistic, potentially sidelining the relational, spiritual aspects of loving God. It could foster an understanding of the law that is rigid rather than dynamic and relational.
3. Misapplication of cultural context: Given the cultural differences between ancient Israel and modern contexts, applying the laws in a direct, literal sense without understanding their symbolic or covenantal function can lead to misunderstandings about their relevance or purpose in contemporary settings.

Summary of Test Case

While the Genre Author approach helps establish the foundational nature of this text as part of the covenantal and legal framework of Israel, it is crucial to balance this with an awareness of its editorial history, its theological richness, and its relational implications for how believers today engage with God's commands.

Theological Development Approach

What Is the Israelite Religion in This Text?

In this text, the Israelite religion is henotheistic—hence my translation of "alone." The Israelites are called to love God with their whole being, integrating faith into every part of life. This religion is centered on a covenant relationship between God and Israel, which is marked by both divine commands and the expectation of Israel's loyalty, holiness, and obedience.

What Theological Themes or Concepts Are Present in This Text?

Several key theological themes emerge from this text:

1. Love for God: The command to love God "with all your heart, soul, and strength" (v. 5) reflects the central importance of devotion and loyalty in the covenantal relationship. While there were other "gods" available to worship, loving Yahweh alone is the central theme here.
2. Covenant and commandments: The text underscores the importance of keeping God's commands and teaching them to future generations, highlighting the covenantal law that governs Israel's relationship with God.
3. Holistic worship: The text emphasizes that devotion to God is not just ceremonial but is also to permeate all aspects of life, living, traveling, and interacting with others (vv. 6–9). This reflects the Israelite belief in a comprehensive relationship with God.

What Role Does This Text Play in the Development of Israelite/Jewish Theology?

This text is foundational for Israelite and Jewish theology because it outlines the central command of loving God with one's whole being, which is repeated throughout Jewish tradition as the essence of the faith. It plays a crucial role in defining the identity of Israel as a people in covenant with God. The Shema (v. 4) becomes a touchstone of Jewish monotheism, and the command to love God integrates both religious and ethical dimensions, helping to shape how Israelites and Jews think about their relationship with God and their duties to others.

How Does This Text Contribute to the Overall Theological Framework of the Tanakh?

This text is pivotal in the Tanakh's theological framework as it stresses the foundation of covenantal relationship with God. It frames all of Israel's laws, worship practices, and behavior within the context of loving God. This love is not abstract but is shown through obedience to God's commands. The text emphasizes that the covenant is not just a legal contract but also a relationship, setting the stage for later theological developments throughout the Tanakh, particularly in the writings of the Nevi'im and Ketuvim.

How Does This Approach Inform Our Hermeneutic of This Text?

If we view the Tanakh as organized by theological development, the Shema (v. 4) serves as a theological pinnacle. The text emphasizes God's unity and the necessity of Israel's exclusive loyalty, forming the core of Israel's faith and shaping the trajectory of later theological reflection, especially in the prophetic literature. It informs our hermeneutic by helping us understand that this text represents the beginning of Israel's national and religious identity, with God as the one true God and the source of moral and ethical conduct. This establishes a foundational theology from which later development flows, guiding our interpretation toward an understanding of Israel's covenantal obligations.

What Are the Benefits of Applying This Approach to This Text?

1. Theological centrality of loving God: This perspective highlights the centrality of love in the relationship between Israel and God. By focusing on loving God with one's whole being, it encourages readers to see faith not as an abstract or peripheral concern but as something that shapes all areas of life.
2. Comprehensive approach to covenant: By emphasizing the relational aspect of the covenant, it reminds us that obedience to God is not limited to ritual observances but should be reflected in all actions, relationships, and attitudes. This has practical applications for daily living.
3. Building a strong identity: The text serves as a foundational statement for Israel's identity, providing a coherent theological basis for understanding their role as a distinct people with specific obligations and duties toward God.

What Are the Potential Problems in Applying This Approach to This Text?

1. Overemphasis on monotheism: Viewing this text as a theological milestone might lead to an overemphasis on the theme of monotheism, depending on one's translation of this Hebrew text.
2. Hermeneutical stagnation: If the text is viewed purely as an introductory theological statement, it may inhibit readings that explore its dynamic role within the ongoing narrative of the Tanakh. Again, if read as "alone," then this text sheds light on the persistent struggle against idolatry portrayed in the narrative passages. But if read as "one" it may cause readers to overlook how this text interacts with later texts.
3. Potential legalism: Viewing the text only as the introduction to Israel's covenantal obligations may lead to a legalistic reading, focusing primarily on rules and duties rather than on the deeper, relational aspects of loving God and others. Much could be said about the application of this text in rabbinic Judaism.

Summary of Test Case

In summary, Deut. 6:4–9 forms a key theological text in the Tanakh, highlighting the centrality of love for God, monotheism, and covenantal obedience. While the text contributes deeply to Israelite theology, there are risks in overemphasizing certain themes or applying it in ways that miss its broader relational implications. It is essential to read this text in light of its evolving theological context throughout the rest of the Tanakh.

Spiritual Guide Approach

What Topic(s) Does this Text Teach Believers?

This text primarily teaches the following key topics for believers:

1. Love for God: The command to love God with one's heart, soul, and strength (v. 5) emphasizes the total, holistic devotion that believers should have toward God.
2. Obedience to God's commands: This text stresses that love for God is demonstrated through obedience to his commandments and passing them down to future generations (vv. 6–9).
3. Covenant faithfulness: The text teaches the importance of maintaining faithfulness to the covenant through daily practices, including teaching and remembering God's commandments (v. 6).

How Do These Topics Relate to Other Sections of the Tanakh?

These topics are closely related to other key themes throughout the Tanakh:

1. Love for God: The call to love God with one's whole being is foundational to Israel's faith and reappears throughout Israel's history, especially in the Ketuvim (e.g., Psalms, Proverbs) and Nevi'im (e.g., Hosea 6:6).
2. Obedience and covenant: The call to keep God's commandments links this text to broader covenantal themes, particularly in the Deuteronomistic History (Joshua, Judges, Kings) and in the Nevi'im, which frequently calls Israel back to covenantal faithfulness.
3. Generational teaching: The emphasis on teaching God's commands to children connects this text with themes of transmitting faith across generations seen throughout the Tanakh, especially in books such as Psalms and Proverbs.

How Does This Approach Inform Our Hermeneutic of This Text?

The Tanakh is viewed as a spiritual guide, and Deut. 6:4–9 serves as foundational teaching for how believers are to live in relationship with God. This text presents the core of Israel's religious and ethical life: a holistic love for God that includes obedience to his commands and a commitment to teach and pass this love and knowledge on to future generations. The text is not only theological but also practical, showing that the believer's relationship with God impacts every aspect of life. As a spiritual guide, the text challenges believers to think about how they can make God's commands a daily part of their lives, integrating faith into all aspects of thought, action, and relationships.

In this view, our hermeneutic of the text should highlight its practical applications. It encourages readers to recognize that loving God is not merely a spiritual or emotional sentiment but also a comprehensive, daily action that includes how we treat others, how we teach our children, and how we organize our lives around the knowledge of God. This approach guides readers to focus on obedience and internal transformation through God's commandments.

What Are the Benefits of Applying This Approach to This Text?

1. Practical devotion: This approach highlights that loving God involves action, a devotion that is not passive but active in every part of life. It encourages believers to live with intentionality in their relationship with

God, seeing all of life as an opportunity to express love for God through obedience and faithful action.

2. Comprehensive obedience: By interpreting the text as a guide for living, readers can grasp that God's commands are meant to shape all areas of life, not just religious rituals. This interpretation promotes a holistic view of faith, where obedience is reflected in actions, relationships, and ethical choices.
3. Generational responsibility: The command to teach God's commandments to future generations encourages the passing down of faith, not only in terms of doctrines but also in practices and examples. This interpretation highlights the importance of community and family in nurturing faith across generations.
4. Spiritual transformation: Focusing on this text as a spiritual guide encourages believers to seek internal transformation through the love of God, knowing that this leads to outward transformation in actions and relationships.

What Are the Potential Problems in Applying This Approach to This Text?

1. Oversimplifying spiritual guidance: Viewing the Tanakh solely as a spiritual guide might lead to oversimplification. Not all of the Tanakh's content is prescriptive for daily living; some parts are historical, prophetic, or wisdom literature that may need more nuanced interpretation. As such, if we read this text only as a spiritual guide, we might fail to fully understand the historical, covenantal, and liturgical context in which it was given. This could lead to misinterpretations about the nature of the commands and their specific application in ancient Israel.
2. Ignoring historical context: Reading the Tanakh primarily as a spiritual guide risks missing the historical context in which these commandments were given. The commands in Deuteronomy were given specifically to Israel, and though they offer spiritual guidance, their application in ancient Israel might differ significantly from their application in the modern world.
3. Neglecting the narrative: Focusing on the practical aspects of the text might divert attention from the broader narrative framework of the Tanakh, in which these teachings emerge. The narrative of Israel's journey and covenant with God shapes the spiritual and theological meaning of these commands.

4. Exclusivity of Israel's covenant: The text's role within the Tanakh could be misapplied in a way that makes it difficult to reconcile with the broader Christian view of faith or other faith traditions. While the love of God is a universal principle, its expression in the Tanakh is tied specifically to the people of Israel, and reading it as purely universal might be problematic.
5. Risk of legalism: Focusing too much on practical obedience to the commandments risks turning the relationship with God into a matter of legalistic performance rather than one based on a gracious relationship with God. The text could be misused to stress outward behaviors without addressing the inner transformation that true love for God demands.

Summary of Test Case

Interpreting Deut. 6:4–9 using the Spiritual Guide approach emphasizes the holistic nature of love for God, showing how this love should be expressed in daily life. This approach highlights practical devotion, obedience, and generational faithfulness. However, careful attention must be given to the historical and covenantal context to avoid oversimplification or misapplication in modern settings.

Messianic Trajectory Approach

What Topic(s) Does This Text Teach Believers?

1. Messiah as the embodiment of covenant love and obedience: The Shema commands a complete, undivided love for God with heart, soul, and strength. Jesus identifies this as the greatest commandment (Matt. 22:37–38), making it a direct link to the Messiah's person and teaching.
2. Messiah as the fulfillment of the law: This text represents the essence of Torah obedience, not just legal conformity but also internalized devotion. The Messiah fulfills this by perfectly obeying and internalizing the law (Matt. 5:17).
3. Messiah as the teacher of God's word: The text commands teaching diligently to children. Jesus, as rabbi, is the ultimate teacher, who embodies and imparts the Torah's heart.

How Do These Topics Relate to the Other Sections of the Tanakh and Ultimately to Christ?

1. Nevi'im—Messiah as prophetic hope: The Nevi'im books continually call Israel back to the Shema's vision of wholehearted love and covenant

faithfulness. Their future hope often includes a coming one who will lead God's people in this love (e.g., Jer. 31:31–34; Ezek. 36:26–27).

2. Ketuvim—Messiah longed for: The Psalms and other wisdom literature express the longing for God's presence and instruction to dwell in the heart, a longing the Messiah fulfills (e.g., Ps. 119's love for the law; Ps. 2's messianic kingship).
3. Christ: Jesus lives out the Shema in perfection, teaches it as the core of the Torah, and makes it possible for believers to love God fully through the Spirit (Rom. 5:5). Thus Jesus Christ is the fulfillment of the Shema's demand for whole-person devotion.

How Does This Approach Inform Our Hermeneutic of This Text?

1. Messiah-centered reading: We interpret the Shema not merely as an ethical directive but also as a pointer to the Messiah, who models and empowers love for God.
2. Progressive revelation: The Shema is foundational in Torah; the Nevi'im shows how Israel failed to embody it, yet anticipated one who would; the Ketuvim longs for intimacy with God, which the Messiah ultimately brings.

What Potential Problems Arise from the Above Question?

1. Anachronism: Reading Messiah explicitly into Deut. 6:4–9 risks ignoring its original context as covenantal instruction to Israel.
2. Flattening of canonical voice: If every text is forced into a messianic mold, we may overlook the richness of Israel's particular covenant experience and ethical obligations.
3. Supersessionism: A messianic lens, if unchecked, might subtly imply that the Torah is valuable only because Christ fulfills it, thus dismissing its intrinsic theological and moral worth in Israel's life.

What Are the Benefits of Applying This Approach to This Text?

1. Theological unity of Scripture: This approach helps believers see a unified biblical story culminating in Christ—from Torah to longing to fulfillment.
2. Christ-centered spiritual formation: It encourages Christians to imitate Christ in loving God with full devotion, not as mere duty but with Spirit-enabled joy.

3. Missional impulse: The Shema's command to teach and live the Word is fulfilled in Christ's Great Commission. Discipleship reflects the Shema's call to transmission across generations.
4. Integration of law and gospel: Rather than viewing law and grace in opposition, this view shows that the law's deepest demands are met and modeled in Christ, inviting believers to walk in step with his life.

What Are the Potential Problems in Applying This Approach to This Text?

1. Historical displacement: Applying a messianic trajectory too strongly may cause readers to lose sight of Israel's story.
2. Over-realized Christology: Assuming that every text must explicitly prefigure Christ might lead to imagined or stretched connections that aren't supported by the text.
3. Neglect of ethical implications: Overemphasis on fulfillment can make believers think the Shema is fulfilled for them rather than calling them to live it through Christ.

Summary of Test Case

Deuteronomy 6:4–9, read through a messianic trajectory, reveals the heart of God's covenant: undivided love and faithful instruction. This love reaches its fullness in Christ, the one who fulfills, teaches, and enables the law. While this approach unites the Scriptures around Jesus, it must be balanced with careful attention to the text's historical and covenantal context.

Sacred Structure Approach

How Does This Text Relate to the Respective Court?

Just as the temple's holy of holies symbolizes the ultimate closeness to God, the text in Deuteronomy emphasizes the spiritual closeness that Israel was to have with God through their obedience and covenantal relationship. In this light, the love of God expressed in this text of Deuteronomy is at the heart of the Israelite/Jewish religion just as the holy of holies is at the center of the temple. The result is that obedience and devotion are spiritual acts that bring believers closer to Yahweh, much like physical proximity to God in the temple.

What Does This Text Espouse as This Temple Court Would?

This text espouses holistic devotion and obedience to Yahweh, which are the qualities required to enter Yahweh's presence, much like the physical proximity granted to the priests and Levites in the temple courts. In a symbolic sense, Deut. 6:4–9 calls all of Israel to be fully devoted to Yahweh, making them spiritually fit to approach his presence, just as only the pure and obedient could physically approach the temple's inner courts and most holy place. The text emphasizes that just as the temple ritual was essential for maintaining one's relationship with God, so loving God with one's entire being—heart, soul, and strength—is essential for maintaining that spiritual closeness.

How Does This Approach Inform Our Hermeneutic of This Text?

In terms of hermeneutics, this analogy suggests a layered or graduated understanding of how obedience to God's commands and a devoted heart allow the believer to enter into deeper communion with God, much like how certain people could access different areas of the temple based on their purity and role. Therefore, this text could be interpreted as a guide to moving closer to God's presence through faithful worship and obedient living, progressively increasing one's closeness to him. We may start at the outside (not yet part of the people of God), but we progressively learn what it means to hold to Yahweh alone and to live this life in a holy way.

What Are the Benefits of Applying This Approach to This Text?

1. Holistic worship: Viewing the text through the Sacred Structure approach emphasizes that true devotion to God involves wholehearted commitment in every aspect of life. The text calls for complete love for God, a devotion that impacts the heart, mind, and body—much as temple worship required specific acts from the people.
2. Spiritual proximity: The temple analogy provides a helpful framework for understanding how obedience and love for God bring believers spiritually closer to him. It reinforces the idea that worship and obedience lead to intimacy with God, akin to how one's proximity to God in the temple was determined by purity and priestly role.
3. A spiritual process of holiness: This approach encourages believers to see their spiritual lives as a journey of becoming more holy and obedient, progressively drawing closer to God through righteous living, much as the temple itself was structured around increasing levels of sacredness.

What Are the Potential Problems in Applying This Approach to This Text?

1. Overspiritualizing the text: Applying the Sacred Structure approach too strictly could lead to the overspiritualization of a text that was originally very concrete and practical in its historical context. Deuteronomy 6:4–9 is about covenant loyalty and obedience in the everyday life of Israel, not just about climbing spiritual levels of closeness to God.
2. Neglecting the larger covenant: Viewing the Tanakh as a temple system could reduce the broader narrative of God's covenant with Israel to a series of ritualized processes. The story of Israel's relationship with God in the Tanakh is far more dynamic than a strict temple hierarchy of access—involving history, prophecy, wisdom, and law.
3. Misapplying temple structure: One potential problem is the temptation to over-apply the temple-court analogy and treat the Tanakh as a mechanical system of increasing access to God rather than focusing on the spiritual principles behind it. Relationship with God in the Tanakh is gracious and relational, not based solely on performance, as temple worship might have been interpreted.
4. Overlooking the centrality of grace: Focusing too much on temple imagery might lead to an understanding of the text that is overly centered on works and obedience as prerequisites for spiritual proximity to God, potentially neglecting the grace and mercy that ultimately defines the relationship between Yahweh and his people.
5. Contextual displacement: The temple courts were a part of Israel's national worship system, and applying a modern or spiritualized version of this framework might create confusion about how we should understand temple worship versus the spiritual obedience that Deuteronomy calls for.

Summary of Test Case

In conclusion, applying the Sacred Structure approach to this text provides a helpful analogy for understanding spiritual proximity to God through obedience, but it must be carefully balanced to avoid overspiritualizing the text and losing sight of its historical context and relational depth.

Torah Conclusion

Deuteronomy 6:4–9, often referred to as the Shema, stands as one of the most theologically rich and spiritually formative texts in the Tanakh. Its profound declaration "Yahweh is our God, Yahweh alone" anchors Israel's identity in exclusive devotion to a singular, covenantal God. Read through multiple interpretive approaches, this text emerges as both a theological cornerstone and a practical guide for the covenant community.

Canonically placed as the final voice of the Torah, the Shema resounds with the urgency of a people needing spiritual clarity and social cohesion in a postexilic or Josianic context. Its final form reflects an effort toward political and religious consolidation intended to preserve Israel's distinct identity amid foreign influence and the trauma of exile. From the perspective of a Genre Author approach, the text belongs to the legal-exhortative tradition through Moses. Whether viewed as directly Mosaic or the result of later redaction, its covenantal genre reminds readers that loving God is not abstract. Theologically, in a world surrounded by competing deities, the call to love Yahweh "alone" with heart, soul, and strength was a theological confession. As a spiritual guide, Deut. 6:4–9 transcends its ancient Near Eastern setting to offer modern readers a robust vision of integrated faith. Messianically, the Shema calls us to live the life of Christ and to find our heart, soul, and being enveloped with Christ. Lastly, viewed through the analogy of the temple structure, this text symbolizes relational intimacy with Yahweh as found in the holy of holies. Unlike the temple, where access was limited, this text democratizes nearness to God: Every Israelite, through love and instruction, is invited into sacred proximity.

In conclusion, each interpretive approach offers unique insights and cautions. Whether the risk is legalism, historical disconnect, or overspiritualization, the central message remains unwavering: Love for God must be total, transformative, and transmittable. As such, the Shema remains the heartbeat of Torah spirituality, the threshold to the Nevi'im's prophetic critique, and the echo resounding in the wisdom of the Ketuvim.

Nevi'im: Unjust Rulers and Invading Chaldeans (Hab. 1–2)

What Is This Text About?

Habakkuk 1–2 consists of a dialogue between the prophet Habakkuk and God. In chapter 1, Habakkuk complains to God about the violence, injustice, and corruption rampant among the people of Judah and asks why God seems indifferent. God responds by revealing that he will raise up the Chaldeans (Babylonians), a ruthless nation, to bring judgment on Judah. In chapter 2, Habakkuk questions how a more wicked nation (the Chaldeans) can be used to punish Judah (God's chosen people), but God assures him that the Chaldeans will ultimately face judgment for their own crimes. The section ends with a series of woes against the oppressors and a call for the righteous to live by faith.

Triple Canon Approach

How Does This Text Fit into This Section?

The book of Habakkuk belongs to the Nevi'im, specifically to the Minor Prophets (also called the Book of the Twelve) in the Hebrew Bible. This text fits into the broader context of prophetic literature, which often deals with themes of judgment, social justice, and divine sovereignty. Habakkuk's unique contribution is that we get a glimpse into a prophet's dialogue with God.

When Was This Section of the Canon Closed?

The book of Habakkuk was likely finalized in the late seventh century BCE, just before the Babylonian conquests of Judah (ca. 605 BCE, culminating in 586). While the original prophecies likely come from this period, the book may have been edited or compiled during the exilic or postexilic periods (6th–5th cent. BCE), when the themes of divine justice and Babylon's fall became more relevant.

In What Historical Period Was This Text Written and Canonized?

The text was written in the context of Judah's decline and the rise of the Babylonian Empire. This was a time of great social and political upheaval: Assyria had fallen, and Babylon was asserting dominance over the Near East. Judah was plagued by internal corruption, with unjust rulers such as Jehoahaz, Jehoiakim, and Jehoiachin oppressing the people. God's revelation to Habakkuk that Babylon would be the instrument of Judah's punishment would have been shocking to the prophet and his audience. Politically and socially Judah was in shambles, and religiously the people struggled to reconcile God's promises with the harsh reality of impending invasion.

Who Compiled This Section?

All the prophetic books were likely compiled by scribes or disciples of the prophets. While Habakkuk himself would have delivered the original oracles, the final form of the text may have been shaped by later editors, particularly during the exilic period when Babylon's dominance and eventual downfall became clearer in hindsight.

What Is the Political Purpose of This Section?

The political purpose of Hab. 1–2 is significant. The text addresses the corruption and injustice in Judah's leadership and society, and it serves as a prophetic warning that God's judgment is imminent. The prophecy about the Chaldeans (Babylonians) is both a message of impending divine retribution and a reassurance that even the mighty Babylonians will not escape God's justice. It also challenges the idea that military power or political dominance equals divine favor, showing that God can use even a wicked nation as an instrument of his will but will ultimately hold all nations accountable for their actions.

How Does This Approach Inform Our Hermeneutic of This Text?

The Triple Canon approach, which looks at how this text was compiled and its context within the broader canon, helps us interpret Hab. 1–2 as part of a larger theological conversation about divine justice. It informs our hermeneutic by emphasizing that God's ways are often mysterious and that his timing and methods of judgment are not always immediately understandable. This perspective helps us see Habakkuk's complaint not as rebellion but as faithful questioning that leads to a deeper trust in God's ultimate plan. It also reminds us that God's use of historical events (such as the rise of Babylon) serves a larger divine purpose beyond immediate political circumstances.

What Are the Benefits of Applying This Approach to This Text?

1. God's sovereignty: Habakkuk 1–2 offers a powerful reminder of God's sovereignty over the nations. It reassures believers that even when unjust rulers or wicked powers seem to prevail, God is still in control and will bring about justice in his own time.
2. Faith amid uncertainty: The call for the righteous to "live by faith" (Hab. 2:4) is a key theological takeaway. It teaches that in times of crisis, when God's ways are unclear, believers must trust in God's plan, even when it seems contrary to human understanding.
3. Divine justice: The text affirms that God's justice is comprehensive. He will not let the wicked escape, whether they are corrupt rulers in Judah or foreign invaders such as the Chaldeans. Both will face judgment in due time.

4. Hope amid judgment: The prophecy is not only about judgment; it also contains a message of hope. God will not allow injustice to persist forever, and the Lord will ultimately bring about the vindication of the righteous.

What Are the Potential Problems in Applying This Approach to This Text?

1. Historical specificity: Focusing too heavily on the historical context of the Chaldean invasion might limit the text's applicability, making it seem like a message for only ancient Judah and not for readers today.
2. Theodicy challenges: The questions raised by Habakkuk about why God allows evil and injustice remain troubling for many, and the answer provided (to live by faith) may not fully satisfy those seeking a more immediate resolution to the problem of suffering.

Summary of Test Case

By situating Habakkuk's dialogue with God in the late seventh-century BCE context of Judah's political corruption and the rise of Babylon, this method clarifies how the book addresses both the immediate problem of unjust rulers in Judah and the larger question of why God uses a more wicked nation as an instrument of judgment. At the same time, reading Habakkuk within the broader prophetic canon underscores its enduring message that God remains sovereign over all nations, that apparent delays in judgment do not negate his justice, and that the righteous are called to live by faith amid uncertainty. Thus this approach shows that Hab. 1–2 is not merely a historical oracle about Babylon's invasion but also a canonical witness inviting readers in every age to wrestle faithfully with God's governance of history and to find hope in his ultimate vindication of the righteous.

Genre Author Approach

What Is the Genre of This Text, and How Does This Genre Accord with This Approach to the Tanakh?

The genre of Hab. 1–2 is prophetic literature, and it appears in the division of the Tanakh traditionally identified as containing prophetic literature, the Nevi'im. It includes dialogue between the prophet and God, visions, and divine pronouncements (esp. the vision of chap. 2). It is not wisdom literature, though it raises moral and theological questions similar to those found in wisdom texts. The content—God's judgment, vision, and dialogue between prophet and deity—fits the prophetic mold.

Who Is the Author, and How Does the Authorship Accord with This Approach to the Tanakh?

The prophet Habakkuk is the attributed author. Little is known about him, but he identifies himself by name (Hab. 1:1), and his role is as a visionary and intercessor. His work is part of the Book of the Twelve (Minor Prophets) in the Nevi'im division, so both the genre and attributed author align with the Nevi'im classification.

How Does This Approach Inform Our Hermeneutic of This Text?

Recognizing Habakkuk as a prophetic book delivered by a prophet encourages readers to interpret it as a divine-human dialogue centered on national fate and divine justice. It cues the reader to expect visions, revelatory speech, and covenantal accountability—key themes in prophetic texts.

What Are the Benefits of Applying This Approach to This Text?

1. Clarifies function and audience: Understanding Habakkuk as prophetic literature situates the text within a national, covenantal context where God addresses Judah's fate and the rise of Babylon.
2. Frames the theological expectation: It highlights the prophet's role as intercessor and visionary, shaping expectations of revelation, not merely philosophical reflection.
3. Provides narrative continuity: This approach aligns Habakkuk with other prophetic voices calling for trust in God amid injustice, especially in light of impending exile.
4. Grounds interpretation in authority: The prophetic Genre Author approach implies a structure of divine origin and public relevance, which shapes a communal and theological reading.

What Are the Potential Problems in Applying This Approach to This Text?

1. Genre rigidity: Reducing Habakkuk to "only prophecy" might ignore the wisdom-like aspects (e.g., questioning God's justice) that enrich interpretation. Pending one's teaching, it may also limit the interpretation to

only future concerns and ignore the immediate concerns of the original hearers in Habakkuk's day.

2. Neglect of literary complexity: The structure may cause interpreters to overlook the poetic, lament, and vision forms in the text, which could yield more nuanced meaning. While the text is prophetic (per the genre), Hab. 1–2 also includes many subgenres.
3. Overshadowing of individual experience: The Genre Author approach tends to emphasize national themes, potentially downplaying personal anguish and existential wrestling in Habakkuk. While indeed the text concerns Judah's demise, one can easily overlook the personal pain of Habakkuk.
4. Limits canonical connectivity: Overemphasis on one genre might limit exploration of intertextual connections with Deuteronomy (chap. 28), Psalms (laments), or Job (theodicy) that broaden interpretive insight.

Summary of Test Case

The Genre Author approach understands Hab. 1–2 primarily as prophetic literature within the Nevi'im, authored by the prophet Habakkuk as a visionary and intercessor speaking to Judah's covenantal crisis. Reading it this way rightly highlights its function as divine revelation about national fate, judgment, and justice, framing expectations of visions, oracles, and God's authoritative word to his people. It helpfully clarifies audience and purpose, links Habakkuk with other prophetic calls to trust God amid impending exile, and grounds interpretation in communal, theologically weighty proclamation. At the same time, if applied too rigidly, this approach risks flattening the book's literary richness—its lament, wisdom-like questioning, and poetic complexity—and may underplay Habakkuk's personal anguish and the broader intertextual ties to Deuteronomy, Psalms, and Job that deepen its exploration of the problem of divine justice.

Theological Development Approach

What Is the Israelite Religion in This Text?

The Israelite religion in Hab. 1–2 is characterized by monotheism, covenant awareness, and deep moral expectation of divine justice. However, it is also a religion in crisis. The text shows Habakkuk's struggle to reconcile God's holiness and justice with the reality of evil and injustice in the world. Contextually Hab. 1–2 shows a late-monarchic context, where prophetic figures question God's involvement in global affairs and the belief in God's sovereign use of nations (e.g., Babylon) for judgment. This stage of religion is focused less on ritual and more on the moral and theological implications of God's actions in history.

What Theological Themes or Concepts Are Present in This Text?

1. Theodicy: This text raises the question Why does a just God tolerate injustice and violence?
2. Divine sovereignty: God raises up nations (even wicked ones) to accomplish divine purposes.
3. Faith as endurance: The statement that "the righteous shall live by their faith" (Hab. 2:4 AT) suggests trust amid unanswered questions.
4. Divine silence: God's delayed action or silence becomes a theological issue, not just an emotional one.
5. Historical judgment: This text teaches that God is not confined to Israel's borders but works through international powers.

What Role Does This Text Play in the Development of Israelite/Jewish Theology?

Habakkuk 1–2 plays a pivotal transitional role in the following ways:

1. It articulates a mature theology of questioning, in which dialogue with God is a legitimate response to divine mystery.
2. It introduces a proto-apocalyptic framework, a vision of future judgment that transcends immediate historical fixes.
3. It deepens Israel's theology of faith and endurance, a theme picked up in postexilic texts and later in Christian theology (e.g., Romans, Hebrews).
4. This text shows Israelite faith as under pressure yet growing deeper rather than collapsing.

How Does This Text Contribute to the Overall Theological Framework of the Tanakh?

1. It expands the range of acceptable faith responses: not just praise or obedience but also lament and protest.
2. It reinforces God's universal justice, not just as Israel's God but as God of all nations and of history.
3. It sets up later theological concepts such as remnant faithfulness, eschatological vision, and delayed vindication.

4. It adds emotional honesty and existential realism to the Tanakh's theology in a manner similar to Job and Ecclesiastes.

How Does This Approach Inform Our Hermeneutic of This Text?

At this point, theologically/cultically speaking, Judah has moved fully into monotheism and yet struggles to accept Yahweh as King supreme. Thus we see a struggle in the prophetic text between the will of man and the Torah of God. In fact, Habakkuk notes that the Torah isn't kept, and justice (if enacted at all) goes forth perverted. So the Israelite religion, which found its high point in Josiah just before Habakkuk's book, is now quickly sliding into decay. The religion that had found unity and obedience resulting in holiness now finds none.

What Are the Benefits of Applying This Approach to This Text?

1. Honors historical and theological complexity: This approach respects the evolving nature of theology, recognizing that later prophetic texts build on and respond to earlier revelations.
2. Encourages canonical interconnectedness: It positions Habakkuk as part of a larger theological arc—from Deuteronomistic covenant theology to prophetic critique and apocalyptic hope.
3. Makes space for doubt and lament: This approach legitimizes Habakkuk's questioning as not rebellion but as part of one's faith development and useful for pastoral and practical application.
4. Highlights human struggle in theological formation: It portrays the whole Tanakh as a human-divine conversation across time, not just a static codebook of truth.

What Are the Potential Problems in Applying This Approach to This Text?

1. Relativizing theological authority: Seeing theology as "developing" might make it seem less authoritative by suggesting that earlier beliefs are outdated or inferior.
2. Imposing later theology: There's a risk of retroactively applying later development that doesn't reflect the theology of this time.
3. Undermines the unity of Scripture: By focusing on theological diversity, this view might downplay the coherence of the Tanakh's central theological claims (e.g., covenant, justice, sovereignty).

SUMMARY OF TEST CASE

In the Theological Development approach, Hab. 1–2 is a witness to Israelite religion in crisis. As such, the Israelite religion is fully monotheistic and covenant-aware, yet struggling to reconcile God's justice and divine "silence." The text calls for faith as endurance amid unresolved theodicy and portrays God's sovereign use of nations in historical judgment. This approach highlights the dynamic, developing nature of Israel's faith and its interconnectedness with Deuteronomy, Psalms, Job, and later traditions, while also risking, if misused, a relativizing of theological authority or an overemphasis on diversity at the expense of scriptural unity.

Spiritual Guide Approach

WHAT TOPIC(S) DOES THIS TEXT TEACH BELIEVERS?

Habakkuk 1–2 addresses several spiritual life topics, including the following:

1. How to bring honest doubts to God: Habakkuk is not condemned for questioning God's justice and timing.
2. Living faithfully during confusion and delay: The call for the righteous to live by faith (Hab. 2:4) offers a spiritual posture of trust in uncertain times.
3. God's sovereignty over global events: Believers are reminded that even oppressive nations (such as Babylon) serve a divine purpose.
4. Waiting with hope: The vision awaits its time. Though it lingers, wait for it; it will come (Hab. 2:3).
5. Warnings against pride and injustice: Woes pronounced against unjust powers show how not to live and what God condemns.

These topics are deeply spiritual, touching on trust, justice, patience, humility, and hope.

HOW DO THESE TOPICS RELATE TO THE OTHER SECTIONS OF THE TANAKH?

1. Relation to Torah (God's laws for life): Habakkuk reflects Torah values (justice, righteousness) but explores what happens when God appears inactive in enforcing those laws. It shows how the Torah's ideals meet life's painful realities, especially when wickedness prevails.
2. Relation to Nevi'im (warnings, encouragement, insight): Habakkuk fits directly here. It warns the proud, encourages the faithful, and gives

insight into divine timing and justice. Its format (dialogue and vision) shows how prophecy can engage human concern and divine response.

3. Relation to Ketuvim (wisdom and comfort): Like Psalms or Job, Habakkuk voices human anguish and theological confusion, offering comfort in solidarity. It mirrors the wisdom theme that not all things make sense immediately.

How Does This Approach Inform Our Hermeneutic of This Text?

This approach invites readers to treat Hab. 1–2 as spiritual instruction for the inner life, not just as historical commentary. This approach emphasizes personal and communal application, especially for those who feel that God is silent. It treats the text as an invitation to bring doubts to God, making it a model for spiritual honesty. It encourages a faith that endures even when circumstances seem to contradict God's promises, and it views the woes against injustice as ethical direction for godly living. In essence, this approach leads us to ask "What kind of spiritual posture does this text call me to adopt?" rather than just "What historical situation is it responding to?"

What Potential Problems Arise from the Above Question?

1. Spiritualizing over contextualizing: The danger is over-allegorizing or ignoring the historical specificity of the Babylonian threat.
2. Misapplication: Believers might wrongly interpret God's use of Babylon as justification for current political oppression or draw unhelpful analogies.
3. Minimizing the communal aspect: Focusing too much on individual spiritual growth could neglect the text's national and justice-oriented messages.
4. Neglecting the prophet's role: Turning the text into a devotional tool might flatten its prophetic authority and reduce it to feel-good spirituality.

What Are the Benefits of Applying This Approach to This Text?

1. Promotes emotional honesty in matters of faith: Habakkuk gives voice to spiritual struggles, validating questions and doubt as part of the faithful life.
2. Encourages perseverance in uncertainty: "The righteous shall live by faith" becomes not just a doctrinal slogan but a lived spiritual reality during periods of waiting.

3. Strengthens hope in God's justice: It reminds readers that evil will be judged, not on our timeline but on God's.
4. Models a life of prayerful engagement: Habakkuk doesn't walk away from God; he prays, waits, and listens—a guide for navigating silence and confusion.
5. Bridges the heart and the mind: The text invites readers to think deeply and feel deeply; it engages both reason and emotion.

What Are the Potential Problems in Applying This Approach to This Text?

1. Risk of over-privatization: Reducing the text to personal spiritual lessons may ignore corporate and national dimensions such as communal injustice and judgment.
2. Ignoring the prophetic role: The prophet's job is to speak God's word to power. Spiritualizing the text too narrowly can obscure that public, justice-driven dimension.
3. Historical flattening: Treating the text purely as a timeless spiritual resource risks erasing the Babylonian crisis and Judah's historical trauma.
4. Prophecy reduced to therapy: There's a risk that the prophetic cry becomes just a therapeutic outlet, not a divine confrontation of injustice and pride.

Summary of Test Case

The Spiritual Guide approach reads Hab. 1–2 primarily as instruction for the inner and communal life of believers. Hermeneutically, this method asks what spiritual posture the text calls forth, inviting believers to bring questions to God, endure divine "silence," and live ethically in hope of God's justice. Its strengths lie in promoting emotional honesty, perseverance, prayerful engagement, and holistic (head–heart) spirituality, but it risks overspiritualizing the book, privatizing its message, minimizing its historical context, and reducing prophetic confrontation of injustice to mere personal therapy.

Messianic Trajectory Approach

What Messianic Topic(s) Does This Text Teach Believers?

Habakkuk 1–2 deals with themes of divine justice, waiting on God, and faith amid injustice. The key messianic topic centers on the righteous living by faith (Hab. 2:4), which becomes a central theological point in the New

Testament concerning the person and work of the Messiah (Rom. 1:16–17; Gal. 3:10–14; Heb. 10:19–38). This text implicitly points toward a future vindication of the righteous and God's ultimate justice, both of which are fulfilled in Christ, who embodies perfect righteousness and enacts final judgment.

How Do These Topics Relate to the Other Sections of the Tanakh and Ultimately to Christ?

1. Torah (Messiah as Torah's fulfillment): The Torah establishes the covenant and legal framework in which righteousness is defined. Habakkuk critiques the failure of justice under this law, highlighting the need for a deeper fulfillment, something that Jesus as the Messiah later accomplishes.
2. Nevi'im (Messiah as prophetic hope): Habakkuk joins other prophetic voices that call for justice and anticipate divine intervention. The expectation of a coming day of the Lord, divine judgment, and restoration of the righteous all echo a messianic hope, which Christ fulfills.
3. Ketuvim (Messiah longed for): The existential tension seen in Habakkuk's lament mirrors the longing for resolution and justice expressed in the Ketuvim (e.g., Psalms, Job). The Messiah is the one who answers this longing by bringing ultimate peace and righteousness.
4. Ultimately Christ: Christ embodies the righteous one who lives by faith and also becomes the object of faith for others. He both endures injustice (like the suffering righteous in Habakkuk's complaint) and promises final justice and restoration, fulfilling the hope implicit in this text.

How Does This Approach Inform Our Hermeneutic of This Text?

This approach invites readers to see Hab. 1–2 not merely as a historical complaint but also as part of a prophetic longing for the Messiah. The text becomes a theological bridge from the failure of worldly justice to the hope of messianic intervention. It sharpens our focus on how the Messiah will redefine righteousness, justice, and faith. Hermeneutically, this allows readers to see the "righteous by faith" theme not only in its historical setting but as a forward-looking theological axis that connects to Christ and the New Testament witness.

What Potential Problems Arise from the Above Question?

1. Over-reading Christ into the text: There's a risk of anachronism, imposing Christian theology into a text that does not explicitly mention or anticipate a specific messianic figure.

2. Minimizing historical context: The original dialogue between the prophet and God regarding Babylonian injustice may be overshadowed or spiritualized, losing its original political and ethical urgency.
3. Ignoring genre and lament: The prophetic lament genre may be flattened into a predictive or theological reading that ignores its poetic and emotional depth.

What Are the Benefits of Applying This Approach to This Text?

1. Canonical coherence: This approach helps readers understand how the text fits into a broader, unified biblical narrative that culminates in Christ.
2. Theological hope: It reinforces the message that God will ultimately bring justice through the Messiah, affirming faith during suffering.
3. Faith-centered living: Highlights the enduring principle that faith is central to righteousness, prefiguring Paul's theological emphasis.
4. Deepens christological reading: Trains believers to see how the longing for justice and righteousness in the Nevi'im finds its answer in the person and work of Jesus.

What Are the Potential Problems in Applying This Approach to This Text?

1. Danger of reductionism: This approach may reduce the prophetic literature to mere messianic pointers, ignoring other theological dimensions (e.g., covenantal warning, communal grief).
2. Loss of diversity: Habakkuk's unique contribution to Israel's theological reflection on suffering and divine justice could be diminished by over-systematizing the messianic lens.
3. Supersessionism: If not nuanced, the Messianic Trajectory approach can lead to supersessionist interpretations, where the Christian fulfillment invalidates the Jewish meaning of the text.
4. Overemphasis on fulfillment: The complex process of theological development in Israel's history could be oversimplified by focusing only on fulfillment in Christ.

Summary of Test Case

The Messianic Trajectory approach reads Hab. 1–2 as part of a forward-looking movement in Scripture that culminates in Christ. It highlights the theme of "the righteous shall live by faith" (Hab. 2:4) as a key messianic axis later taken up in the New Testament, where Christ both embodies perfect righteousness and becomes the object of saving faith. Within the Tanakh, Habakkuk exposes the failure of justice, thus joining the prophets' longing for divine intervention, and resonates with the Ketuvim's cry for resolution, all of which point toward a future, messianic vindication of the righteous and final judgment on evil. This approach offers strong canonical and christological unity and deepens messianic hope. Like other approaches, there is a risk of reading Christ anachronistically into the text, minimizing its historical and literary context, and reducing Habakkuk's message to a mere prooftext for messianic fulfillment.

Sacred Structure Approach

How Does This Section Relate to the Respective Temple Court?

Habakkuk 1–2 belongs to the Nevi'im and therefore aligns with the holy place in the temple structure, where God's word is proclaimed and mediated. This space, occupied by the lampstand (light), the table of showbread (provision), and the altar of incense (prayer), symbolically aligns with the prophetic role of bringing light, provision, and intercession on behalf of the people.

Habakkuk acts as a spiritual mediator by questioning God, hearing his response, and awaiting a vision, all aligning with the prophetic dynamic of intercession and divine communication. This "holy place" encounter is not direct presence (as in Torah), but it is a powerful nearness to God's activity.

What Does This Text Espouse as This Temple Court Would?

As part of the Nevi'im/holy place, this text espouses intimate dialogue between the prophet and God, accessible to those specially called (i.e., the prophets), not the general public. The text embodies the wrestling of faith, the confusion over God's justice, and the prophetic burden to watch, listen, and proclaim God's timing and justice.

Like the priest in the holy place, Habakkuk burns incense (prayer), seeks light (lampstand), and maintains spiritual communion (bread). His message is not veiled, but still requires spiritual sensitivity to understand God's response ("Write the vision . . . so he who reads it may run," Hab. 2:2 AT).

How Does This Approach Inform Our Hermeneutic of This Text?

This approach helps us read Habakkuk not simply as historical or moral instruction but as a mediated word from God—something to be handled with reverence, interpreted prayerfully, and proclaimed courageously. It frames the text as sacred space, not casual critique or philosophical musing. We are invited not just to analyze God's justice but to enter into a space of divine-human conversation akin to temple service.

What Are the Benefits of Applying This Approach to This Text?

1. Sacred encounter: This approach reminds readers that prophetic texts such as Habakkuk are not just informational but are also transformational, inviting reverence and reflection.
2. Prophetic mediation: It also encourages a hermeneutic of listening, like a priest or prophet in the holy place, where prayer, patience, and vision are essential.
3. Spatial theology: This approach helps situate the Nevi'im within the broader narrative of divine access—from presence (Torah) to proclamation (Nevi'im) to invitation (Ketuvim).
4. Liturgical imagination: This approach trains readers to imagine their own Bible reading as a temple act, a movement closer to God's voice and presence.

What Are the Potential Problems in Applying This Approach to This Text?

1. Loss of context: This approach may minimize the very real geopolitical threat and theological protest happening in Habakkuk's day.
2. Elitism: This approach could unintentionally promote a view that only "special" people such as prophets or pastors can interpret or receive God's message.
3. Forced uniformity: Not all prophetic books fit neatly into "holy place" categories; some function more like wisdom or Torah texts.
4. Limiting genre richness: The analogy might ignore the poetic lament and dialogical structure of Habakkuk by emphasizing only ritual roles.
5. Over-allegorization: The Sacred Structure approach may overly spiritualize the text, making it hard to engage with the historical context (i.e., Babylonian threat and Judah's sin).
6. Restricting access: It may imply that such divine dialogue is only for a special class, such as priests or prophets, rather than something the broader believing community can engage with.

7. Reductive framework: It may limit the diversity of prophetic literature to just one function (i.e., "holy place"), ignoring literary, political, and theological dimensions.

Summary of Test Case

The Sacred Structure approach interprets Hab. 1–2 as a "holy place" text within the temple analogy, corresponding to the Nevi'im, where God's word is proclaimed through prophetic mediation. Habakkuk functions like a priest in the holy place, offering prayer, seeking divine light, and depending on God's provision as he questions, listens, and records God's vision. The benefits of this approach include highlighting the transformational, sacred character of prophetic Scripture and situating the Nevi'im within a larger "spatial" theology of access to God. However, there is the danger that the method may overspiritualize the book, minimizing its historical and political context and thus reducing Habakkuk's rich poetic lament to a rigid temple metaphor.

Nevi'im Conclusion

Habakkuk 1–2 presents a unique dialogue, where the prophet dares to question God amid national injustice and foreign threat. Troubled by Judah's moral decay and God's seeming inaction, Habakkuk cries out for divine intervention. God responds, but not with expected comfort. Instead, he reveals that he will raise up the Chaldeans (Babylonians), a ruthless and more wicked nation, to execute judgment on Judah. This confounds the prophet further: How can God use an even more corrupt people as his instrument? In response, God calls for patience and faith, assuring Habakkuk that the Chaldeans too will face judgment. Chapter 2 includes a series of "woes" against oppressors and centers on the foundational principle that "the righteous shall live by their faith" (2:4 AT).

From a Triple Canon approach, Habakkuk's inclusion in the canon reflects Israel's grappling with covenantal consequences and eschatological hope and was likely compiled during the exilic period as a theologically charged reflection on suffering and sovereignty. As prophetic literature, Habakkuk exemplifies the genre with visionary dialogue, divine pronouncement, and moral protest. From a Theological Development approach, this text marks a turning point in Israel's religion—moving from temple-centered stability under Josiah to theological disorientation amid Judah's collapse. Viewed through the lens of the Spiritual Guide approach, Habakkuk models how believers can voice doubt without forfeiting faith. The call to live by faith becomes a spiritual imperative in times of divine silence and societal collapse. In the

Messianic Trajectory approach, Habakkuk's phrase "the righteous shall live by faith" becomes a theological cornerstone echoed in the New Testament (i.e., Romans, Galatians, Hebrews). While the text does not mention a Messiah directly, it anticipates a future where divine justice and righteousness are fully realized in Christ. Finally, through the Sacred Structure approach, Hab. 1–2 aligns with the holy place, a space of mediated divine presence, prophetic vision, and intercessory prayer. The prophet functions like a temple servant, bearing the spiritual burdens of the people and receiving divine revelation.

Taken together, these interpretive approaches show that Hab. 1–2 is far more than a cry for help or a warning of judgment. It is a theological and spiritual masterpiece, presenting a deeply human response to divine mystery and a call to endure with faith in a world where justice is delayed but not denied. Habakkuk affirms God's sovereign control over history, the certainty of divine justice, and the enduring hope that sustains the faithful in every generation.

Ketuvim: The Vanity of Life and Worldly Wisdom (Eccles. 1)

What Is This Text About?

Ecclesiastes 1 is the first sermon in the book of Ecclesiastes, and it introduces the unifying theme of the entire book: the meaninglessness of life when pursued through human effort and worldly wisdom alone. The writer, traditionally referred to as Qohelet or the Preacher, reflects on the cyclical nature of life, noting that human endeavors ultimately lead nowhere, as everything repeats and nothing truly satisfies. Generations come and go, the sun rises and sets, and despite all human striving, "there is nothing new under the sun" (Eccles. 1:9). Qohelet concludes that wisdom, labor, and the pursuit of knowledge are futile since death comes to all, rendering everything vain.

Triple Canon Approach

How Does This Text Fit into This Section?

Ecclesiastes belongs to the wisdom books of the Hebrew Bible, alongside books such as Proverbs and Job. In the context of this canonical division, Eccles. 1 offers a counterpoint to the optimistic wisdom of Proverbs by challenging the idea that life can be understood through human reason or that it follows a predictable moral order. Instead, the Preacher suggests that life's meaning is elusive, and the pursuit of wisdom for its own sake can lead to despair. This chapter establishes the skeptical tone that runs through the rest of the book, questioning the value of human knowledge and achievement.

When Was This Section of the Canon Closed?

Ecclesiastes was likely finalized during the postexilic period (5th–3rd cent. BCE). As a canonical division, the Ketuvim was finalized in the Greek period. For this reason, some scholars suggest that the book reflects the influence of Hellenistic philosophy, which became more prominent after Alexander the Great's conquests in the fourth century BCE. The text's philosophical tone, along with its questioning of traditional wisdom, indicates that it was compiled in a period of cultural and intellectual transition for the Jewish people.

In What Historical Period Was This Text Written and Canonized?

The historical context of Ecclesiastes is probably the postexilic era, when Jewish society was grappling with the tension between traditional values and the new ideas introduced by Greek philosophy. This period was marked by political instability and cultural exchange, which may have led to a sense of disillusionment for many people. The search for meaning in a world that seemed chaotic, despite the restoration of Jerusalem and the temple, could have contributed to the book's emphasis on the futility of worldly pursuits and wisdom. The text reflects a time when traditional religious answers seemed insufficient in the face of broader existential questions.

Who Compiled This Section?

Ecclesiastes was likely compiled by scribes or scholars during the Second Temple period. While traditionally attributed to Solomon, the language and themes suggest that the book was edited by later Jewish thinkers who sought to present a reflective, philosophical view on the meaning of life. These scribes may have incorporated Solomon's reputation for wisdom as a literary device, but the book's content appears to engage with more contemporary issues of the postexilic period.

What Is the Political Purpose of This Section?

Ecclesiastes 1 does not appear to have a direct political agenda.

How Does This Approach Inform Our Hermeneutic of This Text?

The Triple Canon approach, which examines how and why a text was included in the biblical canon, informs our hermeneutic by reminding us that Ecclesiastes is part of a larger body of wisdom literature, which includes different perspectives on life and faith. Ecclesiastes offers a more skeptical or pessimistic view of life than the surrounding ideals of the earthly and divine realms as seen in Greek culture.

What Are the Benefits of Applying This Approach to This Text?

1. Honest reflection on life: Ecclesiastes 1 encourages honest reflection on the nature of life and the limits of human understanding. It acknowledges that life is often filled with uncertainty and frustration, which can resonate with readers facing their own struggles.
2. Humility in human knowledge: The emphasis on the vanity of wisdom reminds us to approach knowledge and understanding with humility. It suggests that human effort alone cannot unlock the ultimate mysteries of life, and we must look beyond our limited perspective.
3. Value of seeking deeper meaning: While the Preacher's reflections may seem pessimistic, they challenge readers to seek deeper meaning in life beyond material success or intellectual achievement. Ecclesiastes encourages readers to consider the transcendence of God and the temporary nature of earthly pursuits.
4. Invitation to trust in God: The ultimate message of Ecclesiastes, though often implicit in chapter 1, is that life without God is futile. The Preacher's relentless questioning points toward the need to find meaning not in worldly wisdom or achievements but in a relationship with the divine.

What Are the Potential Problems in Applying This Approach to This Text?

1. Overemphasis on Greek wisdom: This approach may focus too much on comparison of religions rather than on the wisdom of God articulated by Solomon.
2. Ambiguity of purpose: When focusing too much on the canonizing period, there may grow an ambiguity about the purpose of Ecclesiastes.

Summary of Test Case

Applying the Triple Canon approach to Eccles. 1, we see how the chapter introduces the book's central theme: the vanity and futility of life when pursued through human effort and worldly wisdom alone. Furthermore, through this interpretive approach Ecclesiastes offers a skeptical counterpoint to Proverbs, as it was likely finalized in the postexilic/Greek period and shaped by scribes engaging with both Israel's tradition and emerging philosophical questions.

The Triple Canon approach highlights benefits such as honest reflection on life's frustrations, humility about the limits of human knowledge, and a push to seek meaning in God rather than in achievement. We should recognize and avoid the potential problems of overemphasizing Greek influence and allowing focus on debates about the book's canonicity to obscure its theological purpose.

Author Genre Approach

What Is the Genre of This Text, and How Does This Genre Accord with This Approach to the Tanakh?

The genre of Eccles. 1 is wisdom literature, specifically philosophical or reflective wisdom. It opens with Qohelet's reflections on the vanity (*hevel*) of all things, expressing existential despair and observations about the cyclical nature of life under the sun. It differs from proverbial wisdom in tone and structure, leaning toward skeptical or critical wisdom. Since Ecclesiastes is part of the Ketuvim, a division that includes wisdom books such as Proverbs and Job, its genre does accord with the Genre Author approach. Its reflective and philosophical wisdom fits well in this category, particularly as a counterwisdom or skeptical voice within the wisdom tradition.

Who Is the Author, and How Does the Authorship Accord with This Approach to the Tanakh?

The author is identified as Qohelet (the Teacher/Preacher), son of David, king in Jerusalem (Eccles. 1:1). This author partially accords with the Genre Author approach. While Qohelet is not listed explicitly among biblical "wise men," he is understood to be a wisdom teacher, and the attribution of this book to Solomon places it in the wisdom/other category of the Genre Author approach.

How Does This Approach Inform Our Hermeneutic of This Text?

Recognizing Ecclesiastes as part of the wisdom genre helps interpret its themes of ephemeral existence, human limitation, and the pursuit of meaning. It signals the reader to expect human observation, questioning, and probing rather than divine revelation or prophetic covenantal judgment.

What Are the Benefits of Applying This Approach to This Text?

1. Grounds interpretation in literary context: Understanding Ecclesiastes as wisdom literature helps readers approach it as reflection rather than

revelation and to read it through the lens of human experience rather than prophetic authority.

2. Encourages existential honesty: The Genre Author approach lets Ecclesiastes speak authentically without forcing it into a theological mold. It allows lament, futility, and unanswered questions to be valid theological expressions.

What Are the Potential Problems in Applying This Approach to This Text?

1. Risk of marginalizing the text: Labeling Ecclesiastes as wisdom/other might lead interpreters to dismiss it as less theological or authoritative, especially compared to the Torah or Nevi'im.
2. Overlooking theological depth: Wisdom literature can be viewed as practical, not spiritual, but Ecclesiastes contains deep theological reflection on death, time, God's sovereignty, and life's meaning.
3. Undervaluing canonical context: Over-classifying it as wisdom might prevent readers from seeing its relevance to Israel's broader story (e.g., postexilic identity, loss, or theological reevaluation).
4. Genre stereotyping: Not all wisdom is proverbial. The skeptical tone of Ecclesiastes may confuse readers expecting Proverbs-style certainty and thus require better framing of wisdom subgenres.

Summary of Test Case

By applying the Author Genre approach to Eccles. 1, we see the text as being reflective, philosophical wisdom voiced by Qohelet. Seeing the chapter as skeptical wisdom rather than as prophetic oracle shapes interpretation toward human observation, existential questioning, and exploration of life's vanity (*hevel*) under the sun. The approach helpfully grounds reading in the wisdom tradition, legitimates lament and unresolved questions, and frames Ecclesiastes as honest reflection on human limits and meaning. However, if overemphasized, it can marginalize the book's theological authority and its reflections on God, thus isolating it from Israel's broader canonical story.

Theological Development Approach

What Is the Israelite Religion in This Text?

The Israelite religion in this section is monotheistic, national, and possibly "evangelistic" under the preaching of Solomon. While the religion moved from henotheism to monotheism, it also moved from cultic to reformed in the temple. This temple change was also one of invitation to the surrounding cultures and peoples. Specifically, the Israelite religion espoused in Eccles. 1 is monotheistic, but God is distant (from those not in right relationship), sovereign, and mysterious. As a result, Solomon preaches on the limitations of human actions, the cyclical nature of life, and the fleetingness (*hevel*) of human achievements. This suggests a wisdom-oriented religious expression likely influenced by postexilic realities where traditional theology seemed out of sync with lived experience.

What Theological Themes or Concepts Are Present in This Text?

1. *Hevel* (vanity/fleetingness): All human efforts and accomplishments are ultimately ephemeral.
2. The limits of wisdom: Even wisdom cannot uncover ultimate meaning.
3. The cyclical nature of creation: Nature endures, but human legacy fades.
4. Divine distance or mystery: God is acknowledged but not explained or directly addressed in chapter 1.
5. Human futility: There is a tone of existential frustration in facing life's repetitive cycles.

What Role Does This Text Play in the Development of Israelite/Jewish Theology?

Ecclesiastes critiques naive theology, challenging the idea that righteousness always leads to prosperity. It also expands believers' theological vocabulary by bringing terms such as *hevel* to the forefront as metaphors for life's mystery. In light of the Preacher's *hevel* revelation, Ecclesiastes paves the way for later developments, opening the door to apocalyptic hope, later rabbinic wrestling, and New Testament discussions on meaning and eternity.

How Does This Text Contribute to the Overall Theological Framework of the Tanakh?

Ecclesiastes 1 adds existential realism by balancing the idealism of Proverbs and the legal confidence of the Torah with a real-world theology. Ecclesiastes 1 also introduces ambiguity as a nonresolutionist voice, allowing readers to live in the tension of unanswered questions.

It also democratizes faith by shifting the viewpoint from priest, prophet, or king to a reflective individual navigating life's paradoxes. In this way, the text becomes a means of countering human pride in knowledge, control, or permanence—fostering instead humility before God's mystery.

How Does This Approach Inform Our Hermeneutic of This Text?

This approach calls us to read Eccles. 1 not as a contradiction of earlier theology but as part of the Tanakh's theological maturation. It encourages interpreters to see Qohelet as engaging past theology (like Proverbs and Deuteronomy) with critical reflection. This approach helps us treat Ecclesiastes as a constructive theological voice, not merely skeptical or cynical, and to situate it in a larger theological conversation within Scripture.

What Are the Benefits of Applying This Approach to This Text?

1. Validates honest questioning: This view supports the legitimacy of theological struggle, helping readers who experience doubt or futility to see their questions reflected in Scripture.
2. Encourages a canonical conversation: Ecclesiastes doesn't replace earlier theology but rather interrogates it, encouraging the reader to weigh and synthesize multiple voices across the Tanakh.
3. Highlights theological adaptability: This approach shows how Israelite faith responds creatively to crisis or disappointment, not by abandoning God but by rethinking human expectations.
4. Deepens human engagement with God: This approach presents faith not as simplistic obedience but as intellectual, emotional, and spiritual wrestling.

What Are the Potential Problems in Applying This Approach to This Text?

1. Undermining doctrinal consistency: Theological development can appear to contradict earlier beliefs, leading some readers to feel uncertain about what Scripture teaches definitively.
2. Over-psychologizing the text: Reading Ecclesiastes primarily as a reflection of human crisis might obscure its theological intent and reduce its authority.
3. Fostering relativism: This approach may imply that all theological voices are equally valid, which might undercut convictions about truth or divine revelation.

4. Unclear ethical application: Compared to the Torah or Nevi'im, Ecclesiastes offers few moral imperatives, and this approach might leave readers without clear takeaways for practice.

Summary of Test Case

The Theological Development approach reads Eccles. 1 as a stage in Israel's maturing faith. It portrays a fully monotheistic Israelite religion in which God is sovereign and human life is marked by *hevel*—fleetingness, frustration, and the limits of wisdom. Ecclesiastes 1 challenges simplistic reward-theology, broadens Israel's language for ambiguity and mystery, and democratizes faith by voicing the reflections of an individual sage rather than those of a priest or prophet. This approach encourages us to see Qohelet as engaging earlier texts (Torah, Proverbs, Deuteronomy) in a canonical conversation that validates honest questioning and theological struggle. However, with this method comes the risk of undermining doctrinal clarity by over-psychologizing the book, leaving readers with less concrete ethical guidance than is offered by more directive parts of the Tanakh.

Spiritual Guide Approach

What Topic(s) Does This Text Teach Believers?

Ecclesiastes 1 teaches believers the limits of human achievement, wisdom, and permanence and confronts the repetitive, wearying cycles of life. It introduces the concept of *hevel* (translated "vanity," "futility," or "fleetingness"), expressing the following spiritual themes:

- Dissatisfaction of human striving
- Inability of wisdom alone to provide ultimate meaning
- Mystery and monotony of life under the sun
- Spiritual longing for something more enduring

How Do These Topics Relate to the Other Sections of the Tanakh?

1. Relation to Torah (God's laws for life): Ecclesiastes doesn't contradict the Torah but exposes the limitations of law when life feels incoherent. While Torah offers structure, Ecclesiastes reflects on what happens when the world doesn't reward obedience as expected.
2. Relation to Nevi'im (warnings, encouragement, and insight): Unlike the Nevi'im, with their warnings and calls to action, Ecclesiastes offers a

more reflective tone yet still offers insight, not through vision or judgment but through careful observation of life. It serves as a quiet warning: Even wisdom can become a burden without trust in God.

How Does This Approach Inform Our Hermeneutic of This Text?

This view invites readers to treat Eccles. 1 as a guide for spiritual realism. Instead of reading it as cynical, this framework helps us see the preacher as a spiritual mentor who walks through life's ambiguity and invites readers into relationship with God as the final answer. In this hermeneutic, Ecclesiastes becomes a spiritual detox, clearing out shallow optimism to make room for a deeper, quieter trust.

What Potential Problems Arise from the Above Question?

1. Overspiritualization of skepticism: There's a risk of softening the existential crisis of the text into mere devotional reflection when the text intends to disturb and unsettle.
2. Loss of intellectual integrity: Trying to treat every line as comforting or encouraging may ignore the text's tension and discomfort and thus weaken its spiritual power.
3. Misuse of *hevel* as hopelessness or liberation: Readers might interpret "everything is vanity" as permission to disengage from responsibility or misapply it as ultimate despair.

What Are the Benefits of Applying This Approach to This Text?

1. Validates spiritual disorientation: The text teaches that seasons of questioning, fatigue, and searching are part of spiritual maturity rather than a failure of faith.
2. Exposes idols of achievement and knowledge: Qohelet strips away illusions that wisdom, productivity, or legacy will save us. This leads to a renewed dependence on God.
3. Encourages silence and reflection: Unlike the Torah's commands or the Nevi'im's prophetic calls to action, Ecclesiastes calls for contemplative spirituality, encouraging stillness and thoughtfulness.
4. Comforts the spiritually weary: Those worn out by effort and uncertainty can find solidarity and comfort in a biblical voice that acknowledges life's frustrations.

5. Invites honest spiritual conversation: It makes space for believers to talk with God without pretending everything is okay while still remaining within the life of faith.

What Are the Potential Problems in Applying This Approach to This Text?

1. Risk of therapeutic reductionism: There's a danger of reducing Ecclesiastes to spiritual therapy, ignoring its sharp critiques of worldly ambition and philosophical limits.
2. Disconnection from communal faith: This approach may overly individualize the text, neglecting its value for communal reflection on meaning, justice, and mortality.
3. Marginalizing the fear of God: Later in the book, Qohelet arrives at a reverent conclusion (Eccles. 12:13), but if chapter 1 is spiritualized too soon, we may miss the tension that makes that ending meaningful.

Summary of Test Case

This Spiritual Guide approach reads Eccles. 1 as a manual for "spiritual realism," highlighting the limits of human achievement, wisdom, and permanence and the *hevel*-like frustration of life's repetitive cycles. Furthermore, this approach relates these themes to Torah and Nevi'im by showing how Ecclesiastes probes what happens when obedience and wisdom do not seem to yield the expected outcomes. Hermeneutically, the text is a guide for believers who feel weary or disoriented, validating seasons of doubt and stripping away shallow optimism in order to deepen trust in God. The approach's strengths lie in affirming honest spiritual struggle, exposing the idols of productivity and intellect, and fostering contemplative, reflective faith. Its risks include over-softening the book's theological realities in Qohelet's discourses, especially the eventual powerful call to fear God.

Messianic Trajectory Approach

What Messianic Topic(s) Does This Text Teach Believers?

Ecclesiastes 1 presents the theme of vanity (*hevel*) and the weariness of life under the sun, where all human pursuits seem futile and cyclical. Though the Messiah is not directly mentioned, the absence of meaning and the limits of human wisdom point forward to the need for a redeemer who brings ultimate purpose and resolution. This chapter evokes the longing for a Messiah who transcends the futility of life and offers eternal value.

How Do These Topics Relate to the Other Sections of the Tanakh and Ultimately to Christ?

In considering the Torah, we see a vision of covenantal blessing through obedience. Yet Ecclesiastes acknowledges that even with wisdom (often seen as obedience), futility still reigns. The prophetic literature longs for justice, restoration, and divine presence. In contrast, Eccles. 1 exposes the perceived absence of these realities, which increases the desire for one who will come and break the cycle of futility—a messianic hope.

How Does This Approach Inform Our Hermeneutic of This Text?

This approach invites us to read Eccles. 1 not as pessimistic despair but as a theological tension that demands resolution in the Messiah. The repetitive preachings and perceived futility in Ecclesiastes prepare the heart to recognize its need for transcendent hope. The messianic lens helps us interpret the text as part of a larger yearning, moving from the despair of meaningless repetition to the promise of new creation in the Messiah.

What Are the Benefits of Applying This Approach to This Text?

1. Creates theological coherence: The Messianic Trajectory approach allows Ecclesiastes to participate in the unified longing of the Tanakh, showing a human yearning that Christ fulfills.
2. Highlights human limits: The futility described draws attention to the limitations of human wisdom and effort, helping readers recognize the need for divine intervention.
3. Amplifies Christ's role: This approach accentuates Christ as the solution not only to sin but also to existential despair and purposelessness.
4. Encourages hope: Although Eccles. 1 is bleak, a messianic reading holds out hope that meaning and rest are possible in Christ.

What Are the Potential Problems in Applying This Approach to This Text?

1. Anachronism: Reading messianic themes into every text can be historically and literarily inappropriate, ignoring the original voice and audience. There is no explicit messianic reference in Eccles. 1, so reading it this way can risk overspiritualizing or imposing later theology onto the text. In fact, one would not be aware of the messianic need if not for the New Testament's teachings. It may reduce the value of the

original intent of Ecclesiastes by forcing a Christocentric conclusion where none is suggested. This could lead to neglecting the literary genre and philosophical voice of Ecclesiastes, which thrives on ambiguity and questioning.

2. Oversimplification: The depth and tension of Ecclesiastes may be flattened by hurrying to a messianic resolution.
3. Theological imposition: This approach risks turning every human longing into an automatic prophecy, which may miss the nuanced theology present in wisdom literature.
4. Neglect of genre and purpose: Ecclesiastes 1 is part of a larger philosophical exploration. Overemphasizing messianism may distract from its unique literary function and canonical contribution.

Summary of Test Case

The Messianic Trajectory approach to Eccles. 1 and its portrayal of *hevel*, the futility and weariness of life "under the sun," points to a deep longing for a redeemer who can give lasting meaning. The chapter's exposure of the limits of wisdom, effort, and covenant obedience is read as preparing the heart for the Messiah, who breaks the cycle of vanity and provides eternal purpose. A result of this approach is a theological coherence that highlights human limitation and encourages hope in Christ as the answer to existential despair. This interpretive approach is not without its dangers, however, as it may lead to anachronistically reading explicit messianism into a non-messianic wisdom text, oversimplifying the tensions within the book of Ecclesiastes, and neglecting its unique philosophical genre and original intent.

Sacred Structure Approach

How Does This Text Relate to the Respective Court?

Situated in the Ketuvim, Eccles. 1 parallels the temple's outer court, the place where all Israelites and gentiles could enter and begin engaging with the temple system. This space represents invitation and honest human encounter with the divine, but with rules against engaging further into the court. Like the outer court, Eccles. 1 is accessible in tone and thematic resonance. It voices universal questions such as What is the point of life? and What gain is there in toil? The chapter introduces a raw, almost cynical view of human experience, inviting readers into reflection and honest questioning, which is often the first step toward encountering God. In fact, Ecclesiastes does not use Yahweh as the divine name in the book, making it more approachable to the gentile nonbeliever.

What Does This Text Espouse as This Temple Court Would?

As part of the outer court, Eccles. 1 offers an invitation to all people, not just the righteous or priestly. It gives voice to the human condition in its confusion, fatigue, and search for meaning. It doesn't offer divine answers but rather gives space for inquiry and the beginning of spiritual search. The text allows worshipers (readers) to stand at a distance from God's direct presence and grapple with the futility of life apart from deeper meaning, beckoning them further into the sacred space to find resolution in a deeper relationship with God.

How Does This Approach Inform Our Hermeneutic of This Text?

Interpreting Eccles. 1 using the Sacred Structure approach encourages us to see it not as a stand-alone theological conclusion but as the beginning of a spiritual process. It's where the seeker is welcomed to wrestle with reality before moving closer to the holiness of God's word and ultimately God's presence. It teaches that questioning in the midst of life's problems is not a threat to faith but a necessary step toward realizing the need for a relationship with God. This parallels the journey from the outer court to the holy of holies, which required preparation, honesty, and intention.

What Are the Benefits of Applying This Approach to This Text?

1. Validates doubt and lament: The temple analogy shows that spiritual questioning has a rightful place in Scripture. Ecclesiastes is not a deviation from faith but part of its path.
2. Honors spiritual progression: Just as one progresses through the temple courts, Eccles. 1 shows the starting point of an inner journey toward God.
3. Promotes inclusion and accessibility: The outer court invites everyone, not just the religious elite. Ecclesiastes reflects the broader human experience and offers universal problems to resolve in right relationship with God.
4. Encourages reflection: The outer court is a space for inspection, sacrifice, and consideration like the philosophical and poetic tone of Eccles. 1.

What Are the Potential Problems in Applying This Approach to This Text?

1. Dismissing the text's depth: Viewing it as merely "entry-level" spirituality might keep readers from wrestling with its profound theological insights.

2. Misusing the analogy: The temple-court metaphor, if too rigidly applied, might flatten the genre distinctions or blur the literary intentions of the author of Ecclesiastes.
3. Cultural distance: Readers unfamiliar with temple practices may find the analogy more confusing than clarifying, especially if not properly explained.
4. Imposing structure instead of discovering it: The metaphor might encourage imposing a structure on the text rather than allowing meaning to emerge from it.
5. Undervaluing its sacredness: Readers might mistakenly interpret Ecclesiastes as merely preliminary or less sacred since it dwells in the "outer" court, leading them to undervalue its theological weight.
6. Over-systematization: Trying to force this text into a temple-court framework might oversimplify the theological nuance or complexity of the text.
7. Undervaluing its authority: The model may imply a hierarchical value system, unintentionally suggesting that texts in the Ketuvim are "less authoritative" because of their position further from the holy of holies.

Summary of Test Case

Finally, the test case of the Sacred Structure approach likens Eccles. 1 to the temple's outer court. Because Ecclesiastes is in the Ketuvim and uses general God-language rather than the divine name, the chapter is seen as an "entry space," where anyone—Israelite or gentile, believer or seeker—can voice universal questions about life's meaning, toil, and futility. Hermeneutically, Eccles. 1 is read as the starting point of a spiritual journey: a holy place for doubt, lament, and honest reflection, which ultimately calls readers further toward deeper encounter with God (i.e., deeper into the temple). This interpretive approach does come with the risk of reducing the book to "entry-level" faith and may unintentionally suggest to some that Ecclesiastes (and the Ketuvim) is less sacred or authoritative than texts symbolically closer to the "holy of holies."

Ketuvim Conclusion

Ecclesiastes 1 opens the book with a stark, poetic proclamation: "Vanity of vanities, all is vanity" (1:2). This first chapter introduces the central theme of the entire book: the futility of life and the limitations of human wisdom when pursued apart from God. Qohelet (the Preacher/Teacher), traditionally linked to Solomon, surveys nature and human history, concluding that all human striving is ultimately meaningless. The sun rises and sets, rivers run to the sea only to return, and generations pass without anything truly new happening "under the sun." Qohelet laments that even wisdom and knowledge lead to sorrow rather than satisfaction. In a world where death levels all outcomes, even wisdom cannot shield one from life's inevitable end.

Through the Triple Canon approach, Eccles. 1 offers a voice of spiritual skepticism that exposes the tension between divine truth and human experience. Likely finalized during the postexilic or early Hellenistic period (5th–3rd cent. BCE), Ecclesiastes reflects a world grappling with disillusionment, instability, and the influx of Greek philosophy. As a piece of wisdom literature, Ecclesiastes fits within the wisdom/other category of the Genre Author approach. Its skeptical tone challenges proverbial certainty, offering existential honesty over formulaic answers. Ecclesiastes 1 plays a vital role in the theological development of the Tanakh. The book invites readers to consider how faith in God answers suffering, uncertainty, and intellectual struggle. In the Spiritual Guide approach, Eccles. 1 calls the faithful into deeper reflection, encouraging stillness, humility, and honest questioning. While Eccles. 1 makes no explicit messianic claims, it prepares the way for Christ as the answer to existential despair. Finally, according to the Sacred Structure approach, this text from the Ketuvim is aligned with the outer court of the temple and therefore invites all people—Jew and gentile alike—into the realm of spiritual questioning. Although the Preacher does not offer answers, he does welcome readers into reflection and prepares them to encounter God as the great answer to life's questions.

Ecclesiastes 1 is a theological counterweight to the optimism of Proverbs, a philosophical contrast to the certainty of the Torah, and a spiritual precursor to the messianic hope found in later texts. Whether viewed through the lens of canon, genre, theology, spirituality, messianic anticipation, or temple structure, Eccles. 1 demands that readers pause, reflect, and deal with life's hardest questions.

A FINAL REFLECTION

EXAMINING THE TANAKH through these various approaches enriches our understanding of its depth and complexity. Whether viewed through the historical periods of canonization, distinctive genres and authorship, snapshots of evolving theological beliefs, or the text's role as a guide for spiritual life, each approach reveals vital aspects of the character and purpose of the biblical text. The messianic trajectory highlights the unfolding hope woven throughout the Torah, Nevi'im, and Ketuvim, while the three-court temple analogy offers a powerful metaphor for experiencing the Tanakh as a progressive encounter with God's presence, word, and invitation.

Each of these approaches is beneficial in its own way, providing a unique lens that illuminates a different dimension of the Tanakh's composition, message, and spiritual function. Together they form a holistic view that honors the sacred text's historical development, literary diversity, theological richness, and ongoing relevance. Embracing this multifaceted approach allows readers and scholars alike to engage with the Tanakh in ways that are both intellectually rigorous and spiritually meaningful, appreciating it not merely as a collection of writings but also as a living, dynamic witness to God's revelation and relationship with his people.

Ending this study in the same way we began, I express the following hope and prayer for you as you study God's Word:

- As you approach Scripture using the Triple Canon approach, I hope that you will find assurance in seeing how God has worked throughout the history of God's people to preserve God's word.
- As you employ the Genre Author approach, I pray that you will be encouraged by knowing that God's authors used specific literary forms to convey God's word to us.

- As you view Scripture through the Theological Development approach, may you find rest in the realized Christ as the Yes and Amen of the revealed theology.
- As you use the Spiritual Guide approach, may the Word of God be a lamp to your feet and a light for your path.
- As you follow the Messianic Trajectory approach, may you find Jesus to be the Yes and Amen of the Hebrew Bible.
- Finally, as you view the Tanakh through the Sacred Structure approach, may you find Scripture to be the place where all people are invited into the presence of God, just as the temple was the beacon of hope on Mount Moriah.

BIBLIOGRAPHY

Alexander, T. Desmond. *From Paradise to the Promised Land: An Introduction to the Pentateuch*. 3rd ed. Baker Academic, 2012.

Allen, Leslie C. *A Liturgy of Grief: A Pastoral Commentary on Lamentations*. Baker Academic, 2011.

Alter, Robert. *The Art of Biblical Narrative*. Basic Books, 2011.

American Bible Society. "State of the Bible USA 2023." American Bible Society, 2023. https://1s712.americanbible.org/state-of-the-bible/stateofthebible/State_of_the_bible-2023.pdf.

Bartholomew, Craig G. *Ecclesiastes*. Baker Commentary on the Old Testament. Baker Academic, 2014.

Bartholomew, Craig G., and Ryan P. O'Dowd. *Old Testament Wisdom Literature: A Theological Introduction*. IVP Academic, 2018.

Barton, John. *A History of the Bible: The Book and Its Faiths*. Penguin Books, 2019.

Barton, John. *Reading the Old Testament: Method in Biblical Study*. Westminster John Knox, 1984.

Bauckham, Richard. *The Bible in Politics: How to Read the Bible Politically*. 2nd ed. Westminster John Knox, 2011.

Beale, G. K. *Handbook on the New Testament Use of the Old Testament: Exegesis and Interpretation*. Baker Academic, 2012.

Beale, G. K. *A New Testament Biblical Theology: The Unfolding of the Old Testament in the New*. Baker Academic, 2011.

Beckwith, Roger T. "A Modern Theory of the Old Testament Canon." *Vetus Testamentum* 41.4 (1991): 385–95.

Beckwith, Roger T. *The Old Testament Canon of the New Testament Church: And Its Background in Early Judaism*. Wipf & Stock, 2008.

Beckwith, Roger T. "One Scripture or Many? Canon from Biblical, Theological, and Philosophical Perspectives." *Evangelical Quarterly* 80.1 (2008): 71–72. https://doi.org/10.1163/27725472-08001010.

ben Asher, Aaron. *Sefer Diqduqei ha-Teʿamim*. Edited by Seligmann Baer and Hermann L. Strack. Leipzig: L. Fernau, 1879.

Berkovits, Eliezer. *God, Man and History*. Edited by David Hazony. Shalem, 2004.

Berlin, Adele. *Poetics and Interpretation of Biblical Narrative*. Eisenbrauns, 2005.

Block, Daniel I. *For the Glory of God: Recovering a Biblical Theology of Worship*. Baker Academic, 2016.

Boda, Mark J. *Return to Me: A Biblical Theology of Repentance*. InterVarsity, 2015.

Brettler, Marc Zvi. "The Masoretes at Work: A Tradition Preserved." *Biblical Archaeology Society Library*. n.d. https://library.biblicalarchaeology.org/sidebar/the-masoretes-at-work-a-tradition-preserved/.

Bright, John. *A History of Israel*. 4th ed. Westminster Aids to the Study of the Scriptures. Westminster John Knox, 2000.

Brown, Michael. "It's All About the Messiah." *Ask Dr. Brown* (blog), November 2, 2021. https://archive.askdrbrown.org/library/lineoffireradio/it-s-all-about-messiah.

Brueggemann, Walter. *Genesis*. Interpretation. Westminster John Knox, 1982.

Brueggemann, Walter. *Hopeful Imagination: Prophetic Voices in Exile*. Fortress, 1986.

Brueggemann, Walter. *The Message of the Psalms*. Fortress, 1984.

Brueggemann, Walter. *Theology of the Old Testament: Testimony, Dispute, Advocacy*. Fortress, 2012.

Brueggemann, Walter, and Davis Hankins. *The Prophetic Imagination*. 40th anniversary ed. Fortress, 2018.

Cassuto, Umberto. *A Commentary on the Book of Genesis*. Part 1, *From Adam to Noah*. Varda Books, 2012.

Childs, Brevard S. *Biblical Theology of the Old and New Testaments: Theological Reflection on the Christian Bible*. Fortress, 2011.

Childs, Brevard S. *The Book of Exodus*. Westminster John Knox, 2004.

Childs, Brevard S. *Introduction to the Old Testament as Scripture*. Fortress, 1979.

Childs, Brevard S. *The Struggle to Understand Isaiah as Christian Scripture*. Eerdmans, 2015.

Collins, John J. *Daniel: A Commentary on the Book of Daniel*. Fortress, 1993.

Croy, Casey K. *Sequencing the Hebrew Bible: The Order of the Books*. Sheffield Phoenix, 2021.

Davies, Graham I. "Comparative Aspects of the History of Israelite Religion." *Zeitschrift für die alttestamentliche Wissenschaft* 125.1 (2013): 177–97. https://doi.org/10.1515/zaw-2013-0010.

Davies, Philip R. *Scribes and Schools: The Canonization of the Hebrew Scriptures*. Library of Ancient Israel. Westminster John Knox, 1998.

Davis, Ellen F. *Getting Involved with God: Rediscovering the Old Testament*. Cowley, 2001.

Delitzsch, Franz. *Messianic Prophecies in Historical Succession*. Translated by Samuel Ives Curtiss. Kessinger, 2010.

Dempster, Stephen G. "Canons on the Right and Canons on the Left: Finding a Resolution in the Canon Debate." *Journal of the Evangelical Theological Society* 52.1 (2009): 47–77.

Dempster, Stephen G. *Dominion and Dynasty: A Theology of the Hebrew Bible*. IVP Academic, 2003.

Dempster, Stephen G. "An 'Extraordinary Fact': Torah and Temple and the Contours of the Hebrew Canon." *Tyndale Bulletin* 48.1 (1997): 23–56.

Dempster, Stephen G. "An 'Extraordinary Fact': Torah and Temple and the Contours of the Hebrew Canon, Pt. 2." *Tyndale Bulletin* 48.2 (1997): 191–218.

Edersheim, Alfred. *Bible History, Old Testament*. Hendrickson Academic, 1995.

Fishbane, Michael. *Biblical Interpretation in Ancient Israel*. Reprint, Clarendon, 1989.

Fitzmyer, Joseph A. *The Dead Sea Scrolls and Christian Origins*. Eerdmans-Lightning Source, 2000.

Fox, Michael V. *Proverbs 1–9*. Anchor Yale Bible Commentaries. Yale University Press, 2010.

Gentry, Peter J., and Stephen J. Wellum. *Kingdom Through Covenant: A Biblical-Theological Understanding of the Covenants*. Crossway, 2012.

Goldingay, John. *Old Testament Theology: Israel's Gospel*. Reprint, IVP Academic, 2015.

Goldingay, John. *The Theology of the Book of Isaiah*. IVP Academic, 2014.

Goldsworthy, Graeme. *According to Plan: The Unfolding Revelation of God in the Bible*. IVP Academic, 2002.

Gordon, Robert P. *I & II Samuel: A Commentary*. Zondervan Academic, 1986.

Graetz, Heinrich. *Kohelet, oder der Salomonische Prediger*. Leipzig: C. F. Winter, 1871.

Greenberg, Moshe. *Understanding Exodus: A Holistic Commentary on Exodus 1–11*. 2nd ed. Cascade Books, 2013.

Halbertal, Moshe. *People of the Book: Canon, Meaning, and Authority*. Harvard University Press, 1997.

Hamilton, James M., Jr. *God's Glory in Salvation Through Judgment: A Biblical Theology*. Crossway, 2010.

Harmon, William. *A Handbook to Literature*. Longman, 2012.

Hasel, Gerhard. *Old Testament Theology: Basic Issues in the Current Debate*. 4th ed. Eerdmans, 1991.

Hengel, Martin. *Judaism and Hellenism: Studies in Their Encounter in Palestine During the Early Hellenistic Period*. Wipf & Stock, 2003.

Heschel, Abraham Joshua. *God in Search of Man: A Philosophy of Judaism*. Farrar, Straus & Giroux, 1983.

Heschel, Abraham Joshua. *The Prophets*. Harper Perennial Modern Classics, 2001.

Holtz, Barry W., ed. *Back to the Sources: Reading the Classic Jewish Texts*. Simon & Schuster, 2006.

Japhet, Sara. *I and II Chronicles: A Commentary*. Westminster John Knox, 1993.

Kaiser, Walter C. *The Messiah in the Old Testament*. Rev. ed. Zondervan, 1995.

Kidner, Derek. *Psalms 73–150*. IVP Academic, 2014.

King, Andrew M., Joshua M. Philpot, and William R. Osborne, eds. *The Law, the Prophets, and the Writings: Studies in Evangelical Old Testament Hermeneutics in Honor of Duane A. Garrett*. B&H Academic, 2021.

Kogman-Appel, Katrin. *Jewish Book Art Between Islam and Christianity: The Decoration of Hebrew Bibles in Medieval Spain*. Brill Academic, 2004.

Kugel, James L. *How to Read the Bible: A Guide to Scripture, Then and Now*. Free Press, 2008.

Leiman, Shnayer Z. *The Canon and Masorah of the Hebrew Bible: An Introductory Reader*. Ktav, 1974.

Leiman, Shnayer Z. *The Canonization of Hebrew Scripture: The Talmudic and Midrashic Evidence*. Connecticut Academy of Arts and Sciences, 1991.

Levenson, Jon D. *The Hebrew Bible, the Old Testament, and Historical Criticism: Jews and Christians in Biblical Studies*. Westminster John Knox, 1993.

Levenson, Jon D. *Inheriting Abraham: The Legacy of the Patriarch in Judaism, Christianity, and Islam*. Princeton University Press, 2012.

Levenson, Jon D. *Sinai & Zion: An Entry into the Jewish Bible*. New Voices in Biblical Studies. HarperOne, 1987.

Levine, Baruch A. *Leviticus: The Traditional Hebrew Text with the New JPS Translation*. JPS Torah Commentary. Jewish Publication Society, 1989.

Lieb, Michael, Emma Mason, and Jonathan Roberts, eds. *The Oxford Handbook of the Reception History of the Bible*. Oxford University Press, 2011.

Longman, Tremper, III. *Jeremiah, Lamentations*. New International Biblical Commentary. Hendrickson, 2008.

Longman, Tremper, III. *Job*. Baker Commentary on the Old Testament. Baker Academic, 2016.

Longman, Tremper, III. *Literary Approaches to Biblical Interpretation*. Zondervan, 1987.

Martín Contreras, Elvira, and Lorena Miralles Maciá, eds. *The Text of the Hebrew Bible: From the Rabbis to Masoretes*. Journal of Ancient Judaism. Vandenhoeck & Ruprecht, 2014.

Mays, James Luther. *Psalms*. Interpretation. Westminster John Knox, 2011.

McDonald, Lee Martin. *The Formation of the Biblical Canon*. Vol. 1, *The Old Testament: Its Authority and Canonicity*. T&T Clark, 2025.

Milgrom, Jacob. *Leviticus: A Book of Ritual and Ethics*. Continental Commentaries. Fortress, 2004.

Milgrom, Jacob. *Leviticus 1–16: A New Translation with Introduction and Commentary*. Anchor Yale Bible Commentaries. Yale University Press, 2021.

Milgrom, Jacob. *Numbers: The Traditional Hebrew Text with the New JPS Translation*. JPS Torah Commentary. Jewish Publication Society, 1990.

Moberly, R. W. L. *Old Testament Theology: Reading the Hebrew Bible as Christian Scripture*. Baker Academic, 2015.

Moriarty, Frederick L. "The Habakkuk Scroll and a Controversy." *Journal of Theological Studies* 13.2 (1952): 228–33.

Motyer, J. Alec. *The Prophecy of Isaiah: An Introduction and Commentary*. IVP Academic, 2009.

Mowinckel, Sigmund. *The Psalms in Israel's Worship*. Dove Booksellers, 2004.

Nemoy, Leon. "The Epistle of Sahl Ben Maṣlīaḥ (Appendix: Sahl's Excursus on the Use of Reason in Theology and Law)." *American Academy for Jewish Research* 38/39 (1971): 145–77.

Noth, Martin. *The Deuteronomistic History*. Journal for the Study of the Old Testament Supplement Series 15. JSOT Press, 1981.

O'Connor, Kathleen H. *Lamentations and the Tears of the World*. Orbis Books, 2002.

Ofer, Yosef. "Abraham Firkovich and the Dedication Inscription of the Aleppo Codex." *Hebrew Union College Annual* 76 (2005): 259–72.

Osborne, Grant R. "Testing God's Son: Deuteronomy and Luke 4:1–13." Pages 365–87 in *For Our Good Always: Studies on the Message and Influence of Deuteronomy in Honor of Daniel I. Block*. Edited by Jason S. DeRouchie, Jason Gile, and Kenneth J. Turner. Eisenbrauns, 2013.

Perri, Carmela. "On Alluding." *Poetics* 7 (1978): 289–307.

Reiner, Fred N. "Masoretes, Rabbis, and Karaites: A Comparison of Biblical Interpretations." Pages 137–47 in *International Organization for Masoretic Studies: 1972–1973 Proceedings*. Society of Biblical Literature, 1974.

Rendtorff, Rolf. *The Canonical Hebrew Bible: A Theology of the Old Testament*. Deo, 2006.

Rendtorff, Rolf. *The Problem of the Process of Transmission in the Pentateuch*. Sheffield Academic, 2009.

Richter, Sandra L. *The Epic of Eden: A Christian Entry into the Old Testament*. IVP Academic, 2008.

Riley, Donavon. "How Luther Pointed Me to Christ in the Old Testament." *1517* (blog), November 2, 2018. https://www.1517.org/articles/how-luther-pointed-me-to-christ-in-the-old-testament.

Sacks, Jonathan. *Genesis: The Book of Beginnings*. Vol. 1 of *Covenant & Conversation: A Weekly Reading of the Jewish Bible*. Koren, 2009.

Sailhamer, John H. *Introduction to Old Testament Theology: A Canonical Approach*. Zondervan, 1995.

Sailhamer, John H. *The Meaning of the Pentateuch: Revelation, Composition and Interpretation*. IVP Academic, 2009.

Sailhamer, John H. *The Pentateuch as Narrative: A Biblical-Theological Commentary*. Zondervan Academic, 1995.

Salkin, Jeffrey K. *Righteous Gentiles in the Hebrew Bible: Ancient Role Models for Sacred Relationships*. Jewish Lights, 2008.

Sanders, James A. *Canon and Community: A Guide to Canonical Criticism*. Fortress, 1984.

Sarna, Nahum M. *Exodus: The Traditional Hebrew Text with the New JPS Translation*. JPS Torah Commentary. Jewish Publication Society, 1991.

Sarna, Nahum M. *Exploring Exodus: The Origins of Biblical Israel*. Schocken, 2011.

Seitz, Christopher R. *The Character of Christian Scripture: The Significance of a Two-Testament Bible*. Studies in Theological Interpretation. Baker Academic, 2011.

Seitz, Christopher R. *The Goodly Fellowship of the Prophets: The Achievement of Association in Canon Formation*. Acadia Studies in Bible and Theology. Baker Academic, 2009.

Seitz, Christopher R. *Prophecy and Hermeneutics: Toward a New Introduction to the Prophets*. Studies in Theological Interpretation. Baker Academic, 2007.

Smith, Mark S. *The Early History of God: Yahweh and the Other Deities in Ancient Israel*. 2nd ed. Eerdmans, 2002.

Sommer, Benjamin. *A Prophet Reads Scripture: Allusion in Isaiah 40–66*. Stanford University Press, 1998.

Spellman, Ched. "Metaphors We Read Canonical Collections By: Exploring the Nature and Effect of Canonical Contextuality." *Journal of the Evangelical Theological Society* 65.2 (2022): 261–76.

Sundberg, Albert C., Jr. "The 'Old Testament': A Christian Canon." *Catholic Biblical Quarterly* 30.2 (1968): 143–55.

Sundberg, Albert C., Jr. *The Old Testament of the Early Church*. Harvard University Press, 1968.

Taylor, Joan E. *The Essenes, the Scrolls, and the Dead Sea*. Oxford University Press, 2014.

Thiselton, Anthony C. *The Two Horizons: New Testament Hermeneutics and Philosophical Description*. Eerdmans, 1996.

Tov, Emanuel. *Textual Criticism of the Hebrew Bible*. 3rd ed. Fortress, 2012.

Trible, Phyllis. *God and the Rhetoric of Sexuality*. Fortress, 1978.

Tucker, Gene M. *Form Criticism of Old Testament*. Edited by J. Coert Rylaarsdam. Augsburg Fortress, 1971.

Tucker, Gene M. "Old Testament Theology and Israelite Religion: Problems and Possibilities." *Colloquium* 22.2 (1990): 1–11.

Vermès, Géza. *The Complete Dead Sea Scrolls in English*. 7th ed. Penguin Classics, 2011.

von Rad, Gerhard. *Genesis: A Commentary*. Rev. ed. Westminster, 1972.

von Rad, Gerhard. *Old Testament Theology: A Commentary*. 2 vols. Westminster John Knox, 2001.

Waltke, Bruce K. *An Old Testament Theology: An Exegetical, Canonical, and Thematic Approach*. Zondervan, 2007.

Walton, John H. *The Lost World of Adam and Eve: Genesis 2–3 and the Human Origins Debate*. IVP Academic, 2015.

Walton, John H. *Old Testament Theology for Christians: From Ancient Context to Enduring Belief*. IVP Academic, 2017.

Walton, John H., and Andrew E. Hill. *Old Testament Today: A Journey from Ancient Context to Contemporary Relevance*. 2nd ed. Zondervan Academic, 2013.

Weinfeld, Moshe. *Deuteronomy and the Deuteronomic School*. Reprint, Eisenbrauns, 2014.

Wenham, Gordon J. *The Book of Leviticus*. New International Commentary on the Old Testament. Eerdmans, 2009.

Wenham, Gordon J. *Genesis 1–15*. Word Biblical Commentary. Zondervan, 2014.

Wenham, Gordon J. *Genesis 16–50*. Word Biblical Commentary. Zondervan, 2015.

Wieder, Naftali. "'Sanctuary' as a Metaphor for Scripture." *Journal of Jewish Studies* 8.3–4 (1957): 165–75.

Wright, Christopher J. H. *Knowing Jesus Through the Old Testament*. IVP Academic, 2014.

Wright, Christopher J. H. *The Mission of God: Unlocking the Bible's Grand Narrative*. IVP Academic, 2018.

Wright, N. T. *Jesus and the Victory of God*. Fortress, 1997.

Wright, N. T. *The New Testament and the People of God*. Christian Origins and the Question of God, vol. 1. Fortress, 1992.

Zeitlin, Solomon. "An Historical Study of the Canonization of the Hebrew Scriptures." Pages 164–201 in *The Canon and Masorah of the Hebrew Bible: An Introductory Reader*. Edited by Shnayer Z. Leiman. Library of Biblical Studies. Ktav, 1974.

SCRIPTURE INDEX

INDEX OF SUBJECTS AND NAMES